AMERICAN ECONOMISTS

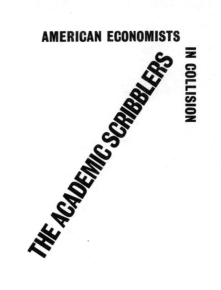

THE ACADEMIC SCRIBBLERS

IN COLLISION

AMERICAN ECONOMISTS IN COLLISION

THE ACADEMIC SCRIBBLERS

William Breit
University of Virginia

Roger L. Ransom
University of California, Riverside

HOLT, RINEHART AND WINSTON, INC.

New York   Chicago   San Francisco   Atlanta
Dallas   Montreal   Toronto   London   Sydney

HB
87
B72

. . . the ideas of economists and political philosophers, both when they are right and when they are wrong, are more powerful than is commonly understood. Indeed the world is ruled by little else. Practical men, who believe themselves to be quite exempt from any intellectual influences, are usually the slaves of some defunct economist. Madmen in authority, who hear voices in the air, are distilling their frenzy from some academic scribbler of a few years back.

—John Maynard Keynes

Preface

This book attempts primarily to capture within the confines of a single volume the most elusive game of all: contemporary economic thought. We undertake this safari through the thickets of modern controversy because of our deep conviction that economics students and intelligent laymen should know more about the individuals whose theories have come to rule their world. The recent observation of Professor A. W. Coats seems particularly encouraging: "Studies of recent economic thought and policy are especially important because the economists' direct influence has latterly been much greater than in most earlier times. . . [W]e urgently need more research into these questions, if only to advance the education of historians, whose notions of the nature and influence of economic ideas are lamentably deficient."

We have attempted to limit the range of our journey in two major ways: (1) The study is largely restricted to the ideas of American economists and (2) we have traced the development of the ideas which have had or are likely to have impact on economic policy. Where non-Americans are discussed in any detail, it is in order to form the backdrop for the American arena of controversy.

Among the most difficult tasks confronting us was the selection of quarry to be included in the study. The writers chosen represent virtually every prominent viewpoint in the American economics profession today. Each of them was, moreover, influential in shaping these views. Because we set out to explore carefully only certain areas of economic thought, many names and topics are omitted from the story. In part this is because of our primary emphasis on policy. Our discussion neglects many of the important technical developments of contemporary economic theory—such areas as mathematical growth models, general equilibrium models, statistical inference, or econometrics. We fully recognize the importance of these developments in providing sophisticated building blocks with which to construct economic policy. We remain convinced, however, that men, not models, are the ultimate determinants of policy. For those who find these omissions serious, we hope that, in spite of the limitations of our approach, we have conveyed some of the diversity, richness, and profundity of contemporary American economic thought.

From the very beginning of the collaboration we determined that it should be, in every sense, a joint project. Although initial responsibility for the several chapters was divided between the two authors, we were able to gain coordination by periodic meetings at the University of Virginia and at the University of California at Berkeley, where we were visiting members of the faculty during the summer quarter of 1968. Both authors consider the thinkers included in this volume to be important economists, but the reader will doubtless detect certain lapses from impartiality. Nevertheless, we believe that each of us helped serve as a check on any over- or underenthusiasm of the other.

Many of our friends and colleagues listened to our ideas and offered helpful advice. We cannot list all of them here, but we want especially to thank James M. Buchanan, William Patton Culbertson, Kenneth G. Elzinga, S. Herbert Frankel, Ivan C. Johnson, John M. Letiche, Roland N. McKean, and Leland B. Yeager for their encouragement and patience. The research assistance of Joseph E. Camp is also gratefully acknowledged, as is a timely subvention from the University of Virgina's Research Committee on Summer Grants.

Over the past several years the students in Breit's seminar in economic thought at the University of Virginia have provided a forum that aided greatly in the development of this work. We must mention, in particular, Evelyn Glazier, Richard Higgins, Joseph Jadlow, Roger Spencer, Robert Tollison, and George Trivoli. Both authors also experimented with parts of this book at the undergraduate level. The enthusiasm of nonspecialists toward the issues raised was a steady source of encouragement.

Moreover, we are deeply indebted to Mrs. Betty H. Tillman. Her ability to turn our illegible script into an acceptable manuscript was truly astonishing.

In the preparation of this work we contacted the living economists included within it, and some of them we bothered continually. Nevertheless, each of them seemed willing to come to our assistance when needed. We hope they will not be too disappointed by the result.

December 1970   WILLIAM BREIT
Charlottesville, Virginia
Riverside, California   ROGER L. RANSOM

Contents

AMERICAN ECONOMISTS

IN COLLISION

THE ACADEMIC SCRIBBLERS

CHAPTER 1

INTRODUCTION

A few years ago a distinguished national magazine asked the following questions of some twenty-seven historians, economists, political scientists, educators, and philosophers:

1. What books published during the past four decades most significantly altered the direction of our society?
2. Which may have a substantial impact on public thought and action in the years ahead?

Although the participants represented wide areas of interests and were invited to submit as many titles as they desired, the book cited most often would scarcely be expected to attract a large reading public and would most certainly not be a likely candidate for sale to a motion picture studio. It was *The General Theory of Employment Interest and Money* by John Maynard Keynes. Among those who voted for it were a political columnist (Walter Lippmann), a philosopher (Sidney Hook), two historians (Allan Nevins and J.H. Plumb), a political scientist (Harry Howe Ransom), and over a half-dozen other representatives of the intelligentsia. This wide-ranging agreement on the importance of a work by an English economist would probably be surprising to the general public, which might have expected the result to favor such authors as Toynbee, Kinsey, or Dr. Spock.

And yet, by almost any standard of influence, the choice seems unerringly right. For this work truly has left its mark on our times as has no other single volume, even leading one writer to christen the period since World War II as "The Age of Keynes." The widely held notion of the necessity for a strongly interventionist state to maintain full employment was unquestionably established in large part by this work.

It would be superficial, of course, to suggest that the "new economics" of post-World War II America is simply the product of one man's ideas. The new economics encompasses much recent theoretical analysis which implies that laissez-faire under free competition will lead neither to an efficient nor to full employment of resources. These ideas involve not only Keynes's concept of inadequate demand but also the wastes of competition, the irrationality of the consumer, and divergencies beteen private and social interests. Such considerations ostensibly lead to the conclusion that free-market capitalism is viable only with the help of an activist government stepping in to maintain demand; to provide goods and services neglected by befuddled, ignorant, or wrong-headed consumers; and generally to levy the taxes and provide the subsidies that would bring about the maximum degree of economic welfare. Keynes was, in the main, silent on such topics as advertising, excess capacity, waste, pollution, congestion, and inadequate provision of public services. Yet these problems are coming to play just as important a role in the exercise of economic policy as is the maintenance of adequate demand. Although August Heckscher has called Keynes's book "the prophetic work which laid the basis for the economics of the welfare state,"[1] others must share in this accomplishment.

But if the general public is only slightly familiar with the name of Keynes, it is even less aware of the names of other economists who helped provide the rationale for the interventionist economic policy of our times. As we shall show, the writings of Thorstein Veblen, Arthur Cecil Pigou, and Edward H. Chamberlin taken together have probably had at least as much influence as Keynes in setting the tone for economic policy in the second half of the twentieth century. These men, along with Keynes, were to shape the thought and policy prescriptions of some of the most influential economists of our time: Alvin H. Hansen, Paul A. Samuelson, Abba P. Lerner, and John Kenneth Galbraith. It will be demonstrated that contemporary economic thought and policy run largely in terms of the arguments and tools provided by these economists.

Yet there is another story to be told in this volume. Revolutions have their counterrevolutions, and upheavals in economic thought are no exception. In American economics the counterrevolution has been led by three important scholars, who happen to have been associated with the University of Chicago. These economists have presented ideas intended to clarify the meaning of neoclassical economics—the body of thought with largely laissez-faire policy implications which was the accepted doctrine before the strictures of Veblen, Pigou, Chamberlin, and Keynes tended to cast it into disrepute. In so doing, they ex-

---

[1] Cited in Rochelle Girson, "Mutations in the Body Politic," *Saturday Review*, August 29, 1964, p. 74.

tended, refined, and drew new implications from these theories in attempting to rebut the interventionist themes of the new economics. It is important that the contributions of Frank Knight, Henry Simons, and Milton Friedman be understood. We shall, therefore, describe some of the intellectual and empirical work associated with these counterrevolutionaries, who have attempted to see economic problems more from the standpoint of pure economic theory and less from that of the political process. The clash and conflicts between the new economists and the new neoclassicists constitute the subject matter of this study. As will probably become clear, whichever school of thought gains ascendancy in the calculable future will be decided as much by the force of its adherents' personalities as by the logic and elegance of their arguments.

It was Keynes who wrote the words about the "academic scribblers" which we have quoted on the frontispiece and which gave this book its title. In the final sentence of his *magnum opus* Keynes warned, "it is ideas, not vested interests, which are dangerous for good or evil." This book is about those academic scribblers who, for good or evil, are influencing the agitators, civil servants, and politicians who will shape economic events today and tomorrow.

PART I

THE PILLARS OF NEOCLASSICAL ECONOMICS

CHAPTER 2

THE INTELLECTUAL GANTRY OF NEOCLASSICAL ECONOMIC POLICY

The economist, like everyone else, must concern himself with the ultimate aims of man.

ALFRED MARSHALL

The policy conclusions dominating the reasoning of most economists during the first 40 years of the twentieth century followed from the logic of what is known as neoclassical economic thought. The date 1871 is used to mark the beginning of this way of thinking about economic problems. In that year two books appeared—one in England, one in Austria—which deviated sharply from the mainstream of classical economics. The Englishman was William Stanley Jevons and the Austrian was Carl Menger.[1] Working independently, they simultaneously discovered (or "rediscovered")[2] a way of thinking which subse-

---

[1] William Stanley Jevons, *The Theory of Political Economy*, 5th ed. (New York: Kelly & Millman, 1957). Original ed. 1871; Carl Menger, *Principles of Economics* (Glencoe, Illinois: The Free Press, reprinted 1950). Original ed., 1871.

[2] Most of the elements of the neoclassical approach were already contained in the work of H. H. Gossen in a book which he published in 1854. This book, almost completely neglected, was soon withdrawn from circulation by the disappointed

quently came to be known as "marginalism." The basic logic of this approach gave to the analysis of political economy a degree of systematization unrivalled by the earlier classical writers. In so doing it marked the transition from "political economy" to "economics." The suffix "ics" is significant, for it decisively arrayed economics along with such subjects as mathematics and physics, as having a rigor equal to the formal and physical sciences.

The Scope and Method of Neoclassical Economics

Neoclassical theory is distinguished from classical doctrine by significant changes in both scope and method. The shift in scope involved a redefinition of the economic problem; the methodological change was the introduction of marginal analysis.

The classical economists saw the economic problem as being essentially "dynamic." The measure of economic welfare to Adam Smith and his followers was the quantity of output. But output was a function of the quantity of labor available and its productivity. The question they presumed to answer was: How can the capital stock be augmented and markets widened so as to increase the productivity of labor, physical output, and therefore, welfare? The neoclassical economists, on the other hand, conceived the economic problem as the attempt to get an optimal result by allocating a *given* quantity of scarce resources among competing uses. Scarcity became the central problem of economics. Jevons stated the problem as follows:

> Given, a certain population, with various needs and powers of production, in possession of certain lands and other sources of material; required, the mode of employing their labour which will maximize the utility of the produce.[3]

Thus there was a marked shift from a concern over the dynamic problem of growth to a concern over the static problem of efficiency.[4]

---

author. Others, (Cournot, Dupuit, Longfield, Senior, and Von Thünen) also were precursors of some aspects of neoclassical thought, but did not develop anything like the systematic presentation of Gossen, Jevons, and Menger. The subject of "lost discoveries" is a fascinating topic all to itself.

[3] Jevons, *The Theory of Political Economy*, p. 267. Note that he desires to maximize the *utility* of the produce, not the physical output itself.

[4] A detailed and excellent discussion of the difference between the classical and neoclassical view of the economic problem is to be found in Hla Myint, *Theories of Welfare Economics* (New York: Augustus M. Kelley, 1962).

Perhaps the most striking feature of neoclassical economics is its concern with changes which involve a slight increase or decrease in the stock of anything under consideration. The meaning and significance of this technique were so well stated by one of the school's leading adherents, Philip H. Wicksteed, that it is worth quoting at length:

> . . . the marginal service rendered to us by any commodity is that service which we should have to forego if the supply of the commodity in question were slightly contracted; our marginal desire for more of anything is measured by the significance of a slight increment added at the margin of our present store. And the importance of this service, or the urgency of this desire, depends . . . on the quantity we already possess. If we possess, or have just consumed, so much of a thing that our desire for more is languid, then additions at the margin have little value to us; but if we possess, or have consumed so little that we are keenly desirous of more, then marginal additions have a high value for us . . . Thus by increasing our supply of anything we reduce its marginal significance and lower the place of an extra unit on our scale of preferences; and suitable additions to our supply will bring it down to any value you please. Thus, whatever the price of any commodity that the housewife finds in the market may be, so long as its marginal significance to her is higher than that price, she will buy; but the very act of putting herself in possession of an increased stock reduces its marginal significance, and the more she buys the lower it becomes. The amount that brings it into coincidence with the market price is the amount she will buy.[5]

The assumption that the utility of a good declined as its stock increased meant that the process described by Wicksteed was an equilibrating one. As the stock of a good changes, the value of additional units change, thus creating a situation where the marginal value is just equal to the price.

This tool enabled the neoclassical writers to solve a problem which beset classical economic thought from Adam Smith onward, namely the paradox of value, or the "diamond-water paradox." Adam Smith had reasoned that since water has greater utility (that is, is more useful) than diamonds, and yet diamonds are more expensive than water, utility could not be a determinant of price. Marginal analysis made it

---

[5] Philip H. Wicksteed, *The Common Sense of Political Economy*, volume 1. (London: Routledge & Kegan Paul Ltd., 1957), pp. 40-41.

blindingly clear that the key factor in the determination of price is the *marginal significance* of having slightly more or less of the item. Although the total utility of water is doubtless greater than the total utility of diamonds, the marginal utility of diamonds is very high (because the stock of diamonds is relatively low) while the marginal utility of water is low (because the stock of water is plentiful). In this fashion, the neoclassicists introduced the role of demand as an important determinant of price.

The Emergence of Economic Man: Consumer Sovereignty

The fact of scarcity creates a necessity for choice and a careful comparing of alternatives. Accordingly, a new view of human nature came into focus in the writings of neoclassical economists. The individual is imagined in a constant process of delicately balancing his marginal expenditures and marginal utilities. This rational, calculating human, who emerges most clearly in the pages of Menger's *Grundsatze*, also appears in most of the works of neoclassical writers including Jevons, Pareto, and Wicksteed.[6] The significance of the notion of the "economic man" is that it provided a rationale for the doctrine of *consumer sovereignty*. This concept implies that, as Adam Smith put it:

> Consumption is the sole end and purpose of all production; and the interest of the producer ought to be attended to, only in so far as it may be necessary for promoting that of the consumer.[7]

Consumer sovereignty provided one of the cornerstones in supporting the laissez-faire policy prescription of neoclassicism. For, granted the maximization of utility as the problem, marginal calculations as the

---

[6] The individual so described has gone by many names in the literature. We refer to him as *economic man*, a term introduced by Pareto. Of course these economists were purposely abstracting from other aspects of man's behavior. That man is multi-motivated was probably understood by all of them. Nevertheless, as Frank H. Knight has complained, ". . . if Menger was aware of the many other men who walk about and variously 'perform in the same skin' as the creature who merely uses means to satisfy needs . . . his *Grundsatze* gives no evidence of the fact." Frank H. Knight, "Introduction to Carl Menger" in Menger, *Principles of Economics*, p. 16.

[7] Adam Smith, *An Inquiry into the Nature and Causes of the Wealth of Nations*, 5th ed., (New York: Random House, Inc., 1937), p. 635. The idea was implicit in classical and neoclassical thought. The term consumer sovereignty was not Smith's, but was introduced into the literature surprisingly late—in 1934—by Professor W. H. Hutt.

tool, and economic man as the actor, the state has little or no role to play. Standards are set by economizing consumers and scarce resources allocated so as to maximize welfare. The specific refinement made in the consumer demand criterion for production is in the concept of cost. Cost is ultimately determined by consumer evaluations. In considering how much of any commodity should be produced, the relevant question is whether it will cover the costs of production. Here again, the use of "margins" comes into play. An increase in the consumption of a commodity by a consumer represents an increase in his welfare or benefit. However, it involves a withdrawal of resources from the production of something else. This means a decrease in the benefit (and hence a cost) to the would-be consumers of the alternative commodity. As long as the benefit is greater than the cost, production of the item in question should be expanded, and where the cost is greater than the benefit, the production should be contracted. The appropriate output is reached where the additional benefit is precisely equal to the additional cost; or as the economist says: where marginal benefit equals marginal cost. At this point, neither an expansion nor contraction of output can increase welfare. But what mechanism guarantees this felicitous result? The answer lies in the neoclassical doctrine of perfect competition.

The Doctrine of Perfect Competition

As in the case of the consumer demand criterion of welfare, the doctrine of perfect competition was already implicit in classical economics. But precision is the keynote of neoclassicism, and thus the doctrine was refined and elaborated. In its refined neoclassical form, there are three major conditions for perfect competition. These are worth listing formally:

1. *Perfect knowledge.* This assures that in a given market at a given time, there will be only one price for identical commodities, and no scope for higgling.
2. *Large numbers.* This assures that no producer or consumer has any appreciable effect on price so that both are price takers rather than price makers in all markets. (Hence collusion among buyers and sellers is ruled out.)
3. *Homogeneous products.* This assures that the products of an industry are perfectly substitutable for one another.

Granted the above mentioned conditions, it should be obvious that the competitive firm can sell any output it desires at the given market price. With even a slight increase in price, it would lose all its customers.

The doctrine of perfect competition is the required corollary of the doctrine of consumer sovereignty. This is true for two reasons. First, only under perfect competition is there a guarantee that the entrepreneur, in the quest for profit, will submit to the will of the consumer. Second, perfect competition assures ideal output, in the sense that marginal benefit is always equated with marginal cost. As we have seen, for the consumer the price of an item is the measure of the importance of an additional cost incurred in producing an extra unit of output. The rationality of the economizing consumer induces him to equate his marginal evaluation of the item to its price. But we can see that the conditions of competition will induce the producer to equate marginal cost to marginal revenue. Since marginal revenue is the addition to total revenue from selling one more unit of product, under perfect competition (where the firm is a price taker), it is also precisely equal to the price of the output. So the producer will expand as long as price is above marginal cost, since the excess of price above marginal cost represents the extra profit that can be made by producing more units. By similar logic, if marginal cost exceeds price, the entrepreneur will reduce output. Thus the producer as an economic man is motivated, under perfectly competitive conditions, to equate price with marginal cost. With consumers and producers so motivated, the conditions of competition create an equilibrium where marginal costs always equal marginal benefits. From a social viewpoint, economic efficiency (or welfare) is then maximized.[8] In short, freedom of choice and competition are the best instruments for promoting the welfare of society. But was there any guarantee that this solution would provide employment for all resources in the economy? This question was answered by Say's Law.

Say's Law and Full Employment Equilibrium

The classical conclusion of automatic full employment rested upon Say's Law of Markets—stated crudely as "Supply creates its own de-

---

8 There is an additional happy property of perfect competition which, for our purposes, we need not consider. Under perfect competition, the division of output among firms will be optimal, that is, output will be produced at minimum possible total cost. The proof of this proposition is handled nicely in Tibor Scitovsky, *Welfare and Competition* (Chicago, Illinois: Richard D. Irwin, Inc., 1951), p. 151.

mand." The fact that inadequate demand could be a cause of unemployment, given the insatiability of human wants, was inconceivable. For if human wants are insatiable, then the money for which men work will be used to help satisfy these wants. Supply will always generate sufficient demand to clear the market through the circular flow of payments from suppliers to consumers or investors. No money would be hoarded, and hence all payments returned to the system in the form of purchases of goods. Saving was possible; however all money saved was invested, since the interest rate would adjust in such a fashion as to induce any idle funds into the market for capital goods. Shifts in demand might create temporary gluts in markets; however these would be adjusted through the movements of wages and prices for each market.

The neoclassical economists refined the explanation of Say's Law by showing the determination of the level of real output through marginal analysis. The American economist John Bates Clark stated this explicitly in his *Distribution of Wealth* published in 1899. Following from the reasoning of the argument regarding the firm's output, it is clear that the producer will never want to offer a worker a wage greater than the value of the added output his labor can produce. Assume that the entrepreneur is hiring additional workers to work with a fixed stock of capital. Under the principle of diminishing marginal productivity, a point is eventually reached where each additional worker adds less to the total product than the preceding worker. The problem is, how many workers will the firm hire? If the firm is attempting to maximize profits under conditions of perfect competition, the firm will add additional workers until the wage paid to the last worker (and therefore all preceding workers, on the assumption that each additional worker is equally skilled) is just equal to the value of the marginal product. This is precisely the same condition as saying that price equals marginal cost.

To prove this, we must ask, what is the marginal cost of adding an additional worker? It is the wage rate that is paid to him divided by the amount that he adds to the total product. For example, if the wage rate is $45 and the worker adds 15 units of output, what is the marginal cost of hiring this worker? It is clearly 45 divided by 15 or $3, because the marginal cost is defined as the addition to total cost of adding only *one* unit of output. If the wage rate is $75 and the worker adds 15 units of output, the marginal cost is $5, and so on.

Assume that the firm, operating in a perfectly competitive market, finds that it can receive $8 per unit of output, and the wage rate is $40. How many workers will the firm hire and how much output will the firm produce? The firm will continue to hire workers and increase output until the last worker adds five units of output. For only at this point does the price of the output ($8) equal the marginal cost of the output (40/5). In other words, the firm will hire workers up to the point where the wage rate is equal to the *value* of the marginal product, that is, price times the marginal product. Or the marginal product equals the real wage (the money wage deflated by the price level). In symbols:

If	$P = MC$	(Price equals marginal cost)
and	$MC = W/MP$	(Marginal cost equals the money wage rate divided by the marginal product)
then	$P = W/MP$	(Price equals the money wage divided by the marginal product)
and	$W = P(MP)$	(The money wage rate equals the value of the marginal product)
then	$MP = \dfrac{W}{P}$	(The marginal product equals the real wage)

Clark applied this reasoning not only to labor markets but to markets for all factors of production. His conclusion was that under perfect competition each factor would inexorably receive a return precisely equal to its contribution. For a factor's contribution to the product was its marginal product, and Clark could demonstrate that each factor would receive a wage equal to the value of this marginal product.

This analysis of the demand for labor, combined with the neoclassical view that the supply of labor is a function of the real wage rate, provides a sophisticated explanation for Say's Law. Full employment is realized where the supply curve of labor cuts the demand curve. In Figure 2.1 we have measured the real wage rate on the vertical axis and the amount of labor on the horizontal axis. The demand curve for labor is given by the curve D_L, and in accordance with Clark's analysis, shows for each quantity of labor the marginal product associated with each worker. The greater the number of workers hired, the lower the marginal product of all workers. On the vertical axis we measure the real wage rate. The curve thus shows, for each real wage rate, the quantity of workers that would be demanded.

The supply curve of labor is represented by curve S_L. It was usually assumed that the greater the real wage rate, the greater the number of workers willing to work. The intersection of the two curves thus gives the uniquely determined point of employment and the average real wage rate corresponding to that volume of employment. This is a position of full employment since there is neither a surplus nor a shortage of labor. If the real wage were to be pushed up to $(W/P)_2$, there would be unemployment in the amount AB. But this could only be temporary since the surplus laborers would bargain to push wages down again to $(W/P)_1$ by cutting money wages. Only an absence of perfect competition, or government interference in the form of minimum wage laws, could cause permanent unemployment by not allowing wages to reach the level at which the two curves intersect. So full employment is the result of a perfectly competitive economy in all factor markets.

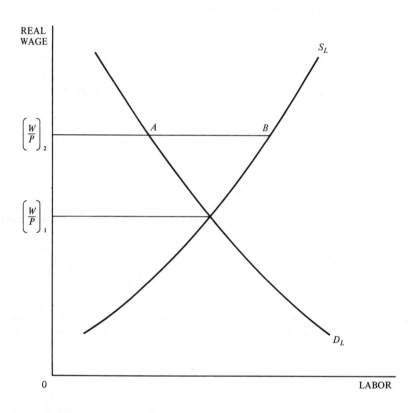

FIGURE 2.1

The reader should note that a cut in money wages was the same thing as a cut in real wages because the price level remained unchanged. The level of money wages did not determine the price level. Rather it was the price level that determined the level of money wages. Then what determined the price level? The answer to this final question was provided by the *Quantity Theory of Money*, which was accepted by virtually every neoclassical writer.

Quantity Theory of Money

Although there were a number of variants of the quantity theory, all of them centered upon the assertion that there was a rough proportionality between changes in the stock of money and changes in the general level of prices in the economy.[9]

The neoclassicists made a fundamental distinction between the *real value* of money and the *nominal value* of money. The real value of money must be expressed in terms of how much a unit of money can buy in the market place; the nominal value of money is expressed in the unit of account (such as a dollar). Quantity theorists insisted that people act to maintain some level of *real balances*, without regard to the nominal value of these holdings.

To see how this behavior affects expenditures, consider the case in which an increase in the stock of money has left people with money balances which—in real terms—they consider to be too large. People will then wish to dispose of their "excess" real balances by increasing expenditures. But, for one person to reduce his money holdings, someone else must increase his, for the nominal stock of money does not change for the community as a whole. Thus, attempts to lower holdings of money will generate an increase in expenditures. Prices will be bid up, lowering the value of a unit of money. With a fall in the value of money, larger nominal balances will be required to meet the desired level of real balances. Pressures to continue expansion of expenditures will be eased. In fact, if there is no change in output, prices will have to rise by exactly enough to make the larger nominal money balances just equal in real terms to the initially desired level of real balances. If rising expenditures elicited an increase in income (production), it would also relieve the pressure to adjust money balances. With higher

---

[9] The roots of the quantity theory go well into the seventeenth century and writers such as David Hume. The earliest formulations argued for the existence of a strict proportionality: a 10 percent increase in the money stock would cause a 10 percent increase in prices. Later writers pointed out some qualifications to such a conclusion. The reader interested in the development of this theory might profitably consult M. Friedman's comments in "Money: The Quantity Theory," *The International Encyclopedia of Social Sciences* (New York: The Macmillan Company and the Free Press, 1968), pp. 432-47. The present discussion draws heavily from Friedman's exposition.

incomes, people would desire larger holdings in real terms. Both circumstances—a fall in the value of money as prices rise, or a rise in real income—return the system to equilibrium. Obviously, the argument can be reversed for a situation in which real balances are less than the desired level.

These relationships between money, prices, and real income can be expressed through the circular flow of payments in the economy. Two explanations are commonly associated with the neoclassical school: the *transactions approach* of the American economist Irving Fisher, and the *cash-balances approach* of the economists at Cambridge, England.[10] Fisher reasoned that since each transaction in the economy consisted of a price coupled with some good or service, the total value of all transactions could be expressed as the product of some "average price" (*P*) times the number of transactions (*T*). At the same time, the sum of all payments in the economy must total the amount of money (*M*) times the *velocity* of money (*V*), which indicated the number of times a unit of money "turned over." He could then express the flow of payments in the economy as:

$$MV = PT \tag{2.1}$$

where V, the transactions velocity, is defined as $\dfrac{PT}{M}$.

Fisher's equation of exchange is nothing more than an accounting identity, given his definition of velocity. To make the equation a useful analytical device, velocity must be viewed as a *behavioral* variable. This is the essence of the quantity theory; for if velocity is stable (or at least predictable), then the relation of the stock of money to income and prices is immediately apparent. The cash-balance approach to the circular flow identity recognizes the crucial role of velocity. The Cambridge group reformulated Equation 2.1 and stated the relationship of money to prices using *income* rather than transactions, and replacing Fisher's *V* with an expression representing the desire of people to hold money balances.[11] They expressed the circular flow of payments as:

---

[10] A third explanation was that of Knut Wicksell, a Swedish economist who wrote at the turn of the century. Wicksell's writing was not as widely read as Fisher or the Cambridge group. It is interesting to note that the "Keynesian" writers today point to Wicksell as the example of the quantity theory, for he came closest to anticipating some of the later developments.

[11] The expression for total transactions (*T*) in Equation (2.1) proved elusive when attempting to empirically study the quantity theory. The development of na-

$$M = kPy \qquad (2.2)$$

Where y is the level of real income, and k is the ratio of money balances to income: M/Py. The demand for cash balances is therefore the reciprocal of velocity. The two are as opposite ends of a seesaw; a rise in the demand for money is tantamount to a decline in the velocity of circulation.

The cash-balances analysis best represents the neoclassical statement of monetary theory by men such as Alfred Marshall and A. C. Pigou. Indeed, it was Pigou's statement of the theory which John Maynard Keynes chose as the stereotype for his assault on neoclassical thought in 1936. The cash-balances equation (2.2), like Fisher's equation (2.1), clearly shows the manner in which money affects prices and income. It says nothing, however, about the equilibrium level of real income in the economy. Given a flexible price level, *any* level of real income (y) can be made consistent with *any* nominal supply of money; people must simply adjust their money balances to bring the real balances to the desired levels. The determination of output, as we have already seen, was left to the interaction of supply and demand in the factor markets of the economy; the quantity theory saw to it that the flows of money payments would automatically let supply create its own demand. Nonetheless, the monetary theory of the neoclassical writers did stress the powerful influence which the level of the money supply could exert on the level of expenditures. And this, they pointed out, meant that the monetary actions of a central bank could have substantial influences on the levels of prices and money income in the economy. Money *was* important.

All these ideas were to find their clearest expression in the writings of one man who can be taken as the exemplar of neoclassical economic thought—Alfred Marshall.

---

tional income accounts made the use of income rather than transactions more useful. Fisher's equation would then be:

$MV = PY$

where Y is total physical output of the economy. Note that the velocity in this equation is income velocity, not transactions velocity.

CHAPTER 3

ALFRED MARSHALL—
Exemplar of Neoclassical
Economic Thought

> . . . *I was led to attach great importance to the fact that our observations of nature, in the moral as in the physical world, relate not so much to aggregate quantities, as to increments of quantities, and that in particular the demand for a thing is a continuous function, of which the "marginal" increment is, in stable equilibrium, balanced against the corresponding increment of its costs of production. It is not easy to get a clear view of Continuity in this aspect without the aid . . . of diagrams.*
>
> *ALFRED MARSHALL*

If one name in the history of economic thought is synonymous with the neoclassical approach—incorporating into one system the chief pillars of neoclassicism—it is that of Alfred Marshall. Marshallian economics came to represent the very best in this new approach to the subject. His great book, *Principles of Economics*, first published in 1890, went through eight editions before Marshall's death in 1924. It became the standard work of reference in the field for thousands of economics students. His work is thought of today as the most orthodox of neoclassicism; yet, as we shall show, it contained the germs of the destruction of the neoclassical model.

However, it is chiefly noted for Marshall's ingenious demonstration of how both costs of production through the supply side of the market (the older classical cost-of-production approach to value) and marginal utility through the demand side of the market (the new subjective utility approach) interacted to determine relative prices. Of course, he was not the first to see the relation between supply and demand in price determination. But he was the one who most effectively synthesized the approaches, showed many of the implications of the analysis, and fashioned many of the analytical instruments that came to make up the economists' tool box. The present subject matter of price theory in terms of its methodology, divisions, terminology, and the conclusions regarding the implication of various economic policies, does not deviate in its essentials from those Marshall developed. The modern conception of the demand curve, the elasticity of demand, the nature of consumer's surplus, the use of long-run and short-run analysis, quasi-rent, partial equilibrium, and comparative statics—all owe much to this pioneering genius of the science of economics. Furthermore, he shares with Jevons the distinction of having developed the technique of marginal analysis.

Alfred Marshall was born in 1842, only 19 years after the death of David Ricardo and eight years after the death of Malthus. He studied at Cambridge where his interests ran primarily to mathematics, but he also had a deep interest in philosophy, especially the works of Kant and Hegel. When still a young man, he wandered around the Alps carrying on his back, not mountain climbing equipment, but a knapsack of books. Reaching a suitable spot he would settle down next to a rock and study the *Critique of Pure Reason*. Eventually he decided that on deep metaphysical questions mankind could never hope to know more than a very little, so he turned to the study of ethics. His decision to move into economics resulted from a vacation in which he "visited the poorest quarters of several cities and walked through one street after another, looking at the faces of the poorest people. Next, I resolved to make as thorough a study as I could of Political Economy."[1] It was on vacations that Marshall seemed to reach the high points of his life. His vacation walks in the Alps gave him a love for the outdoors and until the end of his life he always did his best thinking in the open air. When he taught at Oxford, his study was in a garden, and at

---

[1] J. M. Keynes, "Alfred Marshall, 1842-1924," *Memorials of Alfred Marshall* (New York: Kelley & Millman, 1956), p. 10.

Cambridge he worked on an open balcony; when he visited in Palermo he worked on the roof of a quiet hotel. It was while he sat on the roof of his hotel in Palermo, shaded by a bathcover awning in 1881, that he hit on the idea of elasticity. He was, we are told by Mrs. Marshall, "highly delighted with it."[2]

In 1877 he married his pupil, Mary Paley with whom he collaborated on his first book, *The Economics of Industry*. His first academic post after his marriage was at Bristol and in 1884, he was named Professor of Political Economy at Cambridge, holding this chair for 23 years. His growing fame as an economist drew large throngs of students to his classroom, but his style was best suited to small groups and he did his best to discourage attendance. One of his students provided the following reminiscence of his classroom effect:

> Memory still recaptures the man coming into his room . . . his head bent forward as if in thought, mounting his platform with a little fluster of manner, leaning on his desk, his hands clasped in front of him, his blue eyes lit up, now talking easily, now chuckling over some story, now questioning his class, now pausing impressively, with rapt expression, his eyes in a far corner of the room, now speaking in solemn prophetic tones of some problem of the future —the feeding of India, the prospect of England maintaining her greatness, the banishment of poverty from the world.
>
> He had a singular power of illustration. His mind was stored with facts . . . He dived into the remote past, or drew on recent statistics, on letters in the papers, on some play then being performed, on his own observation. He was never out of touch with life . . . Occasionally he invited questions or remarks, but few people were ever bold enough to speak under Marshall's intent and expectant gaze.[3]

He retired from teaching in 1908 in order to devote his life to writing, but continued to live in Cambridge in the house that he built in Madingley Road called "Balliol Croft." It was here that he died in 1924 within two weeks of his 82nd birthday.[4]

---

2 *Ibid.*, p. 45 n.

3 E. A. Benians, "Reminiscences," *Memorials of Alfred Marshall, op. cit.*, pp. 78-79.

4 For further details of Marshall's life, the reader should consult C. W. Guillebaud, "Editorial Introduction," *Principles of Economics*, 9th variorum ed., (New York: The Macmillan Company, 1961), vol. 1, pp. 3-6; Keynes, "Alfred Marshall, 1824-1924," *Memorials of Alfred Marshall, op. cit.*, pp. 1-65; and A. C. Pigou, "In Memorium: Alfred Marshall," *Ibid.*, pp. 81-90.

Marshall's conception of economic science is indicated by the Latin motto inscribed on the title page of his magnum opus: *Natura non facit saltum*, meaning "nature makes no leaps." He regarded his analysis as being akin to the Darwinian approach in biology and his work is imbued with biological analogies.[5] Throughout his *Principles*, Marshall's objective was to discover the continuities and regularities in economic activities and to measure them.

He took pains to point out his assumptions to his reader and was always keenly aware that the conditions he posited exist solely in a particular institutional framework. The regularities he sought will appear in a largely laissez-faire competitive economy inhabited by utility maximizing consumers and profit maximizing producers. The environment is one of full employment guaranteed by the smooth workings of Say's Law and the quantity theory. Of course, Marshall was careful to point out the multi-motivated facets of man's behavior. But he felt that for purposes of abstraction it is necessary to reduce these motives to a common denominator. The chief group of motives can be measured in terms of money since so large a part of man's actions are involved in the pursuit of a livelihood—that is, in "the ordinary business of life." And although Marshall claimed to eschew any simple explanation of human nature, it is man dominated by acquisitive characteristics that is of central concern. The end result is virtually indistinguishable from the economic man of Jevons and Menger. For while man is motivated by many impulses and often acts irrationally, the actions of individuals in their economic life are most rational and measurable, for their actions are registered in price. To Marshall, therefore, economic laws were simply generalizations about human behavior, which can be measured in terms of money. If it is to be scientific, economics must limit its scope to phenomena that have a price measurement. Hence, value and distribution theory must be its central core. On the basis of the regularities that can be measured, predictions can be made about future events, with only a small margin of error.

It was Marshall's genius to see the limitations inherent in his analysis, to hedge and qualify his statements, and to anticipate criticism. One can find almost anything one looks for in the work. And though his *Principles* was the apogee of neoclassicism, it contained an explicit suggestion of a case for government intervention that went beyond anything allowed for by his neoclassical peers. For he experimented with

---

[5] *Cf.* Alfred Marshall, "Mechanical and Biological Analogies in Economics," reprinted in *Ibid.* (1898), pp. 312-18.

the possibility of improving welfare through a scheme of taxes and subsidies to industries under certain conditions. In so doing he developed a notion that has proved very fruitful in welfare economics—the concept of *consumer's surplus.*

Consumer's surplus is the difference between how much a consumer pays for a commodity and how much he would have been willing to pay rather than do without it. This surplus is an index of well-being. If we could measure it accurately, we would have a test of the amount of welfare our economy generates for consumers. All that would be required is a list of the maximum prices a consumer would be willing to pay for each unit of a good, compared with the price he actually pays. We saw in our discussion of the equilibrium mechanism operative in the consumer market that the marginal utility of a good declines as its stock increases. When translated into a schedule of maximum prices that a consumer would pay for a commodity, this would (when plotted) show a curve going downward and to the right. Measuring price on the vertical axis and quantity demanded on the horizontal axis, as in Figure 3.1, a demand curve is depicted showing the maximum prices a consumer would pay for various units of a good. We can now use this artifice to show consumer's surplus. In our diagram, consumer's surplus at price P for Q units of commodity X would be represented by the triangular area ABP.[6] Such an area would exist for the consumer in competitive markets where he is a price taker for the commodities he purchases. Under competition, producers sell all units of their commodities for a price that just equals the marginal cost of the *last* unit. If the producer could somehow monopolize the industry and force each consumer to pay the maximum price for each unit rather than do without it, then all the consumer's surplus would be diverted to the monopolist. Indeed, it is just this ability of the monopolist to compel a consumer to travel down his demand curve that is one of the major objections of welfare economists to imperfect markets. For if we accept the doctrine of consumer sovereignty, and take the consumer's well-being as our criterion for welfare, then our goal is to

---

6 This area is only an approximation to consumer's surplus unless we make the Marshallian assumption that the marginal utility of money is constant. Marshall assumed that such a small amount of money is spent on each commodity that changes in money's marginal utility can be ignored. Only under this assumption is the area under the demand curve and above the price line precisely the amount of consumer's surplus. On the more technical aspects of consumer's surplus, the interested reader can profitably consult George J. Stigler, *The Theory of Price,* 3rd ed. (New York: The Macmillan Company, 1966), pp. 78-81.

maximize consumer's surplus. Neoclassical welfare economics as developed by Marshall made this welfare criterion explicit.

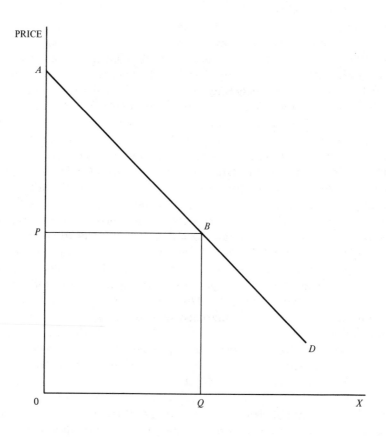

FIGURE 3.1

Now we require only one more Marshallian concept, which, when combined with consumer's surplus analysis, will allow us to see why Marshall was led to suggest a break with the laissez-faire policy conclusions of neoclassicism. This is the notion of average costs. Average cost is the total cost of production divided by the number of units of output. In the long run, a firm may produce under conditions of increasing cost (the usual assumption of neoclassical economics), constant average costs, or decreasing average costs, depending on the existence of what Marshall called "external economies" in the industry in which the firm operates. Such economies are beyond the control of the firm. They depend upon the size of the industry, economy, or world markets. The existence of decreasing average costs was an historical fact, and it was associated with increases in the size of firms and industries. Marshall was searching for an explanation of this phenomenon, but he wanted an explanation that would reconcile the observed existence of decreasing average costs with the existence of perfect competition. It was the doctrine of external economies that enabled Marshall to effect this reconciliation. To Marshall, external economies arise from the "neighborhood effects" of concentrating large numbers of small businesses in the same locality. This concentration leads to a cross-fertilization of ideas, the development of subsidiary and complementary industries, and the availability of specialized labor. Furthermore, the development of communication and transportation facilities also leads to cost reductions for the industry, and they are examples of external economies. There are, of course, other reasons why a firm's average costs might fall as it expands. Marshall summarized these reasons under the term "internal economies," and he minimized their importance. Internal economies are cost reducing factors that result from an expansion of the firm's size, enabling it to achieve greater advantages of large scale production. These economies do not result from the general expansion of the industry or economy as in the case of external economies. Here Marshall noted the ability of an expanding firm to use larger and more efficient machines, to get quantity discounts on large purchases, to enjoy a more extensive division of labor, and to hire better managerial talent. Marshall also noted that easier credit terms were usually available for the larger firm, thus effecting lower average costs for capital.

With all these advantages arising from internal economies, the continued viability of the small firm, and hence of competitive markets, comes into question. But Marshall was optimistic on this subject. Empirical evidence showed that the weaker firms continued to exist in most industries along with the stronger ones, indicating that the latter could not expand their size and output indefinitely. Marshall explained this continued existence of competition in the presence of internal economies on the grounds that few entrepreneurs could be guaranteed a perpetuation of exceptionally skillful management through their heirs. The mortality of the great entrepreneurs maintained free competition. It is in this discussion of the coexistence of decreasing costs and competition that Marshall makes greatest use of his biological analogies. The background for the entire discussion is a uniquely Marshallian concept—namely, the *representative firm*. In turning our attention to an individual firm, Marshall cautions that one must be careful to select a representative firm; that is a "normal" firm, which has had a fairly long life, fair success, managed with normal ability, and with normal access to external and internal economies. He uses the biological analogy of trees in the forest and compares the life cycle of trees to the life cycle of entrepreneurs. Just as trees, business firms grow to maturity and decay. In its early phases of growth, a firm enjoys internal economies; in its later phases, the economies are offset by diseconomies, which limit its ability to experience decreasing costs. Just as no one tree will ever take over a forest, no one firm can expand indefinitely and thereby dominate an entire industry.[7]

But Marshall was not completely satisfied with this explanation and so he added another factor—the possibility of a falling demand curve. If the firm has a partial monopoly position, then the perfectly horizontal demand curve facing the firm under perfectly competitive conditions is no longer applicable. This would mean that price would fall more rapidly than the firm's average costs, thus limiting the firm's expansion. Note that this falling demand curve is incompatible with the assumption of perfect competition.

In effect, Marshall explained the existence of perfect competition with decreasing costs by the simple expedient of assuming it away. For this reason, his suggestion of a falling demand curve was ignored and, as we shall see in Chapter 6, was only rediscovered in the 1930's. Ironically, it was then used to undermine, rather than bolster, one of the key neoclassical pillars.

Although Marshall minimized the importance of internal economies, he strongly emphasized the existence of external economies of scale. As we have seen, this means that each firm in an industry benefits from the general expansion of the industry or economy. But all benefit together. No one firm has any particular advantage over any other in the process. Given the mortality of the able entrepreneurs and the lack of equally competent heirs, the individual firm is limited in its isolated expansion. But all firms in the industry are the beneficiaries of reduced costs resulting from general economic growth. In that way, Marshall ingeniously (or some would say disingenuously)[8] reconciled perfect competition with the historical evidence of decreasing costs.

---

[7] See Marshall, *Principles, op. cit.*, pp. 315-16.

[8] As we have already noted, Marshall had to abandon a rigorous definition of perfect competition. His notion of the mortal entrepreneur replaced by inferior talent disrupts a model in which, by definition, resources are presumed to remain constant, and the notion of a perfectly elastic demand curve is abandoned when the

If in fact there are industries that operate under decreasing average cost conditions because of net external economies, then a possible basis exists for government intervention, which will increase welfare by increasing consumer's surplus. That is, the state might be able to increase consumer welfare by taxing industries operating under increasing cost conditions (where the tax receipts are greater than the loss in consumer's surplus), using the revenue to subsidize decreasing cost industries (where the subsidy is less than the gain in consumer's surplus). It will prove instructive to examine the simple geometry of this proposition.[9]

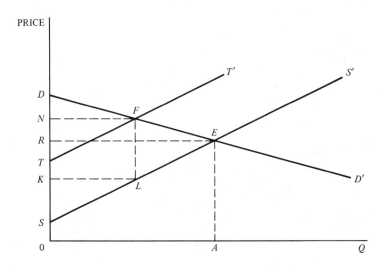

FIGURE 3.2

First, let us examine the case of an increasing cost industry, depicted in Figure 3.2. The fact that this industry operates under increasing costs is represented by the industry supply curve SS', which goes up-

---

existence of quantity discounts is admitted into the model. Why should a firm offer quantity discounts if it can sell unlimited quantities at the prevailing competitive market price? On this, see George J. Stigler, *Production and Distribution Theories* (New York: The Macmillan Company, 1941), p. 82.

[9] The reader uninterested in the purely technical geometry of Marshall's analysis at this point can omit the following discussion without cutting the thread of the general argument. He is advised to turn to page 29.

ward and to the right. This curve is intersected by industry demand curve *DD'* going downward and to the right. In equilibrium the industry produces output *OA* and sells it at price *OR*. Consumer's surplus is the area of the triangle *DER*. Now let us impose a tax on this industry of amount *ST*. That is, each unit of output is now produced at an increased cost of *ST* per unit, and this fact is represented by the supply curve *TT'* lying above *SS'* by the amount of the per unit tax of *ST*. Note that the curve *TT'* now intersects demand curve *DD'* at *F*. Consumer's surplus has clearly been reduced by the amount *NREF*. But in this particular case, the receipts from the tax are *NFLK*, which are greater than the loss in consumer's surplus of *NREF*. So the tax receipts are greater than the loss in consumer's surplus.

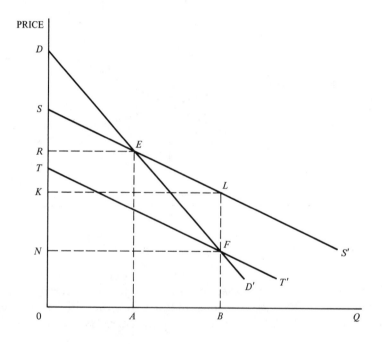

FIGURE 3.3

Now let us see what happens if we use these tax receipts to subsidize a decreasing cost industry, as depicted in Figure 3.3. Here the industry's supply curve *SS'* slopes downward and to the right indicating the presence of decreasing costs. In equilibrium, the industry produces the amount OA and sells it for price OR. Consumer's surplus is DER. Granting a subsidy to this industry of ST per unit of output reduces the supply curve or costs of production per unit of output in the amount ST, and the new supply curve is TT'. But note that consumer's surplus has been increased by the amount $NREF$, since the firm has expanded output from OA to OB. This is clearly greater than the total cost of the subsidy, $NKLF$. Through this expedient, therefore, consumer's surplus has been increased.

Marshall himself considered the above demonstration of rather slight importance. He recognized that his "proof" of the efficacy of government intervention was purely geometrical and depended on the slopes of the curves. Also, it was characteristic of his general reticence to break with the neoclassical model that he noted that indirect effects of taxes and subsidies could more than offset any gains in welfare to be made through their use. "These conclusions," he warned, "do not by themselves afford a valid ground for government interference . . . Much remains to be done . . . in order to discover what are the limits of the work that society can . . . do towards turning the economic actions of individuals into those channels in which they will add the most to the sum total of happiness."[10]

Hints at the direction of economic analysis and policy in the years immediately following Marshall already were contained in his *Principles*. Marshall's suggestion of the downward sloping demand curve as an explanation of the limits to the firm's expansion would have led directly to Chamberlin's monopolistic competition revolution in economics, if its full implications had been then understood. As we shall see, this upheaval had enormous impact on economic attitudes and policy prescriptions, especially in the 1950's and 1960's. Marshall's concept of externalities, although limited to a discussion of pecuniary and technological effects, was picked up by his pupil, A. C. Pigou, whose modification of it led to far-reaching implications regarding government intervention. Pigou also was to develop the Marshallian tax and subsidy scheme into elaborate proposals for modifying the neoclassical approach to economic problems. These in turn were also to have their major impact on policy in the 1960's. Moreover, Marshall's insistence on the view that economic science must proceed on a basis of continuity, on the assumption that "nature makes no leaps" in the Darwinian sense, was to become the watchword of the American institutionalists, who followed Thorstein Veblen in insisting that economics must become an

---

[10] Marshall, *Principles, op. cit.*, vol. 1, pp. 315-16.

"evolutionary science." Economics must rid itself of the pre-Darwinian view of the economic man with inborn and specially endowed propensities for rational calculation. Translated into the economic ideas of the 1960's, the doctrine of consumer rationality was to come under increasing fire, with all the implications for policy that discarding the presumption of consumer sovereignty would entail. And finally, Keynes was later to make Marshall's full employment model only a special case of a general theory of employment. The magnitude of the influence of Keynes's work on later economists and policy makers was to be unparalleled in the entire history of economic thought.

But we are getting ahead of our story. Marshall himself was dimly aware of the cataclysm that lay in store. In 1915, in a letter to one of his former students, he wrote:

> . . . a thousand years hence (1920-1970) will, I expect, be *the* time for historians. It drives me wild to think of it. I believe it will make my poor *Principles*, with a lot of poor comrades, into waste paper. The more I think of it, the less I can guess what the world will be like fifty years hence.[11]

What the world of economic theory and policy became in those 50 years is the subject matter of the chapters that follow.

---

[11] Keynes, *Memorials of Alfred Marshall, op. cit.,* 487-90.

PART II

THE ECLIPSE OF NEOCLASSICAL ECONOMICS

CHAPTER 4
THORSTEIN VEBLEN—
The Abrogation of
Consumer Sovereignty

... history records more frequent and more spectacular instances of the triumph of imbecile institutions over life and culture than of peoples who have by force of instinctive insight saved themselves alive out of a desperately precarious institutional situation, such as now ... faces the peoples of Christendom.

THORSTEIN VEBLEN

The foundations of neoclassical economic science, as outlined in the preceding chapters, are, the reader will possibly agree, formidable. Upon them was constructed a social science second to none in rigor or aesthetic qualities. The use of the tool of "margins" made the apparatus susceptible to manipulation by Euclidian geometry and the differential calculus. It was not long before the time and effort required for proficiency in its highly specialized vocabulary and theoretical techniques restricted the serious study of the economy to the trained specialist. After 1871, the subject emerged from relative obscurity and close association with theology, to a highly professional status.[1]

---

[1] *Cf.* John B. Parrish, "Rise of Economics as an Academic Discipline: The Formative Years to 1900," *Southern Economic Journal,* vol. XXXIV (July 1967), 1-16.

Nevertheless it has always been the case that the received view of economics has had its detractors, who have, in the main, willingly accepted the theoretical apparatus, but used it to turn it on itself. Karl Marx, for example, accepted the tools of classical economics. He simply took it as his task to draw their logical extension. Others, such as the influential American writer, Henry George, suggested heretical policy proposals from the most orthodox of doctrine: Ricardian differential rent theory.

With the neoclassical critics, this acceptance of method and scope was even more complete. Some only claimed to be refining the existing apparatus and, in so doing, asserted they had made its predecessors obsolete. This was true of A. C. Pigou and Edward Chamberlin. Or, as in the case of J. M. Keynes, they have rejected a part of the apparatus while retaining much of the whole. In what follows, we shall see examples of each of these.

But Thorstein Veblen is, in this, as in all else that came within his vision, unique. Reaching intellectual awareness in the heyday of the neoclassical revolution, Veblen was to become its most fervid and, in many ways, most misunderstood, critic. His biting satire and shrewdly perceptive idioms set a standard and style for critical discourse that was not soon reached again by professional economists.

To understand Veblen is to understand the roots of many of the ideas and attitudes of the disenchanted generation of young people today. A photograph of him at the age of 47 shows a heavily moustached man looking much like the portraits of Mark Twain: his long hair parted in the middle, leaning back in his chair holding a lighted cigarette between the thumb and forefinger of his left hand. Cigarettes were his one extravagance; they were supplied to him by one of his former students and cost $3\frac{1}{2}$ cents each. According to Joseph Dorfman,[2] his living quarters were furnished by objects of his own making. His furniture consisted of chairs and tables constructed of dry goods boxes which he covered with burlap. The ritual of making beds was considered a waste of energy, so the covers were merely drawn down over the foot of the bed so that they could be drawn up without much effort at night. A similar attitude prevailed with regard to other mundane household chores. Dishes were washed only when the cupboard was bare of such utensils. As each implement was used it was stacked in a tub, and when the total supply was exhausted the hose was turned on them.

His appearance was generally shoddy. A vivid picture of his de-

---

[2] Joseph Dorfman, *Thorstein Veblen and His America* (New York: The Viking Press, 1934). This book is the definitive full-length study of Veblen's life and works and is the source of most of the material on Veblen's life in this chapter.

meanor is provided by one of his students: "The first time I saw him, ambling along the Quad, with a slouch hat pulled down over his brow, with coat and trousers 'hanging'; with untrimmed hair and moustache creating a general unkempt appearance, I thought he was a tramp."[3] The most obvious traits were a shaggy head of hair and a frizzly beard. Student reminiscences tell of his cast-off-like clothing, his collar several times too large, and a coat and vest that rarely matched. He had a fondness for safety pins: his watch was attached to a piece of black ribbon which was pinned to the front of his vest; and when he sat down in front of his class and drew up his trouser legs, "his sturdy woolen hose was revealed to be held up by equally sturdy safety pins."[4] In a photograph taken of him in 1920 (reproduced as the frontispiece of Dorfman's book) two safety pins can be seen, one attached to the top of his vest, perhaps to be used as a spare in the event of an unforeseen contingency, the other keeping the ends of his collar neatly in place.[5]

He led a life that became legendary with every economist having his favorite "Veblen story." His attractiveness to many American intellectuals and students doubtless derives in part from his anti-Establishment sentiments and style, his refusal to conform to the conventional modes of conduct, and his general sense of helplessness.[6] Many of the film heroes of the long-haired youth of American campuses are admired for the very traits that Veblen possessed. When students applaud W. C. Fields' or the Marx Brothers' high-camp flaunting of middle class conventions (shocking uppity dowagers, putting things over on stuffed shirts), they are approving the irreverent attitudes that Veblen affected.

Born to Norwegian immigrants in 1857 on a farm in Wisconsin, Veblen was seven years old when the family moved to Minnesota.

---

[3] *Ibid.*, p. 274.

[4] *Ibid.*, p. 313.

[5] In this, ironically, Veblen was a forerunner of leisure class fashions. He would doubtless have gotten wry amusement from the fact that safety pin type collar pins later became quite stylish, often being made of 14-karat gold. And, as C. E. Ayres has suggested, Veblen was a "charter member of the do-it-yourself club" having deep respect for mechanical ability and even the simplest skills. C. E. Ayres, "Veblen's Theory of Instincts Reconsidered" in D. Dowd, ed., *Thorstein Veblen: A Critical Reappraisal* (Ithaca: Cornell University Press, 1958), p. 28.

[6] Veblen's anti-Establishment attitude even led him to reject the highest honor that can be given by the American economics profession: the nomination to the presidency of the American Economic Association. In 1925, when the chairman of the nominating committee offered the presidency to Veblen (on condition that Veblen join the association and agree to deliver a presidential address) Veblen refused the offer with the comment, "They didn't offer it to me when I needed it." See Dorfman, *Thorstein Veblen and His America*, p. 492.

Later he attended Carleton College in Northfield. It was characteristic of his father's old world authoritarianism that young Thorstein was never consulted on his choice of school. He first learned that he was to enter Carleton when the family buggy deposited him there. It was at Carleton that Veblen came into contact with economics, at the hands of one of its most distinguished neoclassicists—John Bates Clark. At this time, Clark was working out the principles of his approach to marginal productivity theory of factor prices. Clark, alone among the members of the faculty, liked Veblen. He considered him the most acute thinker among his students, in spite of the fact that at weekly public declamation exercises Veblen delivered papers defending cannibalism and drunkards.

It was at Carleton that Veblen met the girl who was later to become his first wife, Ellen Rolfe, the niece of the President of Carleton, and the daughter of one of the first families of the midwest. After graduation, Veblen entered Johns Hopkins University where he studied philosophy and political economy. One of his teachers was Charles Sanders Peirce and a fellow student was John Dewey, both of whom helped found that distinctly American school of philosophy known as pragmatism. But Veblen was disappointed with Hopkins and stayed less than a year. He then entered Yale, studied under William Graham Sumner, and took his Ph.D. in philosophy in 1884. But he was unable to obtain an academic position. College teachers with a philosophical bent were ordinarily chosen from the ranks of divinity students. So Veblen returned as a failure to his hometown community, where he was to remain seven years.

During this period he read avidly. In Dorfman's words:

> As one pile of books disappeared, he promptly secured another. For days all that one could see of him was the top of his head at the garret window. For intellectual companionship he had his remarkably keen father. He told Ellen Rolfe upon his return from Yale that he had never met his father's intellectual equal. When Veblen was puzzled over some economic problem, he would go out and follow along by his father's plough to talk it over with him. When the day's work was done, Thomas Veblen would leisurely discuss abstruse topics with his son while they smoked.[7]

Veblen and Ellen Rolfe were married four years after his return from Yale. But Veblen still found it impossible to get an academic

---

[7] *Ibid.*, p. 57.

post notwithstanding his Ph.D., his wife's connections, and letters of recommendation from John Bates Clark. Finally, a family council decided that Veblen should reenter academic work if only as a student. His "inactive" period of seven years was difficult to explain to university administrators, and the idea was that he should register at a respectable university and make a fresh start. He decided to enter the field of economics at Cornell University. The chairman of the department was J. Laurence Laughlin, a leading exponent of neoclassical economics. Wearing a coon-skin cap and corduroy trousers, Veblen entered Laughlin's study in Ithaca and announced simply, "I am Thorstein Veblen." That was the first Cornell University knew of his intention to enter. But Laughlin was impressed by the strange young man and was able to secure a special fellowship for him. Veblen remained at Cornell one year, and when Laughlin was appointed head of the economics department at the new University of Chicago, one of the conditions of his acceptance was that he could bring Veblen with him. Veblen was now 35 years old.

At Chicago, Veblen pursued his keen interest in anthropology and induced his better students to read extensively in such works. It was this study that led to his dissatisfaction with a major pillar of neoclassical economics. He wrote one of his students at this time:

> As for the anthropological reading, which I have inveigled you into, I do not know that it will be of much direct use, but it should be of some use in the sense of an acquaintance with mankind. Not that man as viewed by the anthropologist is any more—perhaps he is less—human than man as we see him in everyday life and in commercial life; but the anthropological survey should give a view of man in perspective and more in the generic than is ordinarily attained by the classical economists, and should give added breath and sobriety to the concept of 'the economic man.'[8]

When he was 42 years old he published his first major work, a volume that contained the essence of the arguments he was to make against the classical model of the economy for the rest of his life. The book was called *The Theory of the Leisure Class* and almost immediately catapulted Veblen into fame.[9] Its literary style, as Veblen himself remarked, was polysyllabic. Readers believed him to be a satirist of the most penetrating sort and *aficionados* of language sought him

---

[8] *Ibid.*, pp. 132-33.

[9] T. Veblen, *The Theory of the Leisure Class* (New York: The New American Press, 1953). Originally published in 1899.

out to address their literary clubs. But Veblen always refused. For he was disappointed at the popularity of the work, since he felt that those who praised it most highly had misunderstood its message. Veblen coined many new phrases which were to become part of the vocabulary, words like "conspicuous consumption," "the higher learning," "captains of industry." Not until John Kenneth Galbraith's "affluent society" and "conventional wisdom" did another economist leave his imprint on the language. Dorfman has pointed out that "overnight the language on the university campus changed, and it was said that those who read Veblen could be distinguished by their speech."[10] His old mentor John Bates Clark was delighted at his success and claimed that Veblen had fulfilled his promise.

The Veblenian Dichotomy

The book itself carries out a theme that Veblen had inaugurated in some of his earlier papers on economics. In them he had developed his hunch, derived from his anthropological studies, that every society can be characterized in terms of a dichotomy between those aspects that are dynamic and those that are static. The dynamic qualities of a culture are those that contribute to what he termed "the life process," while those that were static were inhibitory of human life and work. To Veblen, the dynamic aspect was closely related to those activities in which problems were solved through the use of tools, modern science, and matter-of-fact thinking. It is clear that Veblen identifies these activities with the "economic life process" which was "still in great measure awaiting theoretical formulation."[11] An inquiry into this economic life process would deal with the process of cumulative change in society which results from changes in technology—"the methods of dealing with the material means of life." The keynote of all Veblen's thinking was that such tool-using—technological activities derived from man's "instinct of workmanship," "idle curiosity," and the "parental bent." These created a desire within the human breast to see in all human effort and enjoyment an enhancement of life.

The other aspect of culture was represented by those activities which were of an essentially "ceremonial" character. When Veblen speaks of ceremonial behavior, he is talking about the authoritarian, taboo-ridden, emotion-fraught aspect of behavior which is contrary to the life process

---

[10] Dorfman, *Thorstein Veblen and His America*, p. 197.

[11] T. Veblen, "Why Is Economics Not an Evolutionary Science?," *The Place of Science in Modern Civilisation* (New York: Russell & Russell, 1961), p. 70.

and is static by its very nature. These activities of man derived their sanction not from their ability to solve pressing problems, but simply because they are ancient and therefore honorable. The institutions of society have a binding force that derives from the past and are change-resisting because they are linked to the "dawn history" of the tribe. It is from hereditary status that all taboos derive their sanction. Veblen's study of anthropology and of Darwin convinced him that this aspect of behavior (characterized by superstition, teleological thought processes, ritualistic activities) can be projected back to the beginning of human organization, in which certain relationships among men were imbedded in the mores, which the people of the community accept as right and good and which have a tendency to gain priority in order, rank, and importance in social questions.

Just as the "technological" forces were represented by the workmanship proclivity in man's instinctive makeup, the "ceremonial" processes are representative of an opposing instinct, an acquisitive "sportsman-like" propensity in man. It is the clash of opposing instincts in man's nature that has given rise to the dichotomization of culture into dynamic and static elements—that aspect of social life in which tools and instruments are used and that other aspect pervaded by folklore, mana, and mystic potencies.

With this dichotomy, Veblen dissected all behavior and institutions. In his *Theory of the Leisure Class*, Veblen analyzed the consumption patterns of our modern society and found the dichotomy in clear and unequivocal form.

Yet neoclassical economic theory made no such distinction. For in the received doctrine, one kind of expenditure is no less legitimate than any other. An additional dollar spent on the purchase of a diamond bracelet or package of cigarettes is no different in terms of welfare, and therefore efficiency, from an additional dollar spent on insulin by a diabetic. As long as the additional utilities per dollar spent on the items are equated, welfare is maximized. From the point of view of the individual consumer and from the point of view of economic science, there is no question of "waste."

But Veblen rejected the neoclassical notion of the economic man carefully equating his utilities. Furthermore he believed that "waste" is an economic factor which can be analyzed and about which much can be said of a scientific sort. It is only because economics is not an evolutionary science that the neoclassical preconception of man's behavior could have come to dominate the analysis. This framework sees man as an isolated datum, an island of satisfaction. Consumers are supposedly competing for consumer goods by equating their marginal evaluations to prices, and factors of production are moving to the manufacture of those goods and services for which consumers have valued the factors' marginal product highest.

If economic science were couched in terms of "cause-and-effect" Darwinian terms, the static ceremonial elements of consumer behavior would be recognized. For habit and convention, emulation and display, emotion and superstitious irrationality make up much of the motive for consumption:

> Not only is the individual's conduct hedged about and directed by his habitual relations to his fellows in the group, but these relations, being of an institutional character, vary as the institutional scene varies. The wants and desires, the end and aim, the ways and means, the amplitude and drift of the individual's conduct are functions of an institutional variable that is of a highly complex and wholly unstable character.[12]

The neoclassical notion of economic man is based on the psychology of hedonism—the view that man is motivated by the pursuit of pleasure maximization in an isolated state of nature. Veblen's caricature of neoclassical theory's economic man is one of the most quoted examples of his witty, sardonic style:

> The hedonistic conception of man is that of a lightning calculator of pleasures and pains, who oscillates like a homogeneous globule of desire of happiness under the impulse of stimuli that shift him about the area, but leave him intact. He has neither antecedent nor consequent. He is an isolated, definitive human datum, in stable equilibrium except for the buffets of impinging forces that displace him in one direction or another. Self-imposed in elemental space, he spins symmetrically about his own spiritual axis until the parallelogram of forces bears down upon him, whereupon he follows the line of the resultant. When the force of the impact is spent, he comes to rest, a self-contained globule of desire as before.[13]

The Veblenian dichotomy was utilized to show that the neoclassical principles that were outlined in the preceding chapters are not really useful in determining welfare from the point of view of the "life process." For the present enjoyment of goods by a consumer depends not

---

12 T. Veblen, "The Limitations of Marginal Utility," *Ibid.*, pp. 242-43.
13 T. Veblen, "Why Is Economics Not an Evolutionary Science?," pp. 73-74.

so much on rational calculation as on the consumption patterns of others, habit, and the desire for emulative display and conspicuous consumption. Moreover, to Veblen such consumption is wasteful in the sense that it does not serve human life. This judgment is a value judgment, but one that has a scientific basis in the "instinct of workmanship." The competitive advantage of one consumer over another does not satisfy this instinctual craving in man, who must see in all human activities "usefulness" from the point of view of being generically human. Competitive expenditure does not therefore have the approval of conscience and does not square with the notion that consumption must result in a net gain in the fullness of life. So an expenditure is waste if the custom or institution on which it rests can be traced to invidious pecuniary comparisons. Instead of standards in consumption being set by considerations of this life process, they have, through a "contamination" of the instinct of workmanship, come to be determined by the usage of those next above in reputability. This means that ultimately all standards are set by the wealthy leisure class.

In this way Veblen showed that man's sense of beauty is set by wastefulness. The perversion of man's technological proclivity by culture is such that the less well adaptable is an object to its ostensible use, the more beautiful it is. Thus, for example, a machine-made spoon of aluminum has a brute efficiency as compared to a hand-wrought spoon of silver. The latter is conspicuously wasteful and therefore more beautiful. So our sense of costliness masquerades under the name of beauty:

> The high gloss of a gentleman's hat or of a patent leather shoe has no more intrinsic beauty than a similarly high gloss on a threadbare sleeve; and yet there is no question but that all well-bred people . . . instinctively and unaffectedly cleave to the one as a phenomenon of great beauty and eschew the other as offensive to every sense to which it can appeal.[14]

The End of Consumer Sovereignty

What Veblen has done, of course, is to bring into question the whole notion of consumer sovereignty. Once it is recognized that the utility a consumer receives depends on the consumption patterns of others; or that consumer satisfaction depends on habitual patterns of behavior; or that culture has so perverted man's instinct of workmanship that he

---

[14] Veblen, *The Theory of the Leisure Class*, p. 97.

does not know what is good for him; then the view that laissez-faire brings about the maximization of welfare in consumption does not necessarily follow.

If a consumer buys an expensive automobile only in order to receive utility from the emulation of one's neighbors, the individual might be better off if there were a simultaneous restriction of consumption by everyone. Moreover, if his conspicuous consumption of expensive jewelry causes deep dissatisfaction to envious persons, the price paid for the jewels does not reflect the reduction in satisfaction that others have experienced. So under such circumstances relative prices are not a reliable guide to relative satisfactions. This means that the interferences with laissez-faire by the state might increase satisfaction by, for example, taxing the purchase of jewelry and compensating those who lose satisfaction from seeing others display them. When there are external diseconomies in consumption, to allow the allocation of resources at the dictates of consumers no longer can be guaranteed to maximize satisfaction. Thus Veblen, in making economic man into social man upset the policy implications of neoclassical consumption theory.

Veblen went even further in applying his dichotomy in his later critiques of the market economy. In *The Theory of Business Enterprise*,[15] he carried his distinction between "industrial and pecuniary employments" into the distinction between making goods and making money. And in a series of articles published in 1908, he developed the dichotomy into the distinction between industrial processes and business activities. In his book and essays, he made the point that gain from a business investment is often in direct proportion to its retarding effect on the life process of the community. The institution of ownership gives the owner of industrial technology not only the right of use of the economy's material equipment, but also the right of abuse and neglect. Such destructive behavior affords an income to the investor which, like any other income, can be capitalized. This gain can be realized through the "advised idleness" of the industrial plant, a method which does nothing to enhance the livelihood or satisfy the desires of the community. So we find as a common trait of modern life the "capitalization of inefficiency" through misdirecting the industrial process, preventing efficiency, and inhibiting output.

Moreover, a great many enterprises do not have to rely on nonproduction for these dubious benefits. Such establishments as racetracks, saloons, and gambling houses derive their profits for their owners

---

[15] T. Veblen, *The Theory of Business Enterprise* (New York: Charles Scribner's Sons, 1904).

through activities that are suggestive of probable net detriment to mankind.[16]

Furthermore, a large amount of technological equipment is engaged in manufacturing products in which disserviceability is mingled with waste. For example, goods of fashion, proprietary articles, sophisticated household supplies, and advertising enterprise; all of these draw their profits from "skilled mandacity," owing their value to a perverse use of the technology employed. Capital, therefore, is of two kinds: industrial capital, which is technologically serviceable, and ceremonial capital, which is valued in terms of the income which it yields to its owner. The community's evaluation of the latter determines its worth, and so a vast amount of effort is put into advertising in order to influence a favorable consideration. Thus the main interest of the entrepreneur is in making money, not in making goods. And the making of money is often in direct proportion to the amount of disturbance and sabotage to industrial processes that the entrepreneur can create.[17]

Veblen believed that the domination of life and work by business enterprise and industrial sabotage was a transitory phenomenon. For the machine process inculcated into individuals a matter-of-fact, cause and effect way of thinking incompatible with ceremony and superstition. As a new breed of highly trained and specially gifted experts become more and more essential to the operation of business enterprise, "these expert men, technologists, engineers, or whatever name may best suit them, make up the indispensable General Staff of the industrial system; and without their immediate and unremitting guidance and correction the industrial system will not work."[18]

These technological experts will ultimately develop a sense of "class-consciousness" that will lead them to see that the waste and confusion resulting from the management of industrial processes by absentee owners and financial managers could be eliminated by a general strike and the establishment of a "soviet of technicians" who would take no account of absentee ownership. ". . . [T]here is the patent fact that such a thing as a general strike of the technological specialists in industry need involve no more than a minute fraction of one percent of the population; yet it would swiftly bring a collapse of the old order

---

[16] T. Veblen, "On the Nature of Capital," *The Place of Science in Modern Civilisation*, p, 358.

[17] Veblen's analysis of "sabotage" is developed most completely in his *The Engineers and the Price System* (New York: The Viking Press, Inc., 1921), especially chap. I.

[18] *Ibid.*, p. 69.

and sweep the timeworn fabric of finance and absentee sabotage into the discard for good and all."[19]

Veblen's academic career probably was not bolstered by his unorthodox views on business culture. What is more, his lack of discretion in his personal affairs and various amatory scandals involving coeds made his position with university administrators untenable. He moved from Chicago to Stanford to the University of Missouri and eventually to The New School for Social Research. Notwithstanding his international reputation, he never rose above the rank of associate professor.

When he retired to his cabin near Palo Alto, he was lonely and neglected. His finances were in a parlous state. Ill health and an uneasy state of mind plagued him in his final days. On August 3, 1929, he died knowing that he had not set economics on what he considered the right track. But his influence on succeeding generations of economists was to become evermore pronounced, culminating in the mid-twentieth century in the writings of Galbraith, where Veblen's conspicuous consumers and efficiency experts were to reappear in a form and at a time that seemed eminently ripe for them. David Riesman has summarized Veblen's contribution to social science:

> Whatever our debt to the theories Veblen developed, I think we are all in his debt for his way of thinking. Irreverent and catty to the very end, he avoided becoming a substantial citizen, which he defined as one who owns much property. He died insolvent. But the intangible assets that have come down to us, his books and his personal style, have still the power over us that Veblen was all too inclined to disparage: the power of ideas and of personality.[20]

---

[19] *Ibid.*, pp. 81-82.
[20] David Riesman, *Thorstein Veblen, A Critical Interpretation* (New York: Charles Scribner's Sons, 1953), p. 208.

CHAPTER 5

ARTHUR CECIL PIGOU—
Externalities in Production

Wonder, Carlyle declared, is the beginning of philosophy. It is not wonder, but rather the social enthusiasm which revolts from the sordidness of mean streets and the joylessness of withered lives, that is the beginning of economic science.

A. C. PIGOU

Thorstein Veblen's earliest impact was on a generation of young American economists and social scientists who called for radical experimentation and restructuring of property relationships during the Great Depression. Some of them were to prove influential in the New Deal and indeed were to take the name for Roosevelt's administration from Veblen's own works.[1] The early Veblenians took as their text the

---

[1] Disciples of Veblen are generally considered to be members of a school of economic thought called "institutionalism." The label is misleading since it identifies this school with the nontechnological forces which they consider inhibitory of progress, rather than with the technological forces which they consider crucial in contributing to human well-being. But no terms that alternatively have been suggested (instrumentalism, technologism) have "taken." Without doubt, the leading institutionalists in the Veblenian tradition are John Kenneth Galbraith and C. E. Ayres. Ayres's work is noteworthy for being explicitly and avowedly indebted to Veblen, and because it contains a theoretical framework for understanding this approach to the study of the economy. See C. E. Ayres, *The Theory of Economic Progress* (New York: Schocken Books, 1962), and C. E. Ayres, *Toward A Reasonable Society* (Austin: University of Texas Press, 1961).

Engineers and the Price System, calling for a rule of the engineers and technocrats to bring order out of the chaos of the Great Depression. As we shall see John Maynard Keynes's message at this period was equally dramatic. He attempted to show how the capitalist system could be saved from its greatest threat—the revolution of the unemployed masses—through extensive governmental spending policies. While Veblen was working out his ideas on the "imbecile institutions" of the market economy, John Maynard Keynes was studying under a man who was working on problems which seemed less spectacular, but were ultimately to prove just as challenging as Keynes's and Veblen's policies for the survival of the free enterprise system. For no one had yet shown a satisfactory resolution of the conflict between privacy and freedom. To this Cambridge economist, the belching chimneys and car exhausts that contaminate our air, blacken our laundry, and burn our eyes; the waste materials of our fully employed factories that pollute our streams and rivers, killing our fish and wildlife; and the noise of our blaring auto horns and high-powered stereos disturbing the nightly tranquility of our crowded neighborhoods were par excellence the weak link in the neoclassical logic of unfettered individualism.

The economist who considered these disturbing problems in their explicit form and jarred the complacency with which the policy implications of neoclassicism were held was one of the most paradoxical figures in the history of economics. He had the rather odd name of Pigou, but his personality and eccentricities were well suited to the oddness of his name. In truth, there were two Pigous in the professional career of one individual. On the one hand, he was a leading exemplar of the neoclassical school of thought. Indeed, John Maynard Keynes was to use Pigou as the epitome of the neoclassical viewpoint on full employment analysis, which Keynes would set out to annihilate. Pigou himself struck back by referring to Keynes's *General Theory* as "this macedoine of misrepresentations."[2] And to many younger students of economics, Pigou's name is inextricably linked with the "Pigou effect," an argument in answer to Keynes that attempted to rehabilitate neoclassical employment theory by demonstrating its logical completeness under the classical assumptions of wage and price flexibility.

On the other hand, Pigou must be credited with having pioneered the contemporary concern with the untoward social consequences of private actions, and hence with one chief aspect of the contemporary

---

[2] It is characteristic of his objectivity of mind that he was later to change his appraisal of Keynes, although he had been deeply offended.

attack on the laissez-faire model. Pigou raised his disturbing questions as early as 1912 in his book *Wealth and Welfare*.[3] Economists were to wait almost a half-century before realizing that the issues Pigou had grappled with were among the most important facing an opulent economy, indeed were to threaten the very legitimacy of the system. But few economists then understood the nature of the breakthrough in analysis that Pigou had made. The critics of capitalism, until Pigou, had questioned the stability of the system itself and argued for alternative systems of economic order. Frank Knight, alone among the reviewers of Pigou's first edition of *The Economics of Welfare* in 1920,[4] noted the significant fact that Pigou had shifted the debate from the choice between alternative systems of economic order, to the methods of changing and improving the already functioning system. Professor Harry Johnson, in his touching obituary for Pigou, comments that Pigou's analysis, in shifting the argument from revolutionary change to the methods of improving the existing system, "was at once its originality, in the period when Pigou first developed it, and its obvious limitation during the troubled inter-war period which followed its publication. Now that the Keynesian Revolution has been digested, and the political divisions of the thirties and forties have been reconciled in a system of welfare capitalism, economists are becoming increasingly occupied with policy problems of the kind with which Pigou was concerned, and in whose analysis he was the pioneer."[5] John Kenneth Galbraith later was to make us critically aware of the "unevenness of our blessings," popularizing many of the problems Pigou clearly foresaw almost a half-century before anyone else was to take notice.

One of the strangest men in a science noted for its curious personalities, Pigou's character went through an extreme transformation. In his early days he was a gay, joke-loving, social, hospitable bachelor, but he later turned into a rather eccentric recluse. His lifelong friend and colleague, C. R. Fay, explained the metamorphosis as follows: "World War I was a shock to him, and he was never the same afterwards." He had spent most of his vacations from Cambridge in voluntary ambulance work at the front in France, Belgium, and Italy, and was sickened by what he saw. Very early in his career, he recognized the intimate relationship between social and economic problems, reflecting a passion

[3] A. C. Pigou, *Wealth and Welfare* (London: Macmillan & Co., Ltd., 1912).

[4] A. C. Pigou, *Economics of Welfare*, 4th ed. (London: Macmillan & Co., Ltd., 1932).

[5] Harry Johnson, "Arthur Cecil Pigou, 1877-1959," *Canadian Journal of Economics and Political Science*, vol. 26, no. 1 (February 1960), 155.

for both humanistic and scientific concerns. As a student, Pigou displayed a rare ability to excel in both aspects of human knowledge. At the age of 24, he won prizes for two essays, the titles of which give striking evidence of the diverse concerns of the young scholar. One was called "The Causes and Effects of Changes in the Related Values of Agricultural Produce in the United Kingdom during the Last Fifty Years"; the other, "Robert Browning as a Religious Teacher." Two years earlier he had won a gold medal for English verse, with an ode on Alfred the Great. (After the war, with his change in mood, he sold the medal to aid in the relief of starving Georgians.) Upon graduating from King's College, Cambridge, he spent his time lecturing, publishing, and engaging in debate on tariff reform, an issue that was to absorb him until late in life.

A former student has described Pigou's personal appearance in mid-1940's as a tall, straight figure, eccentrically garbed, glimpsed occasionally walking about the countryside or reclining in a deck chair on the grass by the porter's lodge inside Cambridge's front court. He was to remain in his deck chair during Nazi air raids as a defiance to Hitler. Pigou had a well-earned reputation for sartorial economy, appearing in the 1950's at the Marshall Library proudly attired in a pre-World War I suit.

Like many shy personalities who protect themselves by affecting a curmudgeon pose, Pigou's inconsistencies in his prejudices often charmed his acquaintances and proved disarming. Claiming that they lacked the capacity for intellectual integrity, Pigou pretended that he could not tolerate women, foreigners, or politicians. But he made exceptions in each case. He compared women to "that variety of spider which acquires a mate and in due course devours him." Needless to say, Pigou remained a bachelor throughout his life. Yet, he welcomed honeymoon couples to his beautifully situated cottage. Although most foreign economists, and especially Americans, were persona non grata, he was extremely gracious to Alvin Hansen and his wife. And while he taught his undergraduates that "the main purpose of learning economics was to be able to see through the bogus economic arguments of the politicians," he listened with admiration to the speeches of Winston Churchill.[6] Pigou allowed himself to acquire a reputation for being a hermit-like recluse, yet he often invited undergraduates and faculty members to his cottage in Buttermere, taking pleasure in astonishing

---

[6] D. G. Champernowne, "Arthur Cecil Pigou 1877-1959," *Royal Statistical Society Journal*, vol. 122, pt. II (1959), 264.

his visitors by awarding them his war medals for their exploits in hill walking and rock climbing.

He was a stimulating conversationalist, and much like Veblen, a rejector of ceremony in all its forms. Late in his life, when he presided over a meeting of his College in the election of a new Provost, he described the outcomes of the successive returns as though calling a horse race, to the obvious displeasure of the assembled Fellows.

At the age of 30, when he took over the Chair of Political Economy of his beloved mentor, Alfred Marshall, he made a powerful statement of his version of what economics is about:

> If it were not for the hope that a scientific study of man's social actions may lead . . . to practical results in social improvement, I should myself . . . regard the time devoted to that study as misspent . . . If I desired knowledge of man apart from the fruits of knowledge, I should seek it in the history of religious enthusiasm, of passion, of martyrdom and of love; I should not seek it in the marketplace.[7]

But it was to the marketplace that Pigou was to turn his cool and reflective eye.

Externalities and Market Failure

To Pigou, all was not well in the laissez-faire market. Where his neoclassical forebears and colleagues saw efficient allocation, Pigou saw waste. Where the received doctrine spelled out welfare through equating at the margin, Pigou saw that the incorrect use of margins was leading to faulty conclusions. Businessmen, in pursuing their own self interest in the free market economy, were creating "externalities" by which they profited at society's expense, or others in society were profiting at their expense. In the former case, too much product from society's viewpoint was being provided; in the latter case, too little. In order to get a clear grasp of Pigou's argument, it will be necessary to examine the meaning of the term "externality," and the background of its development.

The halcyon environment guaranteed by the neoclassical economic analysis rested in part on the conclusion that, from a social viewpoint, economic welfare is maximized under laissez-faire competitive conditions. In equilibrium, marginal costs equal marginal benefits. The profit maximizing producer is always induced to bear the cost incurred in

---

[7] Johnson, *op. cit.*, 152.

producing an extra unit of product, while the utility maximizing consumer will pay a price just equal to the marginal satisfaction he derives from its consumption. That is why free competition and free choice had such appeal to the neoclassical writers. What man of good will (and a sufficiently libertarian bent of mind) could complain if the costs of production and the benefits of consumption were borne entirely by the parties involved in any transaction? Since the whole is always equal to the sum of its parts, all costs and all benefits being incurred by the individuals in society precisely in proportion to their participation in production and consumption, social welfare is optimized.

But Pigou asked, what if there is a divergence between the private and the social product? That is, what if the private production of a commodity yields social benefits surpassing the purely personal satisfaction yielded to the consumer who buys it? Or, alternatively, what happens to the welfare of society under perfect competition and consumer sovereignty, if the private production of a commodity has negative, unpleasant, disturbing, or other costly effects on innocent third parties? Would not the market mechanism then fail to take the full costs and benefits of production into account? Would not too much of some goods be produced and too little of others (from society's viewpoint)? And, if so, what happens to the esteem with which we learned to view the neoclassical model?

The classical and neoclassical economists had dichotomized the economic system into rigid zones: that area where no restraints should be imposed upon private actions, and that area of extreme cases where the government could intervene. The latter cases were usually summed up under the rubrics of "monopoly" and "paternalism." To Adam Smith, there were certain enterprises such as national defense and those "public institutions, which, though they may be in the highest degree advantageous to a great society, are, however, of such a nature, that the profit could never repay the expense to any individual." But the Master was magnificently vague about the extent of such enterprises and, aside from a few remarks about those institutions that facilitate commerce and instruct the people, there was little elaboration. By the time John Stuart Mill published the very last edition of his *Principles of Political Economy*, he was thought to have been something of a socialist. Yet he still maintained that the only obvious limitation to a laissez-faire policy was in the case of minors and lunatics who were clearly incapable of knowing their own self-interest.

Pigou was not the first to demur. In 1883, a British economist and philosopher, Henry Sidgwick, had broken with the traditional approach. To Sidgwick, a clear-cut boundary did not exist between the areas of governmental action and private enterprise. He fashioned the analytical tool that Pigou was later to sharpen and refine: the distinction and possible divergencies between the private and social net products which create *externalities* or *neighborhood effects*. Sidgwick cast doubt on the proposition that in a competitive laissez-faire system, an individual's claims on wealth will always be exactly equal to his net contribution to society, a result that the neoclassical model had implied. Sidgwick, in elucidating his point, referred to the case of a lighthouse, an example that economists have used ever since to illustrate a good that must be provided collectively if it is to be provided in an amount satisfying society's desires. If a lighthouse is financed privately by a person who produces it for his own consumption, motivated perhaps solely by considerations of his own benefit, he will unintentionally provide external economies or benefits to others. This is what Sidgwick meant when he said the marginal social product may exceed the marginal private product. Since this is the case, and not being able to exclude others from the light's benefits, he may very well hope that some more altruistically minded individual will build the lighthouse, enabling him to act as a "free rider." It follows that the socially optimal number of lighthouses do not get constructed. And so Sidgwick made a case for government intervention, or collective provision of this *public-good*, as later economists were to call it.

Pigou took Sidgwick's lead in this analysis, going far beyond him in developing realistic examples of externalities, and in suggesting a scheme for resolving the serious problems they pose for a free society.

To Pigou, only by eliminating the divergencies between the marginal private and marginal social products, would society's welfare be maximized. He even went so far as to assert that the chief duty of the economist is to identify and eliminate the divergencies.

In the *Economics of Welfare*, Pigou states that his aim is to show that the world of Adam Smith and neoclassical orthodoxy is indeed a dream world. Far from the economic system requiring little state action, the system has performed as well as it has *because* of governmental action. If self-interest promotes human welfare, it is only because human institutions have been designed to bring about this salubrious result. The problem is to determine what government action is still required. In Pigou's words, his task is "to bring into clearer light some of the ways in which it now is, or eventually may become, feasible for governments to control the play of economic forces in such wise as to promote the economic welfare, and through that, the total welfare, of their citizens as a whole."[8]

---

[8] Pigou, *Economics of Welfare, op. cit.*, pp. 129-30.

In his first example of a divergence between private and social products, Pigou refers to the case of railway engines that damage the surrounding woods and crops by emitting sparks. In such an instance, Pigou recommends that the railways should be forced to compensate the crop and forest owners whose property is damaged. Otherwise, the true output of society is incorrectly calculated. For one must reckon the "uncompensated damage" done to the owners of property who have suffered losses due to the action of others over whom they have no control. To Pigou, all that was required was a change in the liability laws requiring compensation for such damages. If the railway is not made liable, it does not take into account the real marginal costs of running an additional train. If it did so, it might in fact decide not to run the train, thus sparing the crops for the use of society. It is the lack of state action, in the form of stringent compulsory liability charges, that is the source of the divergence between private and social products.

A second case of divergence, according to Pigou, comes about because one person, in the course of rendering some service to a second person, incidentally also renders services to third parties, of such a sort that payment cannot be exacted from them.[9] The reader will note that Sidgwick's lighthouse would be an example of such an externality. Pigou chooses a case perhaps more appropriate to an industrial society. He discusses the situation in which a factory owner who, attempting to reduce the air pollution caused by the production of his firm's commodity, goes to the expense of installing a smoke-preventing device. Since he cannot, under the neoclassical laissez-faire model, receive payment for such services, it is unlikely that enough smog prevention will be provided. Thus we must violate the neoclassical policy prescription. Factory owners with chimneys belching smoke should be given bounties to encourage the installation of smokeless smoke stacks. Pigou then turned his attention to the problems of urban blight. He cast a jaundiced eye at the factories in residential areas destroying the amenities of the neighborhood. In Pigou's view, we should not let our obsession with the neoclassical model blind us to the realities of contracted airspace, the disappearing playing room for our children, and the crowded neighborhoods. For the health and efficiency of the families in our cities are being sacrificed to the ideology of the free unfettered market. Only state interference, forcing the appropriate fines and subsidies bringing marginal social and marginal private costs and benefits

---

[9] *Ibid.*, p. 183. Most of this analysis had appeared in Pigou's *Wealth and Welfare* in 1912.

into equality, can right the wrongs, and bring about the results that the neoclassical model was supposed to guarantee. The rules of liability must be clear. Only the state can set the rules and enforce them. Pigou, in attacking the problems of urban blight, polluted rivers and air, and other "uncompensated damages"—problems which seem so pressing in the latter half of the twentieth century—was indeed a man ahead of his time. To those of his contemporaries calling for violent change, his suggestion of fines and subsidies to redress the balance must surely have seemed inadequate palliatives. But Pigou persisted in believing that such governmental action, mild as it seemed to firebrand revolutionaries, was all that was needed to make the classical model relevant for the twentieth century industrial economy. His influence was to be felt later, after the Keynesian revolution had been digested, on such economists as Hansen, Galbraith, and Samuelson. What we call the welfare state today is in no small measure the outgrowth of attitudes and policies prescribed in the *Economics of Welfare*. But if his ideas have had an impact on us, no one would have been more surprised that Pigou. More like Veblen, and less like his student Keynes, he had little hope for the power of ideas to transform our lives. A skeptical man, he stated in his presidential address to the Royal Economic Society in 1939, ". . . the hope that an advance in economic knowledge will appreciably affect actual happenings is . . . a slender one. It is not likely that there will be a market for our produce. None the less . . . we cultivate our garden. For we also follow, not thought but an impulse—the impulse to inquire—which, futile though it may prove, is at least not ignoble."[10]

---

[10] A. C. Pigou, "Reminiscences of Changes in the Economics Profession," *Economic Journal* (June 1939), 221.

CHAPTER 6

EDWARD HASTINGS CHAMBERLIN—The Wastes of Competition

The force of his own merit makes his way.
Inscription under picture of
E. H. Chamberlin, 1916
Yearbook, Iowa City High
School

In 1921, a graduate student at the University of Michigan wrote a paper discussing the ability of railroads to charge discriminatory rates on different classes of freight. He was puzzled why theorists such as A. C. Pigou and Frank Taussig could not agree as to the reason for such rate-making power. The student was Edward H. Chamberlin, and the ideas in the paper were sufficiently original that his professor suggested it be submitted to the *Quarterly Journal of Economics*. It was returned, as Chamberlin noted much later, "no doubt with the highly relevant comment to the effect that it needed more cultivation both intensive and extensive."[1] The details of the argument in the paper are no longer of great concern; what is important is that the young student began questioning the whole structure of value theory at that time, and a decade later, he was to initiate a major revision of economic theory.

---

[1] The comment was written in 1961 when Chamberlin discussed "The Origins and Early Development of Monopolistic Competition Theory," *Quarterly Journal of Economics*, vol. 75, no. 4 (November 1961), 517. Chamberlin's reminiscences in this article provide a very illuminating picture of the development of his ideas.

Away from the halls of academia, the young Chamberlin hardly appeared as one who would become a true innovator in economic theory. He was, in many respects, the stereotype of the "all-around guy." Tall, good looking, and athletic, Chamberlin liked sports as much as his books. He was not, in any sense, a "bookworm." His father had died when Edward was young, and through high school and college he worked as a reporter on the *Iowa City Citizen*. In 1916 he went to the University of Iowa, where he took up the study of accounting.[2] There he came into contact with one of the most influential of economic teachers, Frank Knight.[3] Although they were later to be bitterly opposed to each other on the issues raised by Chamberlin's work, Knight encouraged Chamberlin to teach economics and accept a post to study under Fred M. Taylor at the University of Michigan. When he went to Harvard in 1922 to get his doctorate, Chamberlin had already resolved to write his dissertation on the problems surrounding the competitive model.[4] At Harvard he found a willing supervisor in Professor Allyn Young, who was himself engaged in a debate over similar problems in the 1920's. Chamberlin's thesis was completed in 1927 and six years later its ideas were formulated into *The Theory of Monopolistic Competition*.[5]

Few economists who have achieved the prominence of E. H. Chamberlin have had their work characterized by such a single-minded purpose. Chamberlin's outstanding trait was his tenacity in pursuing a goal. He was an ambitious man who wanted to be remembered for his work in value theory. He once told a friend while working on his dissertation that he was "writing something that's going to change the theory of value." Both his tenacity and his pride are illustrated by the recollections of his lifetime friend, Howard Ellis, when the two were at Michi-

---

[2] The class of 1916 at Iowa City High produced a second outstanding economist. Along with Chamberlin, Howard Ellis, now professor emeritus at the University of California, Berkeley, graduated and went along to the University of Iowa. Both later went on to study at Michigan and Harvard. We are indebted to Professor Ellis for reminiscences on the early years of his acquaintance with Chamberlin.

[3] Knight's influence on his students was extraordinary, as is evidenced by the long list of prominent economists who remain his admirers today. See Chapter 12.

[4] Joseph A. Schumpeter, commenting on Chamberlin's work, notes that it provides "a striking instance of subjective and objective originality." Joseph A. Schumpeter, *History of Economic Analysis* (New York: Oxford University Press, 1959), pp. 1150-1151n.

[5] Edward H. Chamberlin, *Theory of Monopolistic Competition* (Cambridge, Mass.: Harvard University Press, 1933). Chapter III of the initial edition was originally published in the *Quarterly Journal of Economics*; the book has subsequently gone through eight editions with additional appendices added from time to time.

gan where they often argued points of theory. Ellis would feel that a debate on some theoretical point had been settled in his favor, but Chamberlin would return to the issue after several days to try a new angle of attack on the problem.

His work in value theory was not always warmly received; at one point Chamberlin was led to identify an entire "school" of economists who were ". . . distinguished by the zeal with which the theory of monopolistic competition has been attacked. . . ."[6] Through it all, he doggedly continued to cultivate his theory "intensively and extensively." A measure of the success of his effort is that almost every textbook on value theory today utilizes some elements of the Chamberlinian framework derived from the *Theory of Monopolistic Competition.*

Some of the originality of Chamberlin's work has been buried over the years (despite his own attempts to prevent it) by the fact that, six months after the appearance of *Theory of Monopolistic Competition,* the English economist Joan Robinson published her *Economics of Imperfect Competition.*[7] Chamberlin and Mrs. Robinson are usually referred to as the joint discoverers of the analysis of "imperfect" markets, a point which pained Chamberlin no end. His attempt to distinguish his own "product" from that of Mrs. Robinson became almost an obsession with him as his career wore on.[8] While his stress on this point may not have been wholly warranted, there are important differences in the two approaches which we shall return to later.

Chamberlin need not have worried over the recognition his work received. *Theory of Monopolistic Competition* was awarded the David A. Wells prize at Harvard in 1927 as the best thesis in economics that year. Within a decade he was promoted to full professor. In 1951 Chamberlin was elected to the David A. Wells Chair in Political Economy at Harvard, a post he held until his death in 1967.

---

[6] Edward H. Chamberlin, "The Chicago School," in *Towards a More General Theory of Value* (New York: Oxford University Press, 1957), p. 296. The irony of this is that Chamberlin's old mentor, Frank Knight, was a leading figure in this school of thought.

[7] Joan Robinson, *Economics of Imperfect Competition* (London: Macmillan & Co., Ltd., 1933). A third "discoverer" of imperfect competition, Heinrich Von Stackelberg, also treated the question of imperfect markets in a highly original fashion in his *Marktform und Gleichgewicht* (Berlin: Verlag Von Julius Springer, 1934). His work has received far less attention than the other two.

[8] The extent of this preoccupation can be seen in the collection of essays, Chamberlin, *Towards a More General Theory of Value, op. cit.,* published in 1957. Mrs. Robinson is reported to have commented at one point that "I'm sorry I ruined his life."

Problems with the Neoclassical
Theory of the Firm

We have already dealt with the foundations of the Marshallian theory of the firm.[9] It will be recalled that a major difficulty with the postulates of perfect competition involved the cost structure of the firm. If Marshallian "external economies" resulted in a firm realizing *increasing returns* over a very wide range of output, the firm's share of the market might ultimately become large enough to influence the industry price. One of the fundamental conditions of perfect competition—that each firm has an imperceptible influence on supply—would no longer be realized.

Marshall saw the possibility that increasing returns could make perfect competition unworkable. However, his explanations as to why the competitive markets would in fact be likely to survive were not convincing. As a result, the 1920's saw a rising rumble of discontent over the existing theory's inability to explain the case of increasing returns. Economists began to question whether the neoclassical theory of value, which recognized only two market structures—competition and monopoly—was sufficiently broad to allow a meaningful analysis of the movements of prices and output in the "real world." In large part, it was the gap left by these two "ideal" market structures which prompted the work of economists such as Chamberlin, Robinson, and Von Stackelberg.[10] Even more than with most economists of the time, Chamberlin's dissatisfaction with value theory reflected his conviction that Marshallian theory could not answer questions posed by existing market structures in the American economy. This was not surprising: "The theory of pure competition could hardly be expected to fit facts so far different from its assumptions."[11] He did not despair, however,

---

[9] See the discussion of Marshall in Chapter 3.

[10] In 1922, J. H. Clapham questioned the relevance of the Marshallian analysis of increasing returns in his article, "Of Empty Economic Boxes," *Economic Journal*, vol. 32 (September 1922), 305-14. This touched off a long debate by both English and American economists regarding the issues of competition and costs. Mrs. Robinson's *Economics of Imperfect Competition* clearly emerged from the debates in the *Economic Journal*. Chamberlin, on the other hand, insists that his work did not stem from the "increasing returns debate." *Cf.* Chamberlin, "The Origins and Early Development of Monopolistic Competitive Theory," *op. cit.* One should recall, however, that his advisor, Allyn Young, was a major participant in this controversy, and Chamberlin probably felt a good deal of "indirect" influence through him. See P. A. Samuelson, "The Monopolistic Competition Revolution," in Robert Kuenne, *Monopolistic Competition Theory* (New York: John Wiley & Sons, Inc., 1967).

[11] Chamberlin, *Theory of Monopolistic Competition, op. cit.*, p. 10.

since ". . . there is no reason why a theory cannot be formulated which will fit them."[12]

To construct such a theory, Chamberlin began with one of the few noncompetitive cases treated by earlier writers—*duopoly*, or two sellers.[13] The narrow case was easily expanded into a situation which Chamberlin termed *oligopoly*: a market with more than one seller, but one where the actions of a single seller can exert a perceptible influence on market price. The possibility that any firm might have sufficient control over supply to influence the price posed new problems for the equilibrium analysis. In pure competition, the firm paid no heed to its rival's actions since they could not affect the industry price. In oligopoly this is no longer true; therefore, the demand for any given firm's product will depend on the reactions of other firms in response to actions by the initial firm.

Earlier writers had treated this problem of "interdependence" by assuming that each firm would ignore the other firms' actions. This is clearly unrealistic; Chamberlin's solution was to assume that *every* seller "will take account of his *total* influence on price, indirect as well as direct."[14] He then concluded that the resulting equilibrium price and output would be that of a monopolist; for if each firm realizes its total effect on price, it will join with the others to maximize joint profits as a single seller.

Chamberlin's solution to the oligopoly problem is just another special case resulting from a set of assumptions regarding the reactions of a large firm to its rivals. His approach to value theory did, however, lay the foundation for a fundamental change in analysis. Marshall began his analysis with the notion of a "commodity." He termed a group of firms producing that commodity an *industry*, which he proceeded to analyze. Chamberlin shifted the emphasis away from this industry

---

[12] *Ibid.*

[13] A. A. Cournot provided the earliest analysis in 1838 in his *Researches into the Mathematical Principles of the Theory of Wealth*, trans. Nathaniel T. Bacon (New York: The Macmillan Company, 1898). F. Y. Edgeworth was the leading neoclassicist to take up the problem in his article, "Professor Graziani on the Mathematical Theory of Monopoly," *Economic Journal*, vol. 8 (June 1898), 111-14.

[14] Chamberlin, *Theory of Monopolistic Competition, op. cit.*, p. 46. Given his announced objective of constructing a theory which would better fit the "facts" of the "business world," it is interesting to note that Chamberlin's treatment of the issue of interdependence is hardly more realistic than his predecessors'. Clearly, it is unlikely that every firm will be able to assess *all* the indirect and direct effects of a change in output or price. For a compressed discussion of the major theses of oligopoly, see W. Breit, "Approaches to Oligopoly: An Introduction to a Symposium," *Social Science Quarterly*, vol. 49, no. 1 (June 1968), 42-48.

group to the study of the individual demand curve of *each firm*. He distrusted the concept of industry groups, calling such attempts a "snare and delusion" which were "in the highest degree arbitrarily drawn." Far from assisting the analysis, Chamberlin felt they drew attention away from the most important point of focus—the firm's demand curve.

To Chamberlin, the presence of either polar case—monopoly or competition—was rare; he viewed the more general case of *monopolistic competition* as the most prevalent, with instances of oligopoly arising where some firms are large enough to affect total supply.

The emphasis on quantifying market structures in the *Theory of Monopolistic Competition* created an entirely new field of specialization in economics: "industrial organization."[15]

Product Differentiation and the Firm

Chamberlin was struck by the failure of existing theory to take account of the wide variation of products produced within any Marshallian industry. One can easily delineate a "cigarette industry," but the consumer of cigarettes has very strong opinions regarding the relative merits of Camels, Marlboros, Pall Mall, and so forth. The consumer of "automobiles" is similarly able to point out definite tastes as between the various makes and models of automobiles; he chooses among over 100 models from a single manufacturer alone. Clearly, Chamberlin reasoned, a firm is free to manipulate the "products" it sells as well as their price and level of output. In particular, the ability of most firms to "differentiate" their product from that of other firms brought a new dimension onto the decision matrix of the firm.[16] This opportunity was

---

[15] Note the comments by J. S. Bain, "The Impact on Industrial Organization," *American Economic Review*, vol. 54, no. 3 (May 1964), 28-32. An early attempt to pursue the possibilities of Chamberlin's empirical approach to market structure was Robert Triffin's *Monopolistic Competition and General Equilibrium Theory* (Cambridge, Mass.: Harvard University Press, 1940). His use of "cross elasticities," to measure the impact of a change in price by one firm through the change in output of another, pointed out the difficulties of actually measuring the interdependence between firms. The selections by Fellner and Bain in Kuenne, *op. cit.*, provide a recent appraisal of the impact of *Theory of Monopolistic Competition* on the field of industrial organization. William Fellner, "The Adaptability and Lasting Significance of the Chamberlinian Contribution," in Kuenne, *Monopolistic Competition Theory, op. cit.*, pp. 3-30; and Joe S. Bain, "Chamberlin's Impact on Microeconomic Theory," *ibid.*, pp. 147-176.

[16] While his major emphasis—particularly in *Theory of Monopolistic Competition*—was on "product differentiation," Chamberlin also saw other ways in which the "product" was an important variable in the firm's decision matrix. See Edward Chamberlin, "The Product as an Economic Variable," in *Towards a More General Theory of Value, op. cit.*, chapter 6, pp. 105-137.

an important option, for "virtually all products are differentiated, at least slightly."[17] The basis for differentiation is broad indeed, for it is not important that differences in products be real; they may simply be imagined by the consumer. All that matters is that consumers *behave as if* the products are not alike. If they judge the two as being different, they will presumably pay some additional sum to buy the one they like most, regardless of the actual characteristics of the goods.

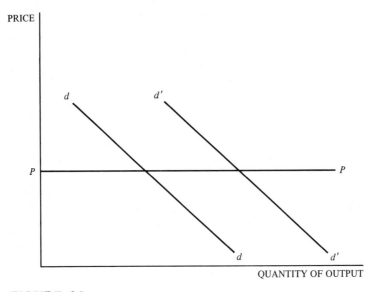

FIGURE 6.1

The importance of product differentiation stems from the effect it has on the demand for a firm's output. We characterized the perfectly competitive firm as being a "price taker"; the price for its output is determined by the industry equilibrium, and it views price as a horizontal line such as *PP* in Figure 6.1. With a differentiated product, the firm would have a demand curve such as *dd* in Figure 6.1, since variations in the price of its "unique" product will now have some impact on the amount demanded by consumers.

Chamberlin emphasized that the degree of product differentiation can be influenced by actions of the firm; the uniqueness of its "product" can be increased through "advertising." Diagramatically, this means that the producer will be able to move the demand curve for his

---

[17] Chamberlin, *Theory of Monopolistic Competition, op. cit.*, p. 57.

"product" to the right (say to $d'd'$) by incurring "selling costs."[18] Firms can now increase their market power through advertising outlays which make consumers prefer their products to other products; the firm is no longer simply a "price taker."

Product Differentiation and Equilibrium

In the neoclassical model, the given price to the firm and the entry or exit of firms from the industry maintained a pressure which kept each firm producing at its most efficient level of production. All "excess profits" were removed.[19] With demand to the firm downward sloping, the firm will be induced to maximize profits by producing at point *A* in Figure 6.2.[20] According to Chamberlin this situation must be temporary, since:

> The extra profit will . . . attract new competitors into the field, with a resulting shift in the demand curve, for the "product" of each seller (*DD* in Figure 6.2) will be moved to the left, since the total purchases must now be distributed among a larger number of sellers. . . . With each shift in the demand curve will come a price readjustment, . . . the process continuing until the demand curve for each 'product' is tangent to its cost curve, and the area of surplus profit is wiped out.[21]

In other words, the demand *to the firm* is reduced by the entry of new firms. The firm's dream of monopoly profits is thus thwarted. Once the rate of profit is reduced back to zero (that is, a normal return), we have the situation of *dd* in Figure 6.2, with the firm now producing at *B*.[22] At *B*, all profits have disappeared. However, each firm produces

---

[18] Chamberlin uses "selling costs" and "advertising" interchangeably. He defined selling costs as those actions which try to "alter the position or shape of the demand curve for a product." Chamberlin, *Theory of Monopolistic Competition, op. cit.*, p. 117.

[19] See the discussion in Chapter 2.

[20] Point *A* is where the difference between average revenue (price) and average cost is greatest. This is equivalent to saying that at *A*, marginal revenue equals marginal cost. However Chamberlin did not employ the terminology of marginal cost and revenue, preferring to work with average quantities.

[21] Chamberlin, *Theory of Monopolistic Competition, op. cit.*, pp. 83-84.

[22] The demand curve must ultimately cease to move at *dd*, since further movements to the left would entail losses to the firms, encouraging exit from the industry. Chamberlin illustrates the relation of the firm and industry demand curves by showing a "path" which the firm demand will follow as it feels the effects of entry and exist. This is omitted from Figure 6.2 for simplicity.

less than a purely competitive firm would, for the competitive equilibrium would be at *C*—where average cost is lowest. Note the paradox; the firm at point *B* has no profits, just as if it were in a purely competitive industry. Yet the price and output are those we would expect from a monopolist. Thus Chamberlin's conclusion: monopolistic competition gives us the disadvantages of monopoly (higher price with reduced output) without giving the firm any profits. The result is the creation of excess capacity on the part of each firm. Price is no longer equated to marginal cost,[23] and the balance between the alternative costs and consumers' desires is upset. Nor is there any pressure for change, since any seller will lose by either raising or lowering price. Profits are just "normal," so there is no incentive for either new entrepreneurs to enter the market, nor existing ones to leave.

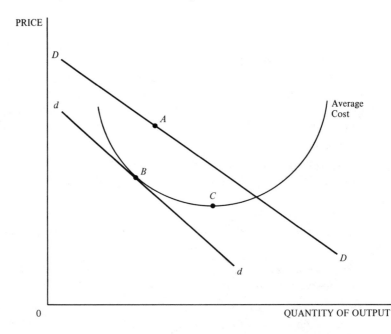

FIGURE 6.2

The introduction of selling cost further complicated the analysis. With free entry into the "group," excess profits cannot persist. If a firm succeeds, through advertising, in shifting its demand curve to the right,

---

[23] This must be so since the marginal cost at *B* is below the average cost. With the demand curve no longer horizontal, the "marginal revenue" will always

it may increase its share of the market. It will be induced to expand output, but its costs—from advertising—will increase. Although the final equilibrium is unclear, Chamberlin concluded that:

> . . . it seems likely that advertising diminishes the discrepancy between actual and most efficient scale of production. But total costs and prices are higher. Selling costs per unit are greater than the decrease in production costs. The resources expended to achieve this result are therefore greater than those saved by achieving it. And, of course, the balance of excess capacity remains.[24]

That is, the firm will move back towards (*C*) as the *dd* curve shifts to the right, but the cost curve will shift up due to the introduction of selling costs. In Chamberlin's view, this upward movement in costs would offset any gains in efficiency realized by moving towards the competitive level of production.

A major appeal of the neoclassical theory of the firm was its simplicity and its implications with regard to efficiency of production. Chamberlin's exposition in the *Theory of Monopolistic Competition* implied that with only a slight change in assumptions—in the direction of greater realism—the competitive solution was no longer ideal. In the "small group" solution (oligopoly), the distortion is greater still. Here Chamberlin concluded that the results depend on the assumptions one makes with regard to firms' reactions in the face of interdependence; a "general solution" does not exist. A major pillar of the neoclassical theory was thus seriously undermined by Chamberlin's assertions. Veblen insisted that advertising would stimulate conspicuous consumption and undermine the rationality of the consumer. This implied that—in Veblen's terms—there is "waste." Chamberlin's point is that even if the consumer acts rationally to adjust his expenditures according to preferences for various "products," advertising leads to the development of excess capacity in the system. Chamberlin's emphasis on the analysis of the firm's demand curve removed the problems surrounding "increasing returns" and competitive industries, since the limit to the size of the firm is set by profit maximizing entrepreneurs facing a downward sloping demand curve; but, at the same time, his work challenged the relevance of the competitive model.

---

be less than price. The firm equates marginal revenue to marginal cost, and both marginal revenue and marginal cost are less than price under monopolistic conditions. See the discussion in Chapter 2.

[24] Chamberlin, *Theory of Monopolistic Competition, op. cit.,* p. 172.

Theories of Monopolistic Competition

We have concentrated our discussion on Chamberlin's analysis of monopolistic competition. One cannot adequately assess Chamberlin's contribution without some reference to Mrs. Robinson's *Economics of Imperfect Competition*. There is little doubt that the two writers intended to approach the same general question: imperfect market systems.[25] Yet it is equally clear that they approached the issue from rather different viewpoints and with rather different objectives.

Chamberlin's analysis contains two major aspects which are either lacking or treated differently by Mrs. Robinson: product differentiation, and his analysis of the equilibrium of the individual firm. While Mrs. Robinson employed differences among products to define industries, she did not recognize product differentiation between firms *within an industry*. In this respect, she followed the neoclassical framework; the product was not a "variable" to be manipulated by the firm. Her analysis rested in large part on the Marshallian analysis of monopoly, elaborating the refinements introduced by the "increasing returns" debate of the 1920's.

In modifying the Marshallian monopoly analysis, Mrs. Robinson merely redefined the Marshallian demand curve to account for the interdependence between firms.[26] She then developed a geometric presentation of the situation in which the additional cost of each unit was just balanced by the additional revenue. Mrs. Robinson's "kit of analytical tools" is an excellent expository device for the general case of industry analysis. It reflects the fact that she was interested in a much broader range of investigation than Chamberlin. She viewed the world as being essentially a group of monopolists, and one of her objectives was to measure the distortion on the distribution of income generated by this power. This is a question which Chamberlin carefully avoided.[27] Her interest in "exploitation" led Mrs. Robinson to

---

[25] Furthermore, they defined the "imperfections" in quite similar terms. See the comparison of the two "problems" posed by the writers given in Triffin, *Monopolistic Competition and General Equilibrium Theory, op. cit.*, pp. 37-42. Triffin is still one of the best references on the subject of monopolistic competition. An excellent —and concise—exposition of the theories is provided in George Malanos, *Intermediate Economic Theory* (Philadelphia: J. B. Lippincott Company, 1962), pp. 501-27.

[26] This is not quite the same treatment as Chamberlin (and Stackelberg) gave to the question of interdependence. Chamberlin thought the firm would know the results of the interaction. Mrs. Robinson deals with an industry where the analytical tool of a demand curve accounts for whatever result interdependence creates.

[27] See, for example, his comments with regard to "exploitation" in "Mrs. Robinson's Recent Visit to Monopolistic Competition," in *Towards a More General Theory of Value, op. cit.*, pp. 307-12.

formulate her model in far more general terms; for example, she was able to extend her reasoning to the market for factors as well as for goods and services.

On the other hand, Mrs. Robinson almost completely ignored the question of the firm equilibrium in a situation of "oligopoly," or few sellers. As she herself pointed out, it was not to her purpose.[28] Her concern was with the industry, and she characterized the firm's demand curve as being a proportional fraction of the industry demand. Chamberlin was concerned with the equilibrium of the firm in oligopoly, but concluded it was not determinate. The real innovator in this area was Stackelberg, who developed the notion of rival strategies by firms in an imperfect market. However, the reactions of the firms—more than the final position of equilibrium—received the largest attention in his model.[29]

The Impact of Monopolistic Competition

Chamberlin's discussion of the roles of advertising and product differentiation represents a major breakthrough in adjusting economic theory to the realities of the "business world," which was unanticipated by the other innovators of imperfect competition. And therein lies his unique contribution, for the discussion of selling costs and market power of advertising led to the development of a new attack on the concept of consumer sovereignty. Chamberlin himself was primarily interested in explaining the firm's attempt to monopolize the market where it had at least some influence over price. One result of this effect was the presence of "excess capacity"; the firm in monopolistic competition would not produce at the efficient level as would the competitive firm.

But Chamberlin did not view this as a wholly undesirable result; the higher prices brought about through selling costs reflect the buyers' desire for increased variety of products. This, he points out, is the basis for the curve *dd* as opposed to the curve *PP* in Figure 6.1: the difference in products is worth something to the consumer. He viewed the monopolistic competition solution, therefore as "a sort of ideal," not a reflection of misallocation.[30]

---

28 Robinson, *The Economics of Imperfect Competition, op. cit.*, p. 21.

29 A more complete discussion of Stackelberg's model is included in the exposition by Malanos, *Intermediate Economic Theory, op. cit.*, pp. 517-27.

30 On this point, see J. M. Cassels, "Excess Capacity and Monopolistic Competition," reprinted in Breit and Hochman, *Readings in Microeconomics* (New York: Holt, Rinehart and Winston, Inc., 1968), pp. 256-66. Originally printed in *Quarterly*

The *Theory of Monopolistic Competition* also provided fuel to those who viewed the success of advertising in influencing consumer wants as undermining the competitive system. If the firm could in fact manipulate demand, then the ability of the consumer to choose rationally between alternatives in the market would be impaired. Such arguments went well beyond the scope of Chamberlin's inquiry, following much more in the vein of Veblen. Nor is it clear that the proposals of men such as Alvin Hansen and John Kenneth Galbraith met with Chamberlin's approval. His attack on the Marshallian theory of value perhaps succeeded too well. Chamberlin himself was a man of massively conservative tendencies; some of his later writings on labor could very nearly be termed reactionary. It is perhaps ironic that his most bitter detractors in the profession were those embracing the philosophy of classical liberalism.

In 1965, E. H. Chamberlin was elected Distinguished Fellow of the American Economic Association. The citation accompanying the award sums up his position in economic thought:

> It is not given to many scientists to reach into the minds of all their fellows and to influence the work of a whole generation, but the author of *Theory of Monopolistic Competition* did so.

Journal of Economics, vol. 51, no. 3 (May 1937), 426-43. For a more recent recognition of this point, see Donald Dewey, *The Theory of Imperfect Competition* (New York: Columbia University Press, 1969), p. 18.

CHAPTER 7

JOHN MAYNARD KEYNES–
Unemployment in Equilibrium

Keynes's intellect was the sharpest and clearest that I have ever known. When I argued with him, I felt that I took my life in my hands, and I seldom emerged without feeling something of a fool.

BERTRAND RUSSELL

John Maynard Keynes is the most redoubtable name in contemporary economic thought, for the upheaval in economic theory in the 1930's is usually associated with him. The appearance of his *General Theory of Employment Interest and Money* in 1936[1] marked an even sharper turning point in the development of economic thought than did the appearance of the marginal analysis of Menger and Jevons 65 years earlier. Keynes was a highly respected economist when he wrote the *General Theory*, and he minced no words in stating the objective of his work:

> . . . the postulates of classical theory are applicable to a special case only and not to the general case, the situation which it assumes being a limiting point of the possible positions of equilibrium. Moreover, the characteristics of the special case assumed by the classical theory happen not to be those of the economic society in which we actually live, with the result that its teaching is mis-

---

[1] John M. Keynes, *The General Theory of Employment Interest and Money* (New York: Harcourt, Brace & World, Inc., 1936). Hereinafter cited as *General Theory*.

leading and disastrous if we attempt to apply it to the facts of experience.[2]

Few economists at the time had a stronger background from which to attack neoclassical theory than did Keynes.[3] Born in 1883, he was the son of a well-known economist, John Neville Keynes.[4] Young Keynes was educated at Eton and later Cambridge, where he received a good deal of individual instruction from both Marshall and Pigou.[5] Although Keynes's first interest was not economics, Marshall saw sufficient promise in his student to write J. N. Keynes: "Your son is doing excellent work in Economics. I have told him that I should be greatly delighted if he should decide on the career of a professional economist."[6] Keynes himself obviously thought he had learned a great deal; when he did not receive top score on a civil service exam he remarked: "I evidently knew more about Economics than my examiners."[7]

His father's eminence as an economist notwithstanding, Keynes came into economics rather gradually; his early interests were in probability analysis and mathematics. Throughout his life, Keynes's career encompassed an extraordinary range of activities in and out of the academic life. His initial position just out of Cambridge was with the India Office for two years. Prompted by Marshall's support, he returned to Cambridge where he was finally appointed lecturer in economics in 1908. His interests remained largely outside economics; his first work in eco-

---

[2] *Ibid.*, p. 3. We noted earlier that Keynes referred to the accepted doctrine of the period as the "classical" rather than "neoclassical" body of thought.

[3] Most of the information in this section is taken from R. F. Harrod, *The Life of John Maynard Keynes* (New York: Harcourt, Brace & World, Inc., 1952), 2nd ed., which is the most authoritative account of Keynes's life. Harrod was quite close to Keynes, and his biography is extremely partial to its subject. Modern readers, wishing to profit from the perspective of 20 years since Harrod's work might prefer Robert Lekachman, *Age of Keynes* (New York: Random House, Inc., 1966). His emphasis on policy makes Lekachman's work an excellent source for the layman; however the author is generally partial to Keynes in his treatment of the material.

[4] J. N. Keynes taught at Cambridge for many years and was a close associate of Alfred Marshall. His *Scope and Method of Political Economy* remains as an excellent statement of the domain of the professional economist today. John N. Keynes, *The Scope and Method of Political Economy* (London: Macmillan & Co., Ltd., 1891).

[5] Pigou had just received a chair at Cambridge. It is interesting to note that two of the men who launched penetrating attacks on the neoclassical system were trained and highly regarded by the most eminent of all neoclassicists, Alfred Marshall.

[6] Harrod, *The Life of John Maynard Keynes, op. cit.*, p. 107.

[7] *Ibid.*, p. 121. Harrod argues that Keynes was probably correct. After all, there were very few examiners who ". . . were capable of understanding such by-play with Marshall." In the opinion of his biographer, Keynes was one of the few.

nomics appeared in 1909.[8] In 1913 Keynes was appointed to the Indian Currency Commission, a post which led him into the Treasury, and eventually in 1919, to the peace conference at Versailles as the representative of the Treasury. Disgusted with the terms of the treaty, Keynes dramatically resigned his position in September 1919, and two months later published his *Economic Consequences of the Peace*.[9] The book strongly protested the imposition of large reparations on Germany and insisted that the terms of the Versailles Treaty could never be enforced. It received wide circulation and catapulted Keynes into the public spotlight, although making him quite unpopular with the government. Fortunately he was offered the editorship of the *Economic Journal* that year—in large part due to support from Marshall. From that point on, Keynes was seldom quiet; by 1936, when the *General Theory* appeared, he was a leading authority on economic theory and policy.

In addition to his academic and government experience, Keynes was a successful financier. His activities as a speculator in the commodity, currency, and stock markets resulted in an estate of $2 million at the time of his death in 1946. As bursar of King's College, he was able to considerably enlarge the endowment.[10] He was a patron of the arts; his wife, Lydia Lopokova, was a ballerina, and at one point he financed a theater group. Nor did he confine his intellectual activities to economics. Keynes frequently engaged in discussion with the "Bloomsbury set," a collection of intellectuals in London, including such people as Lytton Strachey, Duncan Grant, Clive Bell, E. M. Forster, and Virginia Woolf. It was his contact with individuals of this caliber (some of whom he knew as a student at Cambridge) that helped shape the broad intellectual background of Keynes.[11]

---

[8] The work in probability was published in 1920 as: John M. Keynes, *A Treatise on Probability* (Cambridge: Cambridge University Press, 1920). The economics article was: John M. Keynes, "Recent Economic Events in India," *Economic Journal* (March 1909), 51-67.

[9] J. M. Keynes, *The Economic Consequences of the Peace* (New York: Harcourt, Brace & World, Inc., 1920).

[10] Harrod relates that in 1920 Keynes was near bankruptcy; by 1946 his estate was valued at about £450,000 ($2.25 million). Harrod, *The Life of John Maynard Keynes, op. cit.,* p. 297. He enlarged the "free funds" of the college from about £30,000 ($150,000) to £380,000 (about $1.8 million). *Ibid.,* pp. 297, 388.

[11] Recently it has been reported that Keynes, by a familiar caprice of nature, was capable of emotional interest in men. His amorous activities in this regard are evidenced by his letters to Duncan Grant and Lytton Strachey. See M. Holroyd, *Lytton Strachey: A Critical Biography*, 2 vols. (New York: Holt, Rinehart & Winston, Inc., 1968).

Keynes and the Neoclassicists

Keynes was forever advocating policies which ran counter to the "usual" interpretation of monetary thinking; yet, in a real sense he retained much of the outlook of the neoclassical (indeed, the classical) writers. He attacked the laissez-faire policies of the earlier economists but was certainly not an advocate of government intervention. Keynes lacked the faith of his predecessors in the rationality of economic man, but he retained a strong belief in individualism, and there is not in his writings an attack on the neoclassical theory of individual choice. To the extent that the new economics of recent times has a strongly interventionist trend, it did not come directly from Keynes. Although the following remarks of the *General Theory* have been quoted frequently they are often ignored when the implications of "Keynesian" theory are brought up:

> But, above all, individualism, if it can be purged of its defects and its abuses, is the best safeguard of personal liberty in the sense that, compared with any other system, it greatly widens the field for the exercise of personal choice. It is also the best safeguard of the variety of life, which emerges precisely from this extended field of personal choice, and the loss of which is the greatest of all losses of the homogeneous or totalitarian state.[12]

With regard to his own argument for government intervention, Keynes goes on to point out:

> Whilst, therefore, the enlargement of the functions of government, involved in the task of adjusting to one another the propensity to consume and the inducement to invest, would seem . . . to be a terrific encroachment on individualism, I defend it, on the contrary, both as the only practicable means of avoiding the destruction of the existing economic forms in their entirety and as the condition of the successful functioning of individual initiative.[13]

It has been pointed out that the classical economists were interested in the shaping of "better men" through the economic process.[14] Keynes appeared to be concerned that this element was lacking in the society of the mid-twentieth century. In a letter to one of the leading adherents

---

12 Keynes, *General Theory*, p. 380.

13 *Ibid.*

14 See the comment by George Stigler, *Five Lectures on Economic Problems* (London: Longmans, Green & Co., Ltd., 1949), p. 4.

of classical liberalism, F. A. Hayek (commenting on the latter's *Road to Serfdom*), Keynes writes:

> What we need, therefore, in my opinion, is not a change in our economic programmes, which would only lead in practice to disillusion with the results of your philosophy; . . . No, what we need is the restoration of right moral thinking—a return to proper moral values in our social philosophy. . . . Dangerous acts can be done safely in a community which thinks and feels rightly, which would be the way to hell if they were executed by those who think and feel wrongly.[15]

Clearly, then, Keynes does not appear to be a man antagonistic to the free enterprise system. He was a professional economist, rigorously trained in the neoclassical tradition, with broad experience in the applications of that theory to practical policy. Gradually, in the context of the problems facing Britain after World War I, he became convinced that the policy recommendations of the old orthodoxy suffered from serious shortcomings, and this dissatisfaction culminated in the appearance of the *General Theory*. We need not consider the gradual evolution of Keynes's ideas; what is important is that they represented a direct attack on existing economic doctrine by a man already recognized as an eminent economist.[16]

We have already commented on the fact that neoclassical employment theory was largely implicit and not carefully spelled out. This difficulty bothered Keynes when he approached the question of unemployment. The acceptance of Say's Law was so universal that Keynes complained: "the fundamental theory underlying it has been deemed so simple and obvious that it has received, at the most, a bare mention."[17]

The Classical Model

Keynes called his book *The General Theory of Employment Interest and Money*, because he felt that he had developed a truly general

---

[15] Quoted in Harrod, *The Life of John Maynard Keynes, op. cit.*, pp. 436-37. Hayek's *Road to Serfdom* is, by wide agreement, one of the most lucid and articulate statements of the case against state intervention. Friedrich A. Hayek, *The Road to Serfdom* (Chicago: University of Chicago Press, 1944).

[16] The roots of the *General Theory* can be seen in Keynes's earlier works, particularly his *Treatise on Money*, 2 vols. (London: Macmillan & Co., Ltd., 1930). For a concise summary of the development of Keynes's thought to the *General Theory*, see Lekachman, *The Age of Keynes, op. cit.*, chap. 3.

[17] Keynes, *General Theory, op. cit.*, pp. 4-5.

theory in the sense that he could explain all levels of employment, as opposed to the neoclassical theory which concerned itself only with the special case of full employment. As we have seen, the classical conclusion that the equilibrium level of employment was full employment rested mainly upon Say's Law of Markets. The cure for unemployment, in the view of the neoclassical model (which Keynes outlined for purposes of exposition) was to allow real wages to fall, until all workers willing and able to work would be hired. It is the relationship between the money wage and the price level that defines the real wage, and it is the real wage that entrepreneurs look to in deciding the amount of employment they will offer. The possibility that inadequate demand could be the cause of unemployment was brushed aside. For if individuals decide to consume less of their income, they will by definition, be saving more. The fall in consumption expenditure would mean falling profits, wages, and prices, in consumption goods industries. But the increased saving would mean a lower rate of interest and hence a greater amount of investment demanded in capital goods industries. The workers unemployed temporarily in the consumption sector would eventually be reabsorbed in the investment sector. As long as wages, prices, and interest rates are flexible and resources are mobile, then inadequate demand could not be a problem.

If looked at from the point of view of the labor market, the neoclassical model indicates that persistent unemployment could only be a result of some barrier to the fall in the money wage and, given the level of prices, some fall in the real wage. For the fact of unemployment must mean that, at the given real wage, the demand for labor is less than the amount supplied. If workers would take a cut in their money wage, this would mean a cut in their real wage. (The price level would remain constant because the quantity theory of money indicates that the price level is a function of the quantity of money alone, and not the level of money wages.) But the demand for labor and the supply of labor in the neoclassical framework are both functions of the real wage. When the real wage falls, the quantity of labor demanded increases, while the quantity of labor supplied declines. Eventually, full employment would be reached, where the quantity of labor demanded and the quantity of labor supplied were equal. Hence any unemployment must be a result of some barrier to the fall in the real wage, namely, the refusal of workers to accept cuts in their real wage. This being the case, such unemployment was interpreted as being *voluntary unemployment*. Workers simply refused the proffer of employment at a lower real wage. All other unemployment was interpreted as *frictional*: in a complex economy, the number of jobs looking for workers and workers looking for jobs cannot always be instantaneously adjusted to each other. There are frictions or inadequate information, so that at any given time unemployment from this cause would be expected.

But Keynes introduced a new category of unemployment: *involuntary unemployment*. To Keynes, the neoclassical theory of employment was inadequate to explain this category, although it is most significant during a major depression. In order to explain the existence of involuntary unemployment, Keynes required a new theory.

The General Theory

The question that Keynes attempted to answer was: what determines the level of employment and national income at any given time? His answer was: it depends upon the volume of effective demand. Unemployment is a direct result of inadequate effective demand. A theory of effective demand stems from the realization that there are two kinds of people in our economy who do two kinds of things. One group, the workers in already existing factories and shops, produces consumer goods and services; the other group, consisting of workers employed in building new factories and machines, produces investment goods and services. The amount of employment in existing plants depends upon consumer demand which, in turn, depends upon the disposable income or purchasing power people have. But the demand for investment goods is largely autonomous, in the sense that it is independent of purchasing power or income.

The kernel of Keynes's theory of effective demand rests on his notion of the consumption function. That is, as income increases and consumption rises, the latter increases less than does the former. Thus, the volume of investment must be constantly increased to maintain the full employment level of income. Since Keynes believed that consumption patterns are largely fixed, the level of employment, given the consumption function, depends upon investment. But the decision to invest is made independently of the decision to save. The decision to save is made by everybody together deciding how much to consume or not consume in, say, the next year. So all consumers taken together plan to save a certain amount of their income. In the meantime, businessmen are planning to invest so much for the next year. Now it would be the greatest coincidence if the amount that consumers had planned to save was precisely equal to the amount that businessmen planned to invest. And it is precisely the divergencies between these two magnitudes that ultimately determine the volume of employment.

Let us assume that the amount that businessmen plan to invest is greater than the amount that consumers plan to save. In bringing these plans to fruition, the businessmen would find, for example, that their inventories are below the desired level. They would then invest more in inventories generating an increased flow of income and employment. But as income rose in response to the high levels of consumption and investment (since one man's expenditure is another man's income), saving, which to Keynes is a function of income, would rise. And it would continue to rise until it was precisely equal to investment. At this point, anticipated saving and investment would be equal.[18] But note that it is the change in the level of income that brought the two flows into equality.

What happens if the amount that consumers plan to save is greater than the amount that businessmen plan to invest? In that case, since one man's decision not to spend means someone else getting less income, total income in the economy would decline. As inventories accumulate, businessmen cut back their investment, and workers are laid off. Income falls, saving falls, and eventually saving and investment will be equal again at the new lower level of income. This new lower level of income with involuntary unemployment would be an equilibrium level, since there are no forces at work to restore full employment.

But what about competition in the labor market? Would the unemployed workers take cuts in wages that would restore full employment, as the neoclassical model assumed? Not so, says Keynes. For the neoclassical model is correct only as regards the demand curve for labor, but is incorrect regarding the supply curve. That is, Keynes accepted the proposition that the demand for labor is a function of the real wage, and that in equilibrium the real wage is equal to the marginal productivity of labor, as John Bates Clark and Alfred Marshall had maintained. But the trouble was with the neoclassical postulate regarding the supply function of labor. To the neoclassical economists, the supply

---

[18] It is one of Keynes's points that *actual* saving and investment are always equal. But this is purely definitional since income is defined as being equal to consumption expenditures plus investment expenditures. And since saving is defined as the difference between income and consumption, saving equals investment. That is

$$Y = C + I$$
$$\text{since} \quad S = Y - C$$
$$\text{and} \quad I = Y - C$$
$$\text{therefore } S = I$$

Unfortunately, the distinction between anticipated and actual saving and investment was not fully understood by many readers of the *General Theory*. See the discussion in Chapter 8, *infra*.

of labor was a function of the real wage rate. But to Keynes, workers bargain for and react to changes in money wages because they have no control over the real wage. Keynes assumed that the labor supply function has a flat portion at the established money wage rate, implying that workers refuse to take money wage cuts either because of class consciousness, or what is often referred to as the "money illusion." Thus there can exist an unemployment in the labor market. Figure 7.1 depicts such a situation.

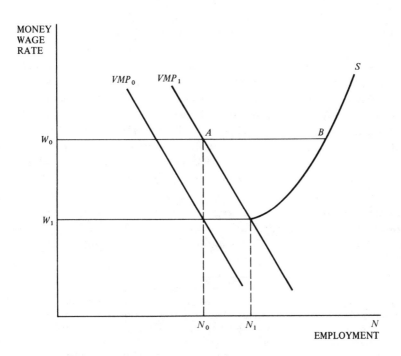

FIGURE 7.1

With a money wage of W_0 and the demand for labor (determined by the value of the marginal product) VMP_1, unemployment exists in the amount AB. To the neoclassical economists, the situation is one of disequilibrium, since the money wage would be cut to W_1, leading to full employment at N_1. To the neoclassical economist, this was true, since the money wage cut (given the price level) would mean a fall in the real wage rate and, therefore, an increase in the quantity of labor demanded and a reduction in the quantity supplied. But Keynes argued that the classical economists are incorrect even within the framework of their own models. Since money wages constitute a large proportion of marginal cost, a cut in the money wage would mean a fall in marginal costs. Since, under conditions of competition, entrepreneurs price at marginal cost, price would fall almost as much as wages. Thus, the fall in the money wage would mean a fall in the real wage, with little or no change in the volume of employment.[19] In terms of our diagram, this would be depicted as a fall in the value of the marginal product as prices fell, that is, a shift to the left of the VMP_1 curve to VMP_0. The volume of employment thus remains at N_0.

Thus, workers have no expedient whereby they can influence the real wage. A cut in the money wage, even within the context of the neoclassical model, means no fall in the real wage. So workers are helpless to affect the amount of employment simply by taking wage cuts. These workers are therefore involuntarily unemployed. For if the offer of employment at wage rate W_0 were made, even though it would mean a lower real wage, workers would be forthcoming, in the amount AB. In the diagram, AB is the amount of involuntary unemployment.

Keynes, in the light of his own theory of employment, would explain the sequence of events resulting from wage cuts differently. His argument was that a cut in the money wage rate would involve a fall in income and therefore in aggregate demand in money terms.[20] This would also be represented by a shift to the left of aggregate demand curve for labor, VMP_1. The lower money wage might therefore be

---

[19] Keynes, *General Theory, op. cit.*, p. 12. It appears that Keynes was of two minds in this matter. By Chapter 19 of the *General Theory*, he admitted that variations in money wages might affect real wages through what has come to be called the "Keynes Effect." Because a fall in wages will be accompanied by a fall in prices, the stock of money in "real" terms increases. Assuming the nominal amount of money is constant, this lowers the rate of interest and increases investment, thereby increasing employment and income. Nothwithstanding this fact, Keynes rejected the manipulation of money wage rates as a policy for increasing employment. For one thing, in capitalistic economies there is no method available to bring about a universal reduction of the money wage rate. Employers must have sufficient bargaining power to push it downward, which they may not have. What is more, even if employers had such power, wages might be reduced in one industry before another, causing great labor unrest and dissatisfaction. Also, falling prices would have adverse effects on debtors. Keynes therefore felt that manipulation of the quantity of money would be a much sounder policy to follow in the event of unemployment. *Ibid.*, pp. 257-71.

[20] Axel Leijonhufvud, *On Keynesian Economics and the Economics of Keynes* (New York: Oxford University Press, 1968), p. 98.

associated with the same volume of employment as before, with unemployment in the amount N_0N_1.

Keynes's Policy Prescriptions

The essence of the Keynesian policy proposals following from this analysis is that instead of waiting for the real wage to fall, monetary and fiscal policy should be employed to increase aggregate demand. This would imply a movement to the right of the VMP_1, until it cut the labor supply function at B. Keynes pointed out that there are a number of ways open to increase aggregate demand. First, there is the possibility of increasing the nominal amount of money. As the money supply increases, interest rates would fall, investment would increase, and income would rise. The VMP_1 curve would move to the right as the price level rose, and the real wage would fall. At B, full employment would be reached. Thus in Keynes's system, "demand determines employment, and employment determines the marginal product (that is, the real wage), not the other way around."[21]

But Keynes admitted the possibility that monetary policy might not be effective in doing the job of bringing about full employment. It is here that he introduced one of his most interesting and original conceptions: the notion of liquidity preference. To Keynes, the quantity theory of money was incorrect in postulating that velocity would be constant in the face of changes in the quantity of money. For with an increase in the supply of money, the quantity of money supplied would be greater than the quantity demanded for speculative purposes at the given interest rate. This would mean that people would buy securities, thereby pushing the rate of interest down and the price of securities up. But as the rate of interest falls, there are increasing numbers of people at the margin who expect it to rise again. Hence, the quantity of money demanded will increase. It is this process that makes the community willing to hold the larger stock of money at lower interest rates. But the increase in the amount of money demanded means that velocity moves in the opposite direction from increases in the quantity of money. Keynes thus denied the simple relationship between increases in the stock of money and increases in the price level, with velocity constant, that the neoclassical model postulated.

Figure 7.2 illustrates Keynes's liquidity preference curve. It shows the quantity of money demanded at various rates of interest. As the

---

[21] Alvin H. Hansen, *A Guide to Keynes* (New York: McGraw-Hill, Inc., 1953), pp. 21-22.

interest rate rises from, say, r_3 to r_4, the quantity of money demanded for speculative purposes declines, since increasing numbers of speculators have come to believe that the interest rate will fall, and those who hold bonds will realize capital gains. So we can interpret a movement up the liquidity preference curve as a movement from money into bonds, and a movement down the curve as a movement from bonds into money. The actual rate of interest is determined by the demand for money for speculative balances, on one hand, and the stock of money (as supplied by the monetary authority) on the other.

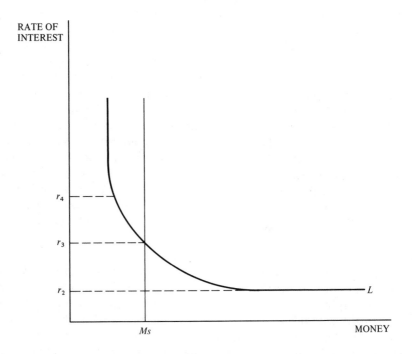

FIGURE 7.2

It is at interest rate r_2 that monetary policy would become completely ineffective in curing a depression. For an increase in the money supply would not lower the rate of interest. The public would be willing to hold the increased money stock at r_2, since expectations are that the interest rate will rise in the future. Thus, no one is willing to hold bonds since they fear capital losses. Once this point is reached (and it should be clear that Keynes considered this situation a *very* special case occurring perhaps in the midst of a great depression), then the government must invest directly in various government projects to cure the unemployment. That is, since interest rates will not fall below this point, there is no way to get more investment from the private sector. Hence direct government investment was recommended. In such a situation, fiscal measures—government tax cutting and spending—rather than monetary measures were called for.[22]

This theory of the rate of interest is decidedly different from that of the neoclassical model. To the neoclassical economist, the rate of interest is not a monetary, but a real phenomenon. It is determined by the demand for capital (which is determined by the marginal productivity of capital) and the supply of saving (which is determined by the thrift of the community). So the rate of interest is a function of real forces: productivity and thrift. Keynes's objection to this theory is that it assumes that the volume of saving is only a function of the rate of interest and is independent of the level of income. To Keynes, saving is a function of income, and in order to determine the volume of saving, we must be able to determine the level of income. But that is precisely what the neoclassical model is unable to do, since according to Keynes, that approach is only able to explain the full employment income, and not all levels of income.

The Multiplier

In working out the implications of government investment to increase the volume of employment, Keynes made effective use of a concept called the *multiplier*. Keynes borrowed this notion from his brilliant pupil, Richard Kahn.[23] It provided a tool which Keynes used to show that deficit financing could provide an increase in income, which was a multiple of the original injection of government spending. The tool it-

---

[22] It should be noted that Keynes also considered monetary policy ineffective in the event that private investment became highly unresponsive to changes in the rate of interest. Keynes believed that when expectations are such that businessmen have had a collapse of confidence in the economy, ". . . moderate changes in the prospective yield of capital-assets or in the rate of interest will not be associated with very great changes in the rate of investment." Keynes, *General Theory, op. cit.,* p. 250. Thus a liquidity trap is not an essential factor in making monetary policy ineffective. A highly inelastic investment demand schedule would have similar implications for policy, requiring direct government expenditures of a fiscal nature.

[23] Richard F. Kahn, "The Relation of Home Investment to Unemployment," *Economic Journal* (June 1931), 173-98.

self can be derived from Keynes's concept of the *marginal propensity to consume,* that is, the change in consumption which is associated with a change in disposable income $(\Delta C/\Delta Y)$. This analysis will perhaps be made clearer with an illustration.

Assume that individuals in an economy have decided to invest $100 billion. The people who receive this $100 billion will regard it as income. Assume that another $500 billion is being provided by the activities of the consumers in spending on consumption. For the economy as a whole, therefore, income is $600 billion, because we know that

$$Y = C + I \tag{7.1}$$

However, consumption is—according to Keynes's theory—a function of income. Let us assume that the marginal propensity to consume $(\Delta C/\Delta Y)$ is 2/3, then

$$C = a + \frac{2}{3}Y \tag{7.2}$$

but $C = 500$ when $Y = 600$

$$500 = a + \frac{2}{3}600$$

$$a = 500 - 400 \tag{7.3}$$

$$= 100$$

Thus the consumption function is

$$C = 100 + \frac{2}{3}Y \tag{7.4}$$

In equilibrium

$$Y = C + I \tag{7.5}$$

therefore

$$Y = 100 + \frac{2}{3}Y + I$$

$$Y - \frac{2}{3}Y = 100 + I$$

$$Y = \frac{1}{1 - \frac{2}{3}}(100 + I). \tag{7.6}$$

If investment is increased by ΔI per period, this will increase the equilibrium income by ΔY

$$Y + \Delta Y = \frac{1}{1 - \frac{2}{3}}(100 + I + \Delta I)$$

$$Y + \Delta Y = \frac{1}{1 - \frac{2}{3}}(100 + I) + \frac{1}{1 - \frac{2}{3}}\Delta I \tag{7.7}$$

$$\Delta Y = \frac{1}{1 - \frac{2}{3}}\Delta I$$

Thus, if the government decides to increase its investment by $10 billion per period, then income will increase by $10 billion multiplied by the multiplier $[1/(1 - 2/3)]$

$$\Delta Y = \frac{1}{1 - \frac{2}{3}}10 \text{ billion}$$

$$= \frac{1}{\frac{1}{3}}10 \text{ billion} \tag{7.8}$$

$$= 30 \text{ billion}$$

Knowing the marginal propensity to consume $(\Delta C/\Delta Y)$, we can derive

the multiplier $\frac{1}{(1 - \Delta C/\Delta Y)}$, and knowing the multiplier, we can estimate

the change in income that will result from any change in expenditure, whether it be consumption, private investment, or government. Note also that the multiplier can work in reverse. A decrease in expenditures of any kind will generate a magnified decrease in income, depending upon the marginal propensity to consume.

Later criticisms of the multiplier centered on the fact that its ultimate effect depends in part on how the government spends the extra money. It is possible that the government expenditure would merely replace what individuals were already spending, inducing them to add this amount to their savings. That is, government spending can divert private spending either into savings or into expenditures that are less attractive. Furthermore, the effect depends on where the money that the government spends comes from. As we shall see in future chapters, there might be considerable differences, depending· on whether the government taxes, prints the money, or borrows from the public.

Keynes's Impact

Keynes's ideas gradually found their way into policy proposals of governments. By the end of the 1930's the New Deal was increasingly relying upon public works expenditures to cure unemployment. In 1946 —a decade after the appearance of the *General Theory*—Congress passed the Full Employment Act, although it said nothing about using "Keynesian" methods to achieve the broad goals set forth in that legislation. Only gradually did government economists openly embrace the new economics. By 1964, however, the Keynesian forces had clearly triumphed when Congress passed a $14 billion tax cut.[24] With the government already running a substantial budget deficit, the main reason for the tax cut was to boost aggregate demand at a time when unemployment was felt to be excessively high. Furthermore, in arguing for the tax cut, government economists stressed the importance of fiscal policy.

The success with which Keynes was able to get his ideas accepted was in no small part due to the forcefulness with which he always stated his views. Keynes was never timid about saying what he believed, and he felt that what he said was important. As he was working on the *General Theory*, he wrote George Bernard Shaw in 1935:

> To understand *my* state of mind, however, you have to know that I believe myself to be writing a book on economic theory which will largely revolutionize— not, I suppose, at once, but in the course of the next ten years—the way the world thinks about economic problems. . . . I can't expect you or anyone else to believe this at the present stage. But for myself I don't merely hope what I say, in my own mind I'm quite sure.[25]

At the time, Shaw—and many others—were probably not convinced; 30 years later, it would appear as though Keynes may have been too pessimistic in his appraisal of the impact of his work.

---

24 H. Stein, *The Fiscal Revolution in America* (Chicago: University of Chicago Press, 1969), esp. chapts. 15, 16, 17.

25 Harrod, *The Life of John Maynard Keynes, op. cit.*, p. 462.

PART III

THE NEW ECONOMICS

CHAPTER 8

ALVIN H. HANSEN—The American Keynes

We have yet to pay proper respect to those who pioneered the Keynesian revolution. Everyone now takes pride in the resulting performance of the economy. We should take a little pride in the men who brought it about . . . The debt to Alvin Hansen is especially great. Next only to Keynes, his is the credit for saving what even conservatives still call capitalism.
JOHN KENNETH GALBRAITH

The *General Theory of Employment Interest and Money* presented a set of ideas which ultimately exerted a profound influence on the direction of economic theory and policy in the United States. However, the effect was not at all sudden, and it did not come directly from Keynes. At the end of World War II, much of what Keynes was arguing remained quite foreign to the average student of economics on this side of the Atlantic. In England his position at Cambridge and his pre-eminence in public life gave Keynes a wide access to interested listeners. At Cambridge he was quickly able to attract a remarkable group of young economists—some of them American—who defended, modified, and expanded the work begun by the *General Theory*. But, in the absence of a leading economist to press the attack in the United States, the impact of these debates was confined to only few places such as Harvard. A substantial number of young economists—many of them affiliated with the second Roosevelt Administration—were impressed by the force of Keynesian arguments. However, the new economics made scant headway into the classrooms of American colleges.[1]

But the delay was short-lived; by 1941, the Keynesian cause in the United States had found a champion who could make himself heard by the entire profession. In that year Professor Alvin Hansen of Harvard University published a book titled, *Fiscal Policy and Business Cycles*.[2] In it, he not only supported Keynes's analysis of the macroeconomic problems of the thirties; he presented a comprehensive scheme of *compensatory finance*, which insisted that the government must implement a continuous policy of stabilization regardless of the position of the revenues and taxes collected. Its theory was rooted directly in Keynes, and Hansen went to some length to support the need for such a policy, by presenting statistical evidence gathered from the preceding decade of economic performance in the United States.

The style of *Fiscal Policy and Business Cycles* hardly matched Keynes's flamboyance or Veblen's biting wit. It was a straightforward, if somewhat pedantic academic approach to an economic problem.[3] As such, it hardly excited the nonspecialist. For the professional economist, the book was an important tract. Alvin Hansen was a leading American economist in 1941, and his comments reflected not only his own views, but those of a growing group of economists (many of them Hansen's own students) who were attacking the pre-Keynesian explanation of the Depression. Hansen's presentation may have been dry, but it was also clear and concise. Henry Simons—an economist who was most certainly *not* one of Keynes's American admirers—noted the book's appearance with considerable misgiving:

> Now, from the ranks of older, distinguished economists, comes Professor Hansen to argue their [Keynesian] case and to espouse their cause. . . . His book is the academic apology par excellence for the inner new deal and all its works. It may well become the

---

[1] The presence of "Keynesians" in the Roosevelt Administration is not to say that the policies in that period were in fact Keynesian. A letter from Keynes to Roosevelt in February of 1937 was very coolly received by the American President. See H. Stein, *The Fiscal Revolution in America* (Chicago: University of Chicago Press, 1969), pp. 108-09. R. Lekachman, in his *Age of Keynes* also notes the unenthusiastic attitude of Roosevelt towards Keynesian finance. Robert Lekachman, *The Age of Keynes* (New York: Random House, Inc., 1966), pp. 112-25.

[2] Alvin Hansen, *Fiscal Policy and Business Cycles* (New York: W. W. Norton & Co., Inc., 1941).

[3] Indeed, portions of the book had appeared in professional journals prior to incorporation into *Fiscal Policy and Business Cycles*.

economic bible for that substantial company of intellectuals, following Keynes and recklessly collectivist, whose influence grows no less rapidly in academic circles than in Washington.[4]

Simons may have exaggerated the immediate impact of this book, but his appraisal that Hansen's espousal of the Keynesian cause was symptomatic of a more general conversion by economists was not so far-fetched.[5] The appearance of *Fiscal Policy and Business Cycles* is a convenient benchmark to denote an appreciable acceleration in the Keynesian movement. When he arrived at Harvard in 1935, Hansen already found an active group favoring the new approach. His own contributions to the debates attracted a steady stream of first-rate students to his Seminar on Fiscal Policy. In the preface of his book, he credits discussions in these seminars with providing an important stimulus towards developing his ideas. Paul Samuelson wrote a mathematical appendix; other prominent economists of today were also present.[6] By the end of the thirties, there were two Cambridges advocating revolution in economics.

Alvin Hansen was at the very center of the American Cambridge, and he remained there for over a quarter of a century. In the formative years of the Keynesian attack, he published a steady stream of books and articles promulgating the new economics.[7] His writing was supplemented by personal appearances when possible. Invited to appear before the Temporary National Economic Committee in May of 1939, he "used this occasion to expound the Keynesian analysis of the great depression from which we were still suffering." The hearings resulted in public debate over the issues raised by Hansen—an event he obviously relished.[8] And, of course, through it all, he continued to instill in stu-

---

[4] Henry Simons, "Hansen on Fiscal Policy," *Journal of Political Economy*, vol. 50 (April 1942), 161-96. Quote on p. 162. For more on Simons and his views on policy, see Chapter 13.

[5] We noted above the reaction of Roosevelt in the late thirties. R. Lekachman—an ardent admirer of Keynes—reaches very much the same conclusion as Simons 25 years later. See Lekachman, *The Age of Keynes, op. cit.*, pp. 126-31.

[6] James Tobin, Paul Sweezy, and John Dunlop are just a few. All of these men reciprocate the credits by citing Hansen as an outstanding teacher.

[7] Hansen ranks three of his books in this era as his most important works: *Monetary Theory and Fiscal Policy* (New York: McGraw-Hill, Inc., 1949); *Business Cycles and National Income* (New York: W. W. Norton & Co., Inc., 1951); and *A Guide to Keynes* (New York: McGraw-Hill, Inc., 1953). All the books deal with his attempts to clarify and expand the Keynesian framework.

[8] A. Hansen, "Keynes After Thirty Years," *Weltwirtschaftliches Archiv*, XCVII, p. 218.

dents an eagerness to explore the implications of the new theory. He was assisted in this by a set of vigorous debates with a colleague at Harvard—John H. Williams. Williams and Hansen together taught the Seminar on Fiscal Policy in the Graduate School of Public Administration at Harvard in the late thirties. As they debated the merits of the emerging ideas in economic theory, they profoundly shaped the thinking of students at Harvard. In the preface to *Fiscal Policy and Business Cycles,* Hansen credits this discussion with sharpening many of the points made.[9] There is little doubt that Hansen had a major role in bringing the Keynesian Revolution in the United States to maturity— or at least to adolescence. By the time he retired from Harvard—but not from the public scene—he had earned the title, the American Keynes.[10]

Our interest in Hansen stems primarily from his ability to place the work of Keynes in the American setting. He was, by contemporary standards, an "orthodox economist" in 1930. His 1927 work on the business cycle was generally accepted as a standard reference in that field.[11] He was well-versed in the British neoclassicists, and also the Swedish writers such as Knut Wicksell. His interest in cycles had led him to carefully study the works of John Maynard Keynes well before the appearance of the *General Theory.*

But this orthodoxy was placed in the context of some uniquely American influences. He was, in a way, the epitome of midwestern American man in the first third of this century. Born in Viborg, South Dakota in 1887, he grew up in an atmosphere of rural America which left an indelible imprint on his personality. He remained in the Dakota territory through his undergraduate college education, which was completed with a B.S. from Yankton College in 1910. Like Veblin and Keynes, he did not rush to the teaching of economics; he was almost 30 when he first met classes at Brown University in the fall of 1916. Two years later he received his doctorate from the University of Wisconsin.

---

[9] Hansen, *Fiscal Policy and Business Cycles, op. cit.,* For comments on the effectiveness of Hansen and Williams, see S. E. Harris, "Alvin Hansen," *Encyclopedia of the Social Sciences* (1968), p. 320. Hansen termed Williams a "consistently able, fairminded critic of Keynesian thinking." Hansen, "Keynes After Thirty Years," *op. cit.,* p. 218.

[10] One should hasten to add that his influence was hardly confined to the United States; Hansen's books on Keynes have been translated in all corners of the globe. To date, ten of his books have been translated into one or more languages; a total of 29 translations.

[11] Hansen, *Business Cycle Theory: Development and Present Status* (Boston: Ginn & Company, 1927). He was also coauthor of a textbook in economics. A. Hansen and F. B. Garver, *Principles of Economics* (Boston: Ginn & Company, 1928).

Hansen's study at Wisconsin was an important part of his development. He was deeply impressed by one of the few uniquely American economists: John R. Commons. At a time when neoclassical theory and policy were in their heyday, Commons argued for an expansion of the functions of government. His view of the economic system—and particularly the plight of the laboring man—led him to reject the idea that free markets alone would bring about the best possible solution. Commons' philosophy was one favoring a "partnership" of government and the market. He did not see government as *interfering* in the economy; its purpose was to assist the operation of the market in a wide variety of ways. Such a view seems conventional enough today; it was not so widespread in the first three decades of this century. Hansen accepted Commons' judgments at the outset of his career. He thus had a far greater disposition towards accepting a larger government role in the economy than most of his contemporaries.[12]

At the time Hansen was studying at Wisconsin, a favorite topic of economics was the "business cycle." Hansen's views on this were significantly influenced by the work of W. C. Mitchell, a student of Thorstein Veblen. Mitchell's approach to the issue of business cycles was inspired by Veblen's mistrust of orthodox theory. Mitchell amassed large amounts of statistical data, which would, he insisted, reveal the reasons for fluctuations without the need for any detailed "theory."[13] Hansen saw no need to ignore theory, but he has always stressed the need for empirical evidence to substantiate any theoretical framework. He was suspicious of the "models" of the business cycle in the same sense that E. H. Chamberlin distrusted the perfect competition model; that is, they were unrealistic. Although he has not been a practitioner of the art of econometrics,[14] Hansen has formulated a considerable number of his ideas from empirical observations.[15]

In the highly specialized academic market of today, we would clas-

---

[12] Commons' views on government action were most pronounced in regard to his own area of economic specialization, labor. Hansen's application of the Commons' legacy stands out most clearly in his very early writings on Keynes and in his latest writings such as *The Economic Issues of the 1960's* (New York: McGraw-Hill Inc., 1960), or *The American Economy* (New York: McGraw-Hill Inc., 1957).

[13] See W. C. Mitchell, *Business Cycles* (Berkeley: University of California Press, 1913).

[14] Econometrics is the application of statistical techniques to investigate propositions in economic theory. Hansen has had little to do with the development of this area.

[15] Most prominent of these is probably his *stagnation thesis* which was postulated on a view of the American economy in the 1930's. More recently, Hansen has employed statistical evidence in his arguments on social priorities.

sify the Hansen of 1930 as a quantitative institutionalist with a strong interest in business cycles. By the end of the great depression, we would have to add the prefix "Keynesian." Hansen's peculiarly American roots in an otherwise rather orthodox background make his conversion to the new economics of considerable interest to the historian of thought. He has, fortunately, provided us with a very complete record of his thoughts in that decade between the stock market crash and the outbreak of World War II. One can see in these writings the gradual erosion of his skepticism as it gives way to enthusiastic support of the new economics.

Certainly his initial interest in Keynes is not surprising. Hansen was, after all, a leading theorist in the area of business cycles in this country. He was convinced that external forces, usually in the form of sharp fluctuations of investment, were largely responsible for business fluctuations. Already uncertain that self-correcting tendencies in a market economy would effectively counter such forces, the catastrophe of the thirties added statistical support for a view that came increasingly to dominate his thinking: an unacceptably high level of idle resources might persist over a long period of time. Keynes's vehement arguments for direct investment were certainly interesting.[16]

Interesting, but not convincing in 1936. Keynes's dry mathematical expositions, showing the need for added investment, did not adequately meet the demand that any government program be in harmony with private investment plans. Commenting on suggestions by Keynes that public works might effectively combat unemployment in 1933, Hansen was hardly taken with the idea:

> The justification of public works must always be something more than that they stimulate investment. . . . It is a mistake to suppose that it makes no difference whether the increase in the rate of investment is undertaken by the government in a program of public works or by private enterprise in an expansion of long range investment. Whenever the government emits a large issue of bonds it weakens the *confidence* in the capital market and therefore postpones, delays, and discourages private investment. . . . A public works policy is in danger of getting unwarranted support from a far too mechanistic interpretation of Keynes' equations. . . . Against

---

[16] Hansen published a large collection of articles and books in the thirties. Perhaps the work which best summarizes his attitude in the period are his essays in *Full Recovery or Stagnation?* (New York: W. W. Norton & Co., Inc., 1938).

implicit faith, derived from the fundamental equations, in the artificial stimulation of investment, we cannot warn too strongly.[17]

Hansen was not yet convinced by the theoretical arguments of Keynes. In fact, his own policy recommendations at the trough of the Depression in the United States followed precisely the neoclassical logic: he advocated wage cuts to restore full employment. It was not a recommendation which found favor in the bulk of the profession.[18] Yet his stand was consistent with a conviction that interference in the private markets was likely to do more harm than good in the long run. One Keynesian precept that Hansen never seemed to accept was the Britisher's dictum that "in the long run we are all dead."

His doubts were only slightly assuaged by the less technical presentation of the *General Theory*. In a review of that volume soon after it was published, Hansen still viewed Keynes's proposals as favoring "artificially contrived measures" of government investment.[19] He did concede, however, that the neoclassical policy recommendations seemed inadequate, and he noted with approval that Keynes "warns us, in a provocative manner, of the danger of reasoning based on assumptions which no longer fit the facts of economic life."[20]

The doubts Hansen expressed towards Keynesian prescriptions were changed in large part by the "facts of economic life" from 1936 to 1938. By 1940 his fear of intervention was pushed aside by the statistics of underemployment; he was criticizing the New Deal for its timidity in generating public works projects to promote expenditures of "a purely salvaging character."[21] His testimony before the Temporary National Economic Committee in 1939 was in a similar vein.[22] Say's Law was a

---

[17] Alvin Hansen and Herbert Trout, "Annual Survey of Business Cycle Theory: Investment and Saving in Business Cycle Theory," *Econometrica*, vol. 1, no. 2 (April 1933), 131-33. The comments were not directed at the *General Theory*, but rather at Keynes's *Treatise on Money, op. cit.*, published in 1930.

[18] On the views of American economists in the early thirties, see J. R. Davis, "Chicago Economists, Deficit Budgets, and the Early 1930's," *American Economic Review*, vol. LVIII (June 1968), 476-82.

[19] A. Hansen, "Mr. Keynes on Underemployment Equilibrium," *Journal of Political Economy*, vol. 44, no. 5 (October 1936), 667-86. Quote on p. 682.

[20] *Ibid.*

[21] Hansen, *Fiscal Policy, op. cit.*, pp. 94-95. Chap. XVIII of *Full Recovery or Stagnation?* shows an earlier (1937) emergence of this conviction that the New Deal was not moving fast enough to boost expenditures on public works.

[22] See *Investigation of Concentration of Economic Power*, Hearings Before the Temporary National Economic Committee, Congress of the United States, 77th Congress, 1st Session.

myth in the context of twentieth century America. Hansen was already reaching beyond Keynes towards an argument that government would have to intervene increasingly to avoid underemployment in the economy.

The path by which Hansen reached agreement with Keynes was influenced rather clearly by his previous background. Those influences were to carry him, and some of his students, well beyond the scope of the *General Theory*. By the time of World War II, Hansen had become profoundly pessimistic about the prospect of private investment opportunities contining to enable full use of resources in the economy. The statistical evidence of the thirties was apparently overwhelming; the long-run prospect for the American economy was stagnation. Hansen's treatment of this question and his pursuit of problems in the postwar era greatly expanded the range of issues which the Keynesian framework had introduced. Before we consider this, however, we must pause to note Hansen's contribution to the theoretical development of the Keynesian system in the United States.

A Guide to Keynes

Alvin Hansen's acceptance of Keynes's views on government investment was, as we have stressed, a gradual transition. The evidence on the economic changes in the 1930's increasingly showed Hansen that the Keynesian framework was a more effective way of looking at the economic problems of a modern economy. But he was quite aware that the *General Theory* had raised as many issues as it had answered. He was not alone. A willing audience of students at Harvard assisted him in his attempts to refine and clarify Keynes's arguments. Though not a particularly forceful speaker, he had a knack for getting to the core of the argument. His statistical analysis was not sophisticated, yet it invariably served to make the point desired. His teaching skill was widely acknowledged; it is not surprising, perhaps, that it was one of Hansen's students—Paul Samuelson—who first presented the profession with a truly "Keynesian" textbook.[23]

By the end of the 1940's, Hansen's attempts at integrating Keynes and the older views of income determination led him to review carefully the Keynesian argument as it appeared in the *General Theory*. In his *Guide to Keynes*, Hansen went through the *General Theory* chapter

---

[23] P. A. Samuelson, *Economics* (New York: McGraw-Hill Inc., 1948). See the discussion in the next chapter on the influence of this text and Samuelson's acknowledgment of a debt to Hansen.

by chapter and took up the issues which had developed from each. Most of his thoughts had been previously published; the *Guide* was primarily a teaching aid to understand Keynes. Its importance as an explanation of the Keynesian viewpoint was substantial. Even today, *A Guide to Keynes* is a frequent companion to the *General Theory* on the bookshelves.[24] Hansen's summary of Keynes is a convenient benchmark to observe the progress of the new economics. By 1953, the quantity theory, which had so thoroughly dominated economic thought 50 years earlier, was no longer the only—or even the dominant—explanation of prices and incomes.[25] Owing in no small part to Hansen's efforts, Keynes had come of age. Not surprisingly, Hansen is proud of his role in this change in attitudes.

Many of the arguments which engaged Hansen's attention in his effort to clarify Keynes seem trivial today. Debates over definitions, heated exchanges involving the explanation of various equilibrium situations, and similar details were all part of the Keynesian "Revolution" during the 1940's.[26]

As we have seen, the *multiplier* is a crucial concept of the Keynesian approach to aggregate economics. It provides the analytical means of showing the effects of a change in aggregate demand. Here again, Hansen provided clear explanations of how the multiplier works. Keynes's treatment of the multiplier involved "an arithmetical multiplier which was tautological."[27] While it was not incorrect, such a view did little to illustrate the interaction of forces providing the new level of income. If the government increases investment in some period, income in that period rises by the amount spent. In succeeding periods, *consumption*

---

[24] When, some years ago, the *General Theory* was put out in paperback in the United States, sales of the *Guide* rose appreciably.

[25] The quantity theory, as we shall see, was never very near extinction. In some areas it thrived and ultimately reemerged in the 1950's to challenge the by then Keynesian "orthodoxy." See Chapter 13 on Simons and Chapter 14 on Friedman.

[26] Keynes had introduced a new way of defining *saving* and *investment* which caused considerable confusion. On the one hand, Keynes argued that *intended* saving—which depended on the level of income—need not always equal *intended* investment—which was largely "autonomous." On the other hand, the total income saved must always be *identical* with the total income invested in any period. This identity of saving and investment was confused by many as an equilibrium condition—that *intended saving* must be identical to *intended investment*. Hansen was one of the earliest to see the pitfalls in Keynes's definitions, and he carefully elaborated the difference between the *accounting identity* and the *equilibrium condition* that saving equals investment *ex ante*.

[27] Hansen, *A Guide to Keynes, op. cit.*, p. 111. We have already discussed Keynes's treatment of the multiplier. See Chapter 7.

must also rise from this added income. While this added income will gradually dwindle to zero, the *total income* resulting from the initial investment will be some multiple of the sum spent. In fact, the mathematical relation is given by the equation

$$k = I + MPC\,(I) + MPC(MPC(I)) + MPC\,(MPC^2(I)) + \ldots = \frac{1}{1 - MPC} \quad (8.1)$$

which is precisely what Keynes's equation said in the *General Theory*.[28] Of course, if the government continues to spend funds equal to (*I*) *each period*, then income will eventually rise by $k(I)$ and remain at the higher level[29]

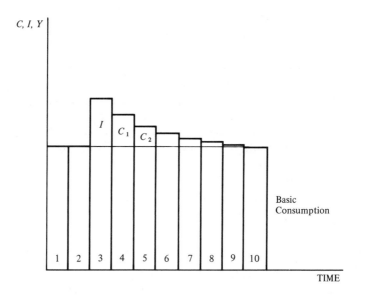

FIGURE 8.1

---

[28] The graphical presentation which Hansen used to explain the equation is illustrated in Figure 8.1. The initial investment (*I*) generates successive increments of added consumption (C_1, C_2 . . .). When added together, the sum will be that of the *General Theory's* equation.

[29] Hansen's corresponding graphical treatment of the phenomenon is illustrated in Figure 8.2. Since the added investment continues, the increments of added consumption pyramid as each successive period elapses. The magnitude of the increase in income for succeeding periods will again work out to be $k(I)$.

$$Y' = Y + \frac{1}{(1 - MPC)}(I) \qquad\qquad (8.2)$$

The multiplier is a cornerstone of the Keynesian analysis. Hansen's careful explanation of the way in which it operates was an important step towards greater understanding of the implications of Keynes.

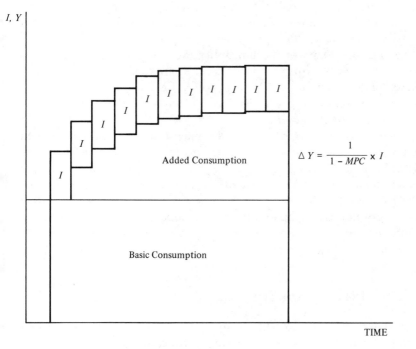

FIGURE 8.2

To be able to use the multiplier as a tool of analysis, one must be able to estimate accurately the "leakages" from the flow of income in each period. In the simple case postulated by the *General Theory*, the only leakage was savings—given by the consumption function. But other leakages—such as taxes—might be far more complex; the estimation of a "tax multiplier" is complicated by the need to know exactly where the tax will generate a leakage.

Furthermore, the decision as to what is done with the savings is not irrelevant. Most economists would agree that a rise in expenditure might induce added investment as well as saving. Then, as the level of expenditure rose, still more investment would be forthcoming. This situation involves the *accelerator principle*. The interaction between the *accelerator* (expressing the effect of a changing rate of consumption on the level of investment) and the *multiplier* (expressing the effects of a change in investment on the level of income) is extremely complex. While it was initially explored by Paul Samuelson in the academic journals, he credits Hansen with first developing the idea.[30]

We have already noted Hansen's blending of statistics and Keynesian analysis to make the arguments more persuasive. His caution regarding the complexity of the multiplier did not prevent him from insisting that it could provide a very useful approximation with which to evaluate policy alternatives. At one point, he felt that J. M. Clark's estimate that the leakages from income flows in the United States amounted to about one third was reasonably close.[31] He employed such rough estimates to point out the magnitudes of the government action which would have been required to avoid slumps such as those of 1929-31 and 1937-38.[32] The importance of such estimates is not so much their accuracy (or lack of it) as their role as an expository device to illustrate the merits of Keynes's approach. Hansen left it to others to develop the complex econometric models which show in detail the interactions of the multiplier-accelerator relationship; he merely pointed out the possibilities.

The Hicks-Hansen Synthesis

The *General Theory* had hardly appeared before economists were vigorously challenging some of Keynes's conclusions. Keynes had insisted that the neoclassical theory of the interest rate was incomplete. His critics soon replied that his own explanation was itself incomplete. Hansen's statement of the debate provides an excellent synopsis of the protagonists as they argued the issue; and we thus quote him in some length:

---

[30] Paul A. Samuelson, *The Collected Scientific Papers of Paul A. Samuelson*, ed. Joseph E. Stiglitz (Cambridge: M.I.T. Press, 1966), vol. 2, p. 1107. For Hansen's own thoughts on the accelerator, see Hansen, *Business Cycles and National Income*, *op. cit.*, chap. 11.

[31] Hansen, *Fiscal Policy and Business Cycles*, *op. cit.*, p. 282. He also cites work by Tinbergen and Kuznets.

[32] *Ibid.*, chap. IV.

According to classical theory the [interest] rate is determined by the intersection of the investment-demand schedule and the saving schedule—schedules disclosing the relation of investment and saving to the rate of interest.

No solution, however, is possible because the position of the saving schedule will vary with the level of real income. As income rises, the schedule will shift to the right. Thus we cannot know what the rate of interest will be unless we already know the income level. And we cannot know the income level without already knowing the rate of interest, since a lower interest rate will mean a larger volume of investment and so, via the multiplier, a higher level of real income. The classical analysis, therefore, offers no solution. . . . In the Keynesian case the money supply and the demand schedules cannot give the rate of interest unless we already know the income level; in the classical case the demand and supply schedules for saving offer no solution until the income is known. Keynes's criticism of the classical theory applies equally to his own theory.[33]

The impasse apparently created by these indeterminants is not, however, irreconcilable, for it involves no logical contradictions within the two economic models. An eclectic approach was soon taken by the English economist J. R. Hicks, who showed that the "Keynesian" and "neoclassical" views could be examined in a single, consistent, economic model. Others hastened to elaborate on this point.[34]

In the United States, Hansen was a leading figure in the theoretical construction of this "synthesis" between the new economics and its predecessors. The "neoclassical synthesis" of Hansen argued that the level of savings might depend on *both* the interest rate *and* the level of

---

[33] Hansen, *A Guide to Keynes*, pp. 140, 141.

[34] J. R. Hicks, "Mr. Keynes and the Classics: A Suggested Interpretation," *Econometrica*, vol. 5 (April 1937), 147-59. While Hicks was the earliest writer to propose a "synthesis" of the two approaches, he was by no means the only one to take an eclectic approach to the problem. Franco Modigliani discussed the two models in his "Liquidity Preference and the Theory of Interest and Money," *Econometrica*, vol. 12 (January 1944), 45-88. Don Patinkin started a whole new controversy with his statement of the neoclassical position in his "Price Flexibility and Full Employment," *American Economic Review*, vol. 38 (September 1948), 543-64. Nonetheless, it is Hicks's formulation of the synthesis which has been most often employed as an expository device comparing the two approaches. Hansen elaborated on Hicks's work in his *Monetary Theory and Fiscal Policy*, *op. cit.* A somewhat different presentation of the "synthesis" was developed by A. P. Lerner in his *Economics of Employment* (New York: McGraw-Hill, Inc., 1951), pp. 117-21.

income. Similarly, the money balances held by the public might vary not only with the rate of interest—Keynes's liquidity preference—but also with the level of income; a possibility not considered in the *General Theory*. Then the "indeterminacy" of both the new and traditional approaches disappears into a more general analytical framework. Hansen was a leading figure in developing such a general presentation in simple terms. It remains, nonetheless, a complex exercise for the nonspecialist, and we present it in an appendix for the interested reader.

Though much of the semantic debate over the construction of an internally consistent analytical framework has been removed through this eclectic approach to "synthesis," basic differences between Keynes and his critics remain. Does a *liquidity trap* exist in the economy? Is the level of investment highly insensitive to the interest rate? These questions remain unanswered by the "synthesized" approach, and in fact are still the subject of some controversy.[35]

Hansen was a leading force in the theoretical developments in income and business cycle theory after World War II. Yet his main interest—and most important influence—has been the formulation of economic policy. Keynesian thought shook the foundations on which pre-Depression economic policy was constructed. The most obvious change which could be seen in the policy recommendations of economists was their loss of faith in monetary policy to correct cyclical disturbances. The experiences of the Depression had convinced the "new economists" that changes in the money supply had little or no effect on the level of demand.[36]

Although he conceded that monetary policy was important, Hansen concurred in the view that it was not nearly enough. The government, he insisted, must be willing to make use of the accelerator-multiplier effect through *direct expenditures*. The system of *compensatory finance* which Hansen suggested was designed to provide for a long-run policy of economic stabilization. Two important prejudices had to be overcome to implement it. The first was the time-honored dictum of the *balanced government budget*. Hansen was one of the most outspoken opponents of the balanced-budget view. He argued for a variable level of taxes and expenditures depending on the needs of the economic system. But if the budget was not balanced, the deficit must be covered. Early in his fight for the new economics, Hansen insisted that internally

[35] See the following chapters on Paul Samuelson, Abba Lerner, and Milton Friedman for comments on the present state of the debate.

[36] Milton Friedman, as we shall see, insists that this view of money in the 1930's is incorrect. Nevertheless, he concedes that even his own mentor, Henry Simons, was deceived by the evidence. See Chapters 13 and 14.

held government debt—so long as it was in some "reasonable relation to income"—was *not* a burden on the economy. Payments for servicing the debt were, after all, paid to ourselves. The government could then finance projects with debt rather than taxes. In this case, aggregate demand could be sustained by the direct investment, while taxes need not rise. The overall effects of the expenditure would depend on who purchased the debt issued by the government. These effects might range from being highly "expansionary," if the bonds were taken by the central bank, to having very little net effect on total spending, if the bonds were purchased by individuals. In the first instance, the effect would be tantamount to printing money; total demand would rise by the amount of the government spending. In the second instance, the government spending might partially replace expenditures which the individuals would have made had they not bought the bonds; the rise in aggregate demand would be dampened. Debt financing was a critical part of Hansen's scheme.[37]

Hansen's concern with debt financing stems in part from his long-run view of the economic stabilization problem. He was not an advocate of "pump-priming" (the theory which argued that, once and for all, expenditures would generate a continuing stream of income). Such "priming" could not succeed in the face of leakages from the income stream. Hansen's multiplier analysis clearly showed that the effects of the priming would die out, unless there were periodic injections of new investment—and, in his view, this would have to come from the government. The long-range nature of such outlays made bonds a more appropriate means of financing than taxes. *Tax policy* was then a major weapon to meet cyclical changes in the level of aggregate demand. From his early Keynesian days, Hansen insisted that a compensatory tax policy was necessary.[38] Thus it is not surprising that Hansen vigorously supported such moves as the tax cut in 1964.

Hansen's compensatory finance reflects his deep conviction that the private sector could not—or would not—maintain a level of investment commensurate with a fully employed economy. To Hansen, the problem of the future on the eve of World War II was *stagnation*.

---

[37] His treatment of debt financing was challenged from both sides. A. P. Lerner, a leading Keynesian, insisted that there was no need to worry about debt financing at all—the internally held debt was irrelevant (see Chapter 10). Henry Simons, a neoclassical supporter, insisted creation of money was all that was required. He refused to say that the level of debt was irrelevant (see Chapter 13). In the intervening years, some economists have raised objections to Hansen's and Lerner's contention that there is no "burden" to government debt.

[38] See in particular his comments on taxes in *Fiscal Policy and Business Cycles, op. cit.*

Maturity and Affluence: The Stagnation Thesis

In December of 1938 Hansen delivered the presidential address to the American Economic Association at their annual meeting. He used the occasion to elaborate on a theme which had been gradually emerging in his writings over the past decade. His thoughts reflect very well the combinations of influences on his background:

> The business cycle was *par excellence* the problem of the nineteenth century. But the main problem of our times, and particularly in the United States, is the problem of full employment. . . . Not until the problem of full employment of our productive resources from the long-run standpoint was upon us, were we compelled to give serious consideration to those factors and forces in our economy which tend to make business recoveries weak and anaemic and which tend to prolong and deepen the course of depressions. This is the essence of secular stagnation—sick recoveries which die in their infancy and depressions which feed on themselves and leave a hard and seemingly unmovable core of unemployment.[39]

Although the events of the Great Depression loomed large in his analysis, Hansen did not make his pessimistic prediction on the basis of the 1930's alone. He felt that earlier periods of stagnation—such as the 1890's—provided supporting evidence of the recurring difficulties of stagnation.[40]

His approach to the question of long-run unemployment and "secular stagnation" was very much in keeping with what Hansen viewed as the classical treatment of the problem:

> . . . fundamental to an understanding of this problem are changes in 'external forces,' if I may so describe them, which underlie economic progress—changes in the character of technological innovation, in the availability of new land, and in the growth of population.[41]

Thus, the "stagnation thesis" came to be identified with Alvin Hansen. The term "stagnation" is perhaps an inaccurate description for

---

[39] Alvin Hansen, "Economic Progress and Declining Population Growth," *American Economic Review*, vol. XXIX, no. 1 (March 1939), 4.

[40] See his comments in Chap. I of *Fiscal Policy and Business Cycles, op. cit.,* pp. 13-19.

[41] *Ibid.,* p. 4.

Hansen's views as they ultimately emerged, for it implies a certain inexorable tendency towards a stationary condition that is not, in fact, implied by Hansen's approach. As he viewed it, as an economy reached "economic maturity," there would be a growing gap between the actual level of output and the "potential level of output." Current output might be increasing, but there would be a tendency for it to fall further and further behind the path of potential output.

The stagnation thesis was never really spelled out in any of Hansen's writings. It represents a "theme" which runs through his investigations of conditions in the 1930's and his theoretical reasoning about the Keynesian system.[42] He began with the broad proposition that the principal variable assuring full employment is investment. He was not optimistic over the prospects for investment following the Depression; three factors would hinder expansion of opportunities:

1. Population expansion—a major impetus to investment in the past —had slowed markedly in the 1930's.
2. The opportunities afforded by the settlement and exploitation of new areas were gradually dying out without being replaced by new opportunities.
3. Technological change, which might counteract these tendencies, did not seem to be doing so. Hansen was very pessimistic about the appearance of new technologies, noting that such changes tended to come in "spurts." He did not see a new industry on the scale of automobiles or railroads arising to fill the needed investment outlets.

Hansen, in short, foresaw a declining demand for capital investment in the mature economy. This would be coupled, moreover, by the increase in the propensity to save. The result would be a persistent tendency for desired saving to exceed desired investment. The interest rate, moreover, would not cure the excess supply of loanable funds. The *rate of profit*—which he considered the prime determinant of invest-

---

[42] The AEA address is probably the best statement of the underlying forces behind stagnation, but it does not spell out the notion of a "gap" between actual and potential output very clearly. This appears in his testimony before the Temporary National Economic Committee and in his comments in Part IV of *Full Recovery or Stagnation?* His remarks in "Some Notes on Terborgh's 'The Bogey of Economic Maturity,'" *Review of Economics and Statistics*, vol. 28 (February 1946), 13-17, are addressed towards some difficulties in interpreting the concept of stagnation. A concise summary of Hansen's position relative to other theories of secular stagnation is given in Benjamin Higgins, "Concepts and Criteria of Secular Stagnation," in *Income, Employment, and Public Policy* (New York: W. W. Norton & Co., Inc., 1948), pp. 82-107.

ment—would remain low due to the lack of investment opportunity. This explains the emergence of a "gap" between actual income and that income which could be "potentially" produced with the resources at hand.[43]

It was in the context of these gloomy predictions that Hansen formulated his *compensatory finance*. His program was intended to be a comprehensive set of government projects which would continuously fill the "gap" between potential and actual income. If one accepts the arguments of the stagnation thesis, the need for compensatory finance is strengthened. Not everyone was willing to do so; was it clear that stagnation was the main problem after 1945?

Stagnation and U.S. Economic Growth

The stagnation thesis was, on the one hand, a set of empirical observations concerning the outlook for investment opportunities, and on the other, a framework for evaluating the performance of the economy. Much of the force of the argument came from the statistical data extrapolated from the thirties. It is hardly surprising that people in 1940 took Hansen's unduly pessimistic prediction of a growing gap between actual and potential output seriously. The three decades of economic growth since that time have somewhat altered our perspective. There has been a remarkable rise of new industries and a technological acceleration which far surpasses the rate of earlier periods. Population growth turned sharply upward following the prolonged dip of the 1930's, removing the pillar of Hansen's statistical predictions.[44] Nor is

---

[43] The clearest presentation of this argument by Hansen is in Chap. XIX of *Full Recovery or Stagnation? op. cit.* It is interesting to note the extent to which he relies on Wicksell's analysis of interest and profits to explain the inability of the interest rate to stimulate investment.

[44] Hansen's concern over the behavior of population is nevertheless currently shared by many economists viewing the future growth patterns in the United States today. The importance of the demographic variable in long-run growth on the basis of a more thorough historical analysis than Hansen's can be found in R. A. Easterlin, "Economic-Demographic Interactions and Long Swings in Economic Growth," *American Economic Review*, vol. LVI, no. 5 (December 1966), 1063-1104. Opinion as to the future path of population is less certain. By 1964 the "baby boom" in the United States appeared to be falling off, moving us closer to the pattern envisioned by Hansen in 1939. Preliminary returns from the 1970 census have caused a drastic reduction in population estimates to the year 2000. However, J. J. Spengler paints a decidedly "Malthusian" picture of population and economic growth in the world as a whole in his presidential address to the American Economic Association in 1965. J. J. Spengler, "The Economist and the Population Question," *American Economic Review*, vol. LVI, no. 1 (March 1966), 1-24.

there any evidence that Hansen's fears regarding the "capital saving" nature of invention have in fact materialized. One is tempted to conclude that, like Malthus' prognostications over a century before, Hansen's prediction grossly underestimated the forces toward growth in the modern market economy.

However, the stagnation thesis is not disproven by evidence of growth in actual income; the nagging question—whether the economy has in fact lived up to its potential growth path—persists. By its nature, the stagnation thesis, with its criteria of a hypothetical alternative, is not easily susceptible to empirical verification. Causal empiricism will not provide an unambiguous answer. Difficulties of testing the theory do not remove the relevance of the question posed by the hypothesis. Certainly the problems of possible retardation in a mature economy remain a highly important issue in policy today. Consider, for example, the arguments employed by John F. Kennedy in his quest for the White House. Failure of the Eisenhower Administration to initiate policies which would maintain an "optimum" rate of growth was a major indictment of the Republican Administration in 1960.

Hansen was not one of the leaders in exploring the mathematical growth models which could be constructed from the Keynesian framework.[45] He did, however, become an early proponent of extending the Keynesian framework to deal with the issues posed by inadequate investment opportunities persisting over long periods of time, not just the business cycle. He was, in a sense, returning economics to the problems posed by the classical economists. Writers of the early period such as Smith, Ricardo, and Mill were also concerned with the long-run prospects for growth. But, as we have seen, their acceptance of Say's Law obviated the need to measure performance other than the actual growth path.[46] In the classical system, the actual rate was the optimum rate, for the economy was always tending toward full employment.

The arguments of Keynes and the evidence supporting the stagnation thesis (in 1939) provided a basis for arguing that the government should supplement private investment efforts to avoid having insuffi-

---

[45] Such models have become increasingly sophisticated in recent years. In the present volume, we have chosen to pass over the mathematical developments in growth theory. The basic contribution towards making the Keynesian system into a growth model was put forward by Roy Harrod and Evsey Domar in 1939. Their formulation of a supply function, based on the marginal propensity to invest, and a demand function, involving the marginal propensity to save, set up the general identity which is present in most aggregate growth models.

[46] See Chapter 2.

cient levels of aggregate demand. Yet even in 1938, as he discussed the problems of stagnation with his colleagues in the American Economic Association, Hansen was quite cautious in advocating large scale government investments. He warned that:

> . . . public spending is the easiest of all recovery methods, and therein lies its danger. If it is carried too far we neglect to attack those specific maladjustments without the removal of which we cannot attain a workable cost-price structure, and therefore we fail to achieve the otherwise available flow of private investment.[47]

The prosperity of the postwar years indicated that the pessimistic picture he painted in 1938 was not developing as predicted. In part, Hansen conceded that this reflected his error in accurately foreseeing trends in population and innovation. But the failure of the "gap" to appear in the statistics also reflected what he felt were some substantial changes in the economic system. Writing in 1957, he contended that:

> The stagnation of the thirties forced us to undertake a remodeling of our economic system. We have equipped the economic machine with cushions which tend to stop the headlong crash into depressions. The consumption base has been broadened and made stronger. . . . The *extensive* forces having weakened, we have done a good deal to strengthen the forces making for *intensive* expansion.[48]

The combination of institutional change—including an expanded role for government—and appearance of new sectors of vigorous growth had apparently greatly *reduced* the problem of stagnation as Hansen had originally posed it. Yet, in 1960 Hansen stated the case for *added* government intervention far more vigorously than he had in the thirties:

> Our budgets, far from being too large, have been too small—too small in terms of needs, too small in terms of growth, and too small in terms of pushing the economy towards full employment and the most economical utilization of capacity.[49]

The threads of the stagnation thesis are still clearly visible, but one could hardly defend so strong an endorsement of added government

---

[47] Hansen, "Economic Progress and Declining Population Growth," *op. cit.*, p. 14.

[48] Hansen, *The American Economy, op. cit.*, p. 31.

[49] Hansen, *Economic Issues of the 1960's, op. cit.*, p. 67.

action on the basis of the earlier model of secular stagnation; something new had been added.

Hansen and the Social Imbalance Hypothesis

Alvin Hansen had been one of the early economists to recognize the application of Keynesian analysis to the question of underemployment in the economy. From the late 1930's on, he had been hammering away on the theme of government actions to ensure full employment in the United States. By the mid-1950's it appeared that this problem had been largely solved. Hansen turned to new areas of economics.[50]

Viewing the postwar changes in the economy, Hansen became convinced that the underlying basis for consumption in the United States had gradually shifted to the point where consumption was no longer generated by the "needs" of the individual; it was generated by the advertising of firms in the economy. Markets were "created" by the "distortion" of values in the society to promote the production of goods which were not really needed by the consumers. He sounds remarkably like Veblen when he insists that:

> A not inconsiderable part of our productive resources is wasted on artificially created wants. Instead of the durable and quality products that are prized more and more as the years go by, we deliberately create things we soon tire of—things that an effervescent scheme of social values quickly renders obsolete. Never before has there been so great a waste of productive resources on things that have little or no inherent value.[51]

In addition to Veblen, it is clear that Hansen was influenced by his colleague, E. H. Chamberlin. To Hansen of the 1960's:

> . . . it is difficult to see how an economist who has been instructed in the theory of monopolistic competition can still adhere to the consumer sovereignty dogma. Nowadays consumers no longer act on their own free will. The demand curve is no longer the product

---

[50] His change in emphasis is illustrated by a conversation related to us by Professor John Letiche. During a visit to Berkeley in the early fifties, Hansen inquired of Letiche what criticism he would make of his work. Letiche replied that it seemed as though Hansen was repeating himself in his works on employment theory. "You're right," Hansen replied, "and I intend to do something about it." He was just past 60 at the time that he started in this new direction.

[51] Hansen, *Economic Issues of the 1960's, op. cit.*, pp. 46-47.

of spontaneous wants. It is manufactured. . . . Consumer wants are no longer a matter of individual choice. They are mass-produced.[52]

In short, Hansen had concluded by 1960 that the cure for stagnation which had emerged was perhaps no better than the disease. For to avoid the stagnation, the economy must "manufacture" wants to "create" the demand for the production of goods which have very little "inherent value." And so we arrive at his support of the "social imbalance hypothesis," which was independently developed by one of his colleagues, John Kenneth Galbraith. The necessary link between the stagnation view of the 1930's and Hansen's contemporary views is Chamberlin and monopolistic competition. The prospects for investment only expand due to the distortion of wants generated through market imperfections and advertising. Economists instructed in *The Theory of Monopolistic Competition* could easily be led to accept Hansen's basic premise that consumer sovereignty is dead. By insisting that—due to the manipulation of demand—the composition of goods produced in an imperfect market represents misallocation, Hansen is able to come to the sweeping conclusion that:

> . . . an optimum rate of growth can not be reached without a change in the social values which permit a better use of our productive resources.[53]

And, indeed, this pattern of social values will, "if long pursued make us a second rate country."[54]

His comments on the "optimum rate of growth" again return us to the basic concepts behind the stagnation thesis, for Hansen's interpretation of the term stems from his view which holds that there is a significant deviation between the current level of production and the "optimal" level. The emphasis from monopolistic competition is that the *composition* of output, as well as its absolute level, must be considered in applying the criteria of "potential" performance.

Hansen's espousal of the social imbalance hypothesis in the 1960's is no more surprising than was his espousal of Keynes. Perhaps the outstanding feature of Hansen as an economist has been his pragmatism.

Alvin Hansen was 69 when he retired from Harvard in 1956. Born

---

[52] *Ibid.,* pp. 75-76. As we noted in Chapter 6, Chamberlin did not share this interpretation of his work.

[53] *Ibid.,* p. 47.

[54] *Ibid.*

only four years after Keynes, his birth date would seem to place him in the same generation. Yet, intellectually we think of him as a major force in post-Keynesian economics, where his most influential work has appeared. And his imprint on the generation which followed was significant. Hansen is one of those scholars whose mark on economic thought appears through the students he taught as well as the books he wrote. A roll call of economists influenced by Hansen would include many of the most prominent men in the profession today. And they would represent many diverse areas of study. Two names will suffice to illustrate the diversity of interests which could be spurred on by Hansen's work. Paul Samuelson, perhaps the leading theorist of the new economics, and John Kenneth Galbraith, a modern critic of economic theory à la Thorstein Veblen, both give considerable credit to Hansen in shaping their present views.

Like Marshall, Hansen could inspire in his students intellectual curiosity, which is the aim of every teacher. For 30 years, Alvin Hansen sat at the apex of academic thought in the United States, and he used those three decades to help shape a school of thought in economics which—more than any other single group—dominated the formulation of economic policy in the postwar period.

Appendix: The Hicks-Hansen Synthesis

The demonstration through graphical analysis that the Keynesian and neoclassical views of aggregate economic behavior could, in fact, be shown within a single economic model is worth noting in some detail. This appendix relies heavily on the reader's knowledge of the techniques of graphical analysis of equilibrium situations.

THE *I-S* CURVE

We begin with the behavior of saving and investment in the capital market. Figure 8.3A shows the relation of investment and saving to the interest rate. As the interest rate (r) falls, investment (I) will increase while saving (S) decreases. Instead of a single saving curve, there is a "family" of schedules; one for the relation of r and S at each level of income (Y), (S_{Y1}, S_{Y2}, and so on).[55] At the points where desired sav-

---

[55] The investment function could also be made responsive to income by showing a "family" of investment curves. The logic of the argument remains unchanged, although the solution is more complex. The reader should recall that the saving curve *implies* a consumption function. Thus Keynes's consumption function enters Figure 8.3 via the family of saving curves for each level of income.

ing just equals the desired investment (*A, B, C* in Figure 8.3A), the market will be in equilibrium. At combinations such as (r_1, Y_1), (r_2, Y_2) and (r_3, Y_3), there is no tendency for excess saving or investment to develop. We can plot these points on another graph. (Fig. 8.3B) to derive what is termed the "*I-S* Curve." The *I-S* curve shows all the possible combinations of interest rates and levels of income where the capital market is in equilibrium. At points off the *I-S* curve of Figure 8.3B, we will not have a situation where intended saving equals intended investment; there will be pressure on *r* and *Y* to move back to a combination on the *I-S* curve.

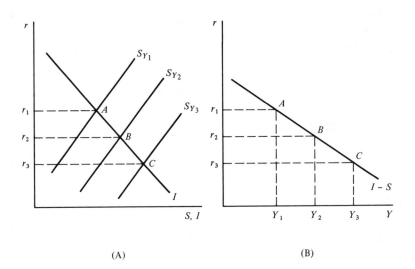

(A)   (B)

FIGURE 8.3

THE *L-M* CURVE

Using the same technique, we can derive a relationship which shows the demand for money balances (liquidity preference) at every level of income and interest rate. Figure 8.4A shows the typical Keynesian liquidity preference schedule. As with Figure 8.3, we show a "family" of liquidity preference curves (L_{Y1}, L_{Y2}, and so on); one for each level of income. The level of the money supply—determined by the monetary authorities—is fixed at the vertical line M_S. We can now determine the equilibrium points (*X, Y, Z* in Figure 8.4A), where the demand for money balances exactly equals the supply of money balances for every combination of interest rate and income. We now plot these points in Figure 8.4B to derive the *L-M* Curve. The *L-M* curve of Figure 8.4B shows those combinations of interest rate and income where the demand and supply for money is in equilibrium. The reader should note that the *L-M* curve will *shift*, if the money supply set by the authorities is changed. The effects of monetary policy as well as fiscal policy can thus be analyzed by this presentation.

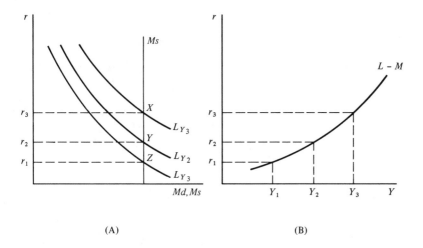

(A)   (B)

FIGURE 8.4

EQUILIBRIUM OF THE *I-S* AND *L-M* CURVES

Neither the *I-S* nor the *L-M* curve alone can give the equilibrium interest rate or the level of income. For equilibrium in the economy to exist, *both* the capital market and the money market must be in equilibrium. Combining the *I-S* curve and the *L-M* curve on a single graph will show that unique combination of interest rate and income which will produce such a result. This is shown in Figure 8.5. At any point other than *E*, there will be a tendency for change in one or both of the markets. Suppose, for example, that the interest rate rose to *r'* with income still at Y_e. At *r'*, people will wish to hold less money (Figure 8.4A); unless income *rises*, the demand for money balances will be less than the supply of money, creating a downward pressure on *r*. In the capital market, the increase to *r'* to the interest rate will cause a lower level of investment to be forthcoming, while the supply of saving (at Y_e) would increase. Unless income *falls*, the supply of saving will exceed the demand for investment, again creating a downward pressure on r. Clearly, unless the underlying curves change their position, only at E will there be no tendency for the level of income and the interest rate to change. The indeterminancy of the two approaches has been removed.

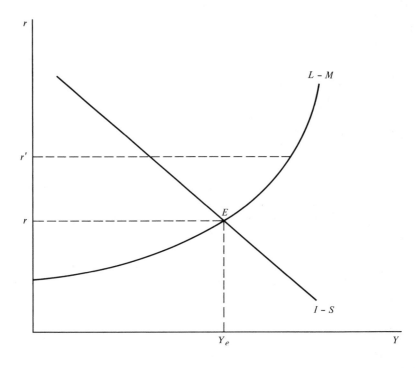

FIGURE 8.5

CHAPTER 9

PAUL A. SAMUELSON—

Economic *Wunderkind* as

Policy Maker

*In the long run, the economic scholar
works for the only coin worth having—our
own applause.*

PAUL A. SAMUELSON

In 1935 a brash young student from the University of Chicago appeared at Harvard. His enthusiastic response to the challenge of the Keynesian Revolution eventually led him to Hansen's seminar in fiscal policy. Twenty years later Paul Samuelson had replaced his teacher as the dean of the new economics. His influence on the economics profession can be seen over an enormous range of topics. As President of the American Economic Association in 1961, he addressed himself to the problem of briefly summarizing his career:

> My own scholarship has covered a great variety of fields. And many of them involve questions like welfare economics and factor-price equalization; turnpike theorems and oscillating envelopes; nonsubstitutability relations in Minkowski-Ricardo-Leontief-Metzler matrices of Mosak-Hicks type; or balanced-budget multipliers under conditions of balance uncertainty in locally impacted topological spaces and molar equivalences.[1]

---

[1] Virtually all of Samuelson's professional publications up to 1964 have been collected in *The Collected Scientific Papers of Paul A. Samuelson*, ed. Joseph Stig-

He went on to say that: "My friends warn me that such topics are suitable merely for captive audiences in search of a degree—and even then only after dark."[2]

Such a description hardly seems to fit a man whose comments can frequently be found in *Newsweek* and the *New York Times*. Paul Samuelson has chosen his words carefully for each audience; his is a familiar name to the introductory student of economics as well as those in search of higher degrees. In fact, the better part of an entire generation of economists has been introduced to economics through Samuelson's textbook—which to date has run through eight editions.[3] Not since Marshall's *Principles*—which also went through eight editions— has a single book so dominated the field. The parallel between the two economists could be pushed further, for each sought to bring together diverse theories of economic thought. Marshall tried to mesh the classical writings with the marginalist revolution. Samuelson was one of the first economists to put Hansen's synthesis of Keynes and the "classics" in a simple and readable form. The success of his textbook is shown not only by the almost two million copies sold; but also by the imitation it has encouraged in competitors.

Samuelson's rise to the top of the economics profession was extraordinarily rapid. Born in 1915, he grew up in Indiana and attended the University of Chicago from which he received his B.A. in 1935. In the course of the next 25 years, he won virtually every honor that the profession could offer him. By the time he was 32—in 1947—he was awarded the first John Bates Clark Award for the most distinguished work by an economist under 40. Twenty-three years later he was the first American to receive the Nobel prize in economics.

When he left Harvard in 1941 as a young Ph.D., he was already a distinguished member of the profession. He had been elected to the Society of Junior Fellows, a position which elevated him into the upper strata of academic circles in Cambridge. Not that he needed much assistance; 11 of his articles had already appeared—with additional bylines already being processed. His work as a graduate student includes some of his best contributions to the field: three articles on the theory of consumer choice later were expanded into a new approach to that

---

litz (Cambridge: M.I.T. Press, 1966). We shall cite Samuelson's work from these volumes whenever possible. One might note in support of his comments that the two volumes contain 129 articles on topics ranging from mathematics to policy and economists. The quote is from *Collected Papers*, No. 113 "Economists and the History of Ideas," p. 1499.

2 *Ibid.*

3 Paul A. Samuelson, *Economics* 8th ed. (New York: McGraw-Hill, Inc., 1970). The first edition appeared in 1948.

problem.[4] Two more dealt with the gains from international trade and laid the groundwork for pioneering analysis of factor returns and trade.[5] And, of course, it was as a graduate student in Hansen's seminar that he developed his contribution on the multiplier-accelerator principle.[6] Small wonder that he found it an exciting time to be an economist:

> To have been born as an economist before 1936 was a boon—yes. But not to have been born too long before!
> *Bliss was it in that dawn to be alive,*
> *But to be young was very Heaven!*[7]

And, of course, all this time he was busily writing a thesis at Harvard. Finished in 1941, it won the David A. Wells Award as the outstanding economics dissertation at Harvard that year. In 1947 it was published as *Foundations of Economic Analysis.*[8] Twenty years later, *Foundations* remains a basic contribution to the area of mathematical economics. In an era when academic promotion was generally slow, Samuelson had become a full professor at MIT when he was 32.

Well before he finished his work at Harvard, it was clear that Samuelson was one of the brightest young economists in the United States. There seemed little question that he would have no trouble getting an appointment at the school of his choice. He made it clear that Harvard was his choice. However, precocity is not always a virtue in the academic establishment; Samuelson's youth, brash personality, and Jewish background all worked against him. Despite his glittering credentials, he was not retained by the department at Harvard. This disappointment was met with characteristic audacity. Determined to remain in Cambridge in spite of the rebuff, Samuelson took a position with the relatively unheralded economics department at MIT. By the end of the 1940's, MIT ranked with the best departments in the country.[9] To be

---

4 Samuelson, *Collected Papers,* papers 1-4, pp. 3-36.

5 *Ibid.,* papers 60-61, pp. 775-91.

6 *Ibid.,* papers 82-83, pp. 1107-22. See the discussion in Chapter 8.

7 *Ibid.,* No. 114, p. 1517. The piece originally appeared as a part of collected essays honoring John Maynard Keynes on the tenth anniversary of the *General Theory*'s appearance.

8 Paul A. Samuelson, *Foundations of Economic Analysis* (Cambridge: Harvard University Press, 1947). Hereinafter cited as *Foundations.* The impact of this work was noted by the committee awarding Samuelson the Nobel prize in 1970.

9 Ranking academic departments is a highly subjective game. A recent study by Allan Cartter concluded that in graduate economics Harvard ranked first and M.I.T. second. Samuelson's reaction was "Like Avis, we try harder." He must be right; of the top five departments in the Cartter study (Harvard, MIT, Chicago, Yale, and Berkeley) only MIT rose from obscurity to the top between 1940 and 1960. See Allan Cartter, *An Assessment of Quality in Graduate Education* (Washington, D.C.: American Council on Education, 1966).

sure, one man does not by himself create a great department. Yet few would deny that it was Samuelson's presence at MIT that enabled them to attract the people which propelled the department into national prominence so quickly.

Paul Samuelson has written in so many areas with great proficiency that it is impossible to do justice to his contributions in a single brief chapter of the present book. Moreover, much of his work has been in the realm of "pure theory," highly abstracted from the world of economic policy and difficult to simplify to the level of an elementary analysis for the nonspecialist. This is particularly true of his work in mathematical economics, and the developments in this area represent one of the major technical achievements of economics during the postwar era. Samuelson's *Foundations* carefully discussed the methodology of mathematical economics and then explored a variety of economic theorems using the techniques developed. His mathematics of income determination—already alluded to in the work of Hansen—provided substantial impetus to the exploration of properties of the Keynesian system. Finally, he is credited with developing pioneering thoughts on the question of a theory of government expenditures.

His virtuosity as a mathematician notwithstanding, Samuelson was also one of the most articulate spokesmen for the new economics of the Kennedy-Johnson administrations. His ability to develop straightforward explanations of economic phenomena—illustrated by the success of his text—made him a leading voice in the policies of recent years. It is on these views which relate to policy that our attention will be focused. But to do this, we must first note Samuelson's methodological views on the use of mathematics and economics.

Mathematics and Economic Analysis

Samuelson has always advocated the use of mathematics as a means to explain and explore the economic problem. He is hardly the first to do so. After all, the marginal analysis of the late nineteenth century was based on the examination of incremental changes which Jevons expressed using calculus. Walras, in his *Elements of Pure Economics,* used mathematics to explain equilibrium in all markets of the economic system simultaneously.[10] Both Keynes and Marshall were well versed

---

[10] Leon Walras, *Elements of Pure Economics,* translated by William Jaffe (Homewood, Ill.: Richard D. Irwin, Inc., 1954). Originally published in 1874. Samuelson feels that Walras and Augustin Cournot carried the development of mathematics in economics to a highly sophisticated level by the turn of the twentieth century. At that point, he claims the study was interrupted by the "verbal" tradition of the English economists at Cambridge.

in the use of mathematics as a "shorthand" to express economic relations. Samuelson wished to use mathematics for much more than a mere device to clarify verbal arguments. It could, he felt, reveal aspects of economic theory which could not be seen by intuition alone. Most economic problems are concerned with the maximization or minimization of some variable (welfare, costs, profits, and so on). If the basic behavior (such as a firm maximizing returns) is postulated as a *mathematical problem,* then one can derive important theorems by exploring the properties of this mathematical statement of the problem.

Such a view represents a distinct break with the neoclassical approach of Marshall, who regarded the role of mathematics in a secondary position. It was Marshall who warned the profession against wasting time putting literary propositions into mathematical form. In the opening pages of *Foundations,* Samuelson insists that this dictum should be "exactly reversed"; it is the effort of converting *essentially mathematical* propositions into *literary* form that is wasteful and "involves . . . mental gymnastics of a peculiarly depraved type."[11] Marshall's use of mathematical appendices was usually imprecise. Writing in 1967, Samuelson insisted that: "The ambiguities of Alfred Marshall paralyzed the best brains in the Anglo-Saxon branch of our profession for three decades."[12] He does not agree with those who see Marshall's loose treatment as an asset proving that "it's all in Marshall." After all, the entire vocabulary of economics can be found in the dictionary.[13]

Samuelson's break with the literary tradition of Marshall employed mathematical techniques which were fairly sophisticated. (Or at least they were viewed as such by economists in 1947. It is perhaps an indication of the acceptance of Samuelson's position on the role of mathematics in economics that today almost any graduate student would be expected to handle the contents of *Foundations* with relative ease.) We shall not reproduce the specific proofs in detail here; in many cases, they rigorously verified propositions derived from marginal analysis. The purpose in developing such rigorous mathematical proofs was to establish once and for all the validity of a set of *basic theorems*

---

[11] Samuelson, *Foundations, op. cit.,* p. 6.

[12] Paul A. Samuelson, "The Monopolistic Competition Revolution," in *Monopolistic Competition Theory,* ed. Robert E. Kuenne (New York: John Wiley & Sons, Inc., 1967), pp. 105-38. Quote on page 109.

[13] He hastens to add that not all economists agree with this rather harsh judgment of Marshall. However, ". . . it is significant that Marshall's remaining defenders . . . tend to be those satisfied with perfect competition as an approximation to reality." *Ibid.,* p. 113, n.9.

in economics. Samuelson felt that it was time for someone to do this, so that redundant literary proofs of these propositions would cease to appear in the literature.

His presentation of a theorem was not confined to a simple statement and proof; he wished to construct corollaries to explore and discover any additional inferences from the original hypothesis. It is important that these corollaries be in a form which could yield *operational hypotheses*—propositions which can be empirically verified in the real world. Thus, through the use of *comparative statics*—examining the change between an existing point of equilibrium and a new point of equilibrium—one can make inferences as to the direction of change, even though the equations may not yield the exact magnitude of that change. To be sure, Samuelson in 1947 was not overly sanguine concerning the prospect of such analysis yielding unambiguous results. Using a very simple Keynesian model of income determination, he found that the possible number of changes is so great that, in the absence of empirical evidence on the values of parameters such as the marginal propensity to consume, very little could be inferred regarding the eventual outcome.[14] However, 20 years of development in computer technology and refinement of empirical techniques (along with improved data) have reduced the limitations on this approach.

One of the most original areas of Samuelson's *Foundations* was his treatment of consumer welfare. He argued that a theory of demand based on the concept of marginal utility was fruitless, because it could not generate any hypotheses which were empirically observable. He therefore introduced the notion of *revealed preference.* Rather than postulating some unobservable field of "tastes" or "utilities," he developed an approach based on the *actual choice* made by the consumer. Much of this work has remained outside the domain of the introductory text,[15] yet it bears on a question of considerable interest: the meaning of index numbers.

We encounter index numbers in a wide area of economics. The "cost of living index" and similar measures of inflationary trends in the economy are based on the measures of price changes through index numbers. Such indices are supposed to reflect changes in welfare resulting from fluctuations in the aggregate level of prices. Can such effects be *exactly* measured—even in theory? Samuelson points out that most of the discussion of index numbers involves the *statistical theory*

---

14 Samuelson, *Foundations, op. cit.,* p. 24.
15Including the latest edition of Samuelson's own text, *Economics, op. cit.*

of their construction; not the *economic meaning* of the resulting index. Using the logic behind revealed preference, he demonstrates that there will always be some bias which will make even the most "ideal" index number subject to ambiguity.[16] A conclusion that index numbers are ambiguous leads to doubt concerning other measures of welfare—such as money income over time. Given changes in prices, how can we assess the comparison of income between periods—or between countries with differing prices?[17] The shortcomings of the measures do not lead us to abandon them; but it is useful to demonstrate logically the extent to which they are constrained by *theoretical limits* irrespective of the data shortcomings.

The *comparative statics* approach to these problems does not, of course, consider the *dynamic adjustments* involved in reaching the new equilibrium. This omission is significant, because the path by which equilibrium is reached may determine whether or not the system will ever get there. The situation may be one of unstable equilibrium which will "explode" when jarred by a change. In such a case, the comparative statics analysis is inadequate.[18]

Samuelson was, of course, aware of such problems. In the second part of *Foundations*, he turns to the dynamics of income determination in the context of the newly emerging Keynesian econometric models. It is in this area that he developed his formulation of the multiplier-accelerator phenomenon with Alvin Hansen.[19] He credits Hansen with supplying the idea of the accelerator to him, claiming simply to have extended Hansen's suggestion and "proceeded to analyze its algebraic structure."[20] This is hardly a trivial contribution; it illustrates Samuelson's approach to economic theory through mathematics. By setting up a Keynesian model of income determination involving second-order

---

[16] This proof is one of the most important demonstrations in *Foundations*. The interested student should be able to follow the logical argument on pages 146-53; Samuelson then employs inequalities to rigorously demonstrate the impossibility of constructing a perfectly "true" index number.

[17] Samuelson discusses these points in his essay, "Evaluation of Real Income," *Collected Papers, op. cit.*, no. 77, pp. 1044-72.

[18] For an excellent graphical treatment of the problems of dynamic equilibrium, see Kenneth E. Boulding, "Samuelson's Foundations: The Role of Mathematics in Economics," *Journal of Political Economy* (June 1948), 187-99.

[19] Samuelson, *Collected Papers, op. cit.*, papers 82, 83, pp. 1107-22. It is in this article written in 1939 that Samuelson makes use of his invention of the so-called "Keynesian Cross" or 45 degree line diagram to depict the determination of the level of national income. This device has become the standard approach when initiating beginning students into macroeconomics.

[20] *Ibid.*, p. 1123.

difference equations, Samuelson was able to explore the interactions of the multiplier-accelerator relationship. Hansen had contented himself with postulating values for the propensities to consume and invest. His estimate of the marginal propensity to consume was, for example, taken from a statement by J. M. Clark.[21] By establishing a more formal mathematical model, Samuelson was able to show the reaction of income to changes in investment with a variety of values for the parameters in the model. He discovered that Hansen's choice of a marginal propensity to consume of 0.5 accidentally produced a steady cyclical fluctuation. Other values would produce cycles which might "explode" into runaway growth (or stagnation) or a "dampened" cycle which would die out of its own accord.[22]

Despite his influence in the construction of mathematical models to explain the economic problem, Samuelson has remained largely apart from the growing trend to apply statistical tools of analysis to the analysis of the economy. "Econometrics"—the empirical application of economic theory through statistical inference—is an area in which Samuelson has not written. He has, to be sure, been instrumental in helping to develop techniques such as linear programming and apply them to the theory of the firm.[23] Yet he clearly prefers to apply his mathematical analysis to investigation of the "pure" economic theory; he has done very little applied work in econometrics.

In addition to his preferences for theory, Samuelson's reluctance to engage in empirical work also reflects his early skepticism regarding the ability of econometric models to predict future economic events. The failure of many econometric models immediately after WWII to

---

[21] Such casual empiricism was typical of Hansen's approach, as we have noted. Commenting on the formulation of the multiplier-accelerator model, Samuelson credits Hansen's *Full Recovery or Stagnation?* (New York: W. W. Norton & Co., Inc., 1938), as having a very "refreshing impact at the time." Samuelson, *Collected Papers, op. cit.*, p. 1123, n.2.

[22] Samuelson himself did not push his investigation further. More recently, another of Hansen's students, James Duesenberry, has used a similar approach to the question of fluctuations by considering the interaction of fluctuations and economic growth with the parameters observed for the U.S. economy. See James Duesenberry, *Business Cycles and Economic Growth* (New York: McGraw-Hill, Inc., 1958).

[23] A paper written by Samuelson in 1949 for the RAND Corporation, but not published until the appearance of the Stiglitz volume, is acknowledged to be one of the clearest and most concise statements of the use of linear programming and maximization of profits by the firm. See "Market Mechanisms and Maximization," *Collected Papers, op. cit.*, No. 33, pp. 425-92. With Robert Dorfman and Robert Solow, Samuelson wrote an early text on linear programming: *Linear Programming and Economic Analysis* (New York: McGraw-Hill, Inc., 1958).

forecast events accurately illustrated the limited tools at hand. Samuelson's own experience as a prognosticator of events in 1944 did little to increase confidence in the new techniques. In that year he published a two part article in the *New Republic* titled: "Unemployment Ahead."[24] The text was as pessimistic as its title implied; Samuelson forecast a serious slump in employment at the end of hostilities.

He was hardly alone in such a view. But he was wrong, and critics were able to jump on his boldness in publishing such a forecast as events unfolded. To those who saw Samuelson as the young "wunderkind," his error gave a feeling of smug satisfaction. Moreover, critics of his mathematical approach in *Foundations* were able to point out that the most brilliant expositor of that school of thought had stumbled in predicting postwar economic adjustment. Even a friendly reviewer of *Foundations* such as Kenneth Boulding was unable to resist pointing out the episode.[25] Ten years later Samuelson was still skeptical of the powers of economic prediction: ". . . I must admit that forecasting experience of the last two decades does not give one high confidence in the accuracy of such estimates."[26] Not until the election of John Kennedy did he again assert policy suggestions based on future economic trends. Even then he shied away from reliance on econometric models.

The Theory of Public Expenditure

As the levels of government activity rapidly expanded in the mid-1950's, the issues surrounding "social" and "private" costs raised by A. C. Pigou returned to the forefront of economics. The existing economic theory of government expenditure was ill-equipped to deal with the challenge posed by these problems. The vast bulk of attention in public finance had focused on *taxation* rather than *spending*. Pigou's own treatment of externalities—such as his road congestion example which we

---

[24] Paul A. Samuelson, "Unemployment Ahead," *New Republic*, September 11, 1944, pp. 297-99, and September 18, pp. 333-35.

[25] As Boulding said: "Samuelson gives a brilliant mathematical analysis of the dynamics of the Keynesian system (p. 276-83). His skill in analyzing the variables of this system did not, however, enable him to avoid very substantial errors in forecasting when he tried to apply the system to problems of the transition [after World War II]." Boulding, "Samuelson's Foundations: The Role of Mathematics in Economics," *op. cit.*, p. 189.

[26] Samuelson, *Collected Papers, op. cit.*, No. 101, "Economic Forecasting and National Policy," p. 1334.

shall examine in Chapter 12—dealt with these phenomena largely in terms of taxes and subsidies to equalize *private* and *social* costs.

Samuelson plunged into this vacuum in 1954 with a brief note entitled "The Pure Theory of Public Expenditure."[27] He sought to integrate the existing theory of taxation with the relatively unexplored question of allocating government expenditures. As he later noted, his effort was meant as "the culmination of a century of writing on public expenditures."[28] His own contribution was to develop a unified analysis which demonstrated that a solution to the allocation of government spending did in fact exist. Unfortunately, the brevity and mathematical notation of the initial argument tended to obscure its contribution to the debate. As one critic noted:

> Mathematical shorthand may permit a three page article, but a few more words would have added many readers, some of them capable of subsequent contribution to the theory.[29]

Samuelson's argument started from a fundamental distinction between two types of goods. First is the *private consumption good*, "which can be parcelled out among different individuals."[30] Consumption of these goods by someone will imply that there is less for someone else. At the other extreme is the *public consumption good*, "which all enjoy in common in the sense that each individual's consumption of such a good leads to no subtraction from any other individual's consumption of that good."[31] An immediate problem arose from this dichotomy, for it

---

[27] *Ibid.*, No. 92, "The Pure Theory of Public Expenditure," pp. 1223-25.

[28] Paul A. Samuelson, "Pure Theory of Public Expenditure and Taxation" (Mimeographed M.I.T., 1967), p. 2. Hereinafter cited as "Pure Theory . . . Taxation." He specifically acknowledged the extensive work done by Knut Wicksell at the turn of the century and more recent writings by Erik Lindahl and Richard Musgrave. Musgrave's text, *The Theory of Public Finance* was one of the first to bring together the elements of expenditure and taxation theory in a single treatment. Richard Musgrave, *The Theory of Public Finance* (New York: McGraw-Hill, Inc., 1958). Musgrave drew, of course, upon Samuelson's work on public goods.

[29] S. Enke, "More on the Misuses of Mathematics in Economics: A rejoinder," *Review of Economics and Statistics* (May 1952), 132. Critics also complained that it was presumptuous of Samuelson to label his views as "the" theory of public expenditure. Samuelson acknowledged the critics by providing "Diagrammatic Exposition of a Theory of Public Expenditure," in *Collected Papers, op. cit.*, pp. 1226-32. In his 1967 paper, Samuelson admitted that the form of his early presentations—even the graphical exposition took only ten pages—may have contributed to confusions of issues in the subsequent debates. Samuelson, "Pure Theory . . . and Taxation," *op. cit.*

[30] Samuelson, *Collected Papers, op. cit.*, p. 1223.

[31] *Ibid.* In the text Samuelson terms public goods "collective consumption goods."

was apparent that the vast majority of goods were not exclusively in *either* category. Eventually this led Samuelson to restate his definition of a public good simply as "one that enters two or more persons' utility."[32] Rather than the two "polar" cases, this leaves us with a "knife's edge of a private good case and with *all* of the rest of the world in the public good domain by virtue of involving some 'consumption externality.' "[33]

But why does the market fail to properly allocate the public goods? Samuelson's answer goes back to the *free rider problem* of Sidgwick and Pigou: ". . . *with public goods [the consumer] has every reason not to provide us with revelatory demand functions.*"[34] Consumers hide their true desire for these goods, since they know that if someone else produces them, everyone will be able to consume them. This *consumption externality* is the crux of Samuelson's formulation of the theory of public expenditures.[35] If consumers behave in this fashion, is there any possible solution to the allocation of public goods? Samuelson begins with an "individualistic approach," in which he attempts to determine the optimum distribution of goods—private and public. Such a situation would formally be stated as one where:

1. no additional gains can be realized from trading goods of any sort among people; and
2. no additional output can be realized through a shift of resources to other goods.[36]

The point of his initial argument was to show mathematically that there was an optimal solution—although it was not unique. A more re-

---

[32] Samuelson, "Pure Theory . . . and Taxation," *op. cit.*, p. 17.

[33] *Ibid.*

[34] *Ibid.*, p. 10.

[35] It is interesting to note that Pigou preferred to treat market failure as arising from each producer's decision matrix separately leading to suboptimal public goods *production*. On the other hand, Samuelson attacks the problem the other way around. He analyzes the consumer's decision matrix and shows that a suboptimal *demand* for public goods can be expected. Of course, the two approaches lead to the same result: market failure. Thorstein Veblen was also concerned with consumption externalities. But he approached them not from the point of view of consumers demanding inadequate amounts of public goods, but on the contrary, demanding the wrong goods of all kinds—public and private. Thus, for example, Veblen would see no reason for public centers of higher learning to engage in any less wasteful activities than private. Such an approach represents a far more general attack on the neoclassical model than that of Samuelson and Pigou.

[36] Stated in terms of the marginal analysis discussed earlier (Chapter 5), these conditions would imply that the *marginal social value* of all goods was identical; and that the *marginal social cost* of production for all goods was identical.

cent exposition of the issue serves to point out just how unlikely it is that an economy would in fact ever reach such a position.[37] The argument is as follows:

1. We first must assume the existence of a "referee" or computer who is able to obtain accurately the true preferences for all individuals. From here it can construct "pseudo-demand functions" for *all* goods.[38]

2. The government now provides each consumer with some lump sum of income which is in addition to his income from ownership of inputs (wages, profits, and so on).

3. Each person now engages in exchange of all goods—public and private—at some range of prices for private goods and "pseudo-tax prices" for consumption of public goods.

4. The referee-computer can now determine the optimal distribution and production of goods through an appropriate juggling of the income subsidies and the "pseudo-tax prices" of public goods. (The allocation of private goods is, of course, simultaneously determined by the market prices which were considered in the problem.)

Samuelson's construction of a "pseudo-market equilibrium" using an abstract mathematical model is another example of the way in which mathematics can explore beyond the boundaries of intuition. Unfortunately, the outcome in this case is not very encouraging to those who seek answers to the issues surrounding government expenditure theory. For whatever its relevance to computer science, Samuelson's model has *no* relevance to market behavior.[39] In fact, far from giving a solution to the question, it provides a "corrosive nihilism" which seems "needed to puncture the bubble of vague and wishful thinking in these matters."[40] Having shown market failure, Samuelson points out that theorists have provided very little additional insight into the questions of collective decisions which lie behind government expenditures.

---

[37] This section is taken from Samuelson, "Pure Theory . . . and Taxation," *op. cit.*, especially the appendix of that paper. Essentially the same logical argument is in his earlier writings. All the presentations are highly abstract, and we shall eschew detailed discussion of the model here.

[38] The demand functions are *pseudo* in that they could never be actually measured in the market due to the incentive of the individual to hide his true preferences for a public good.

[39] *Ibid.*, p. 10.

[40] *Ibid.*, p. 16.

The highly abstract nature of the discussion of public goods inevitably raises the question of whether such a model can provide insight into the policy proposals of the real world. To point out its relevance, we shall consider some of the issues raised by critics since Samuelson's initial statement of the problem in 1954.

One of the most troublesome points involved the nature of the consumption externality in public goods analysis. To a considerable extent, this could be removed by effective "exclusion" devices, which prevented other consumers from enjoying the public good.[41] The question of whether or not the good is a public good then turns upon the cost of excluding consumers. Where such costs are very high—as in national defense—the good will be classified as a public good; where such costs are quite low—as in the case of television—the good approaches a private good.[42] However, Samuelson insists that the use of such exclusion devices does not remove the inherent incentive on the part of the consumer to hide his preferences for the good. Even if exclusion devices allowed us to achieve the "pseudo-prices" of his omniscient computer, "it still pays that last man to dissemble and hide his true liking for the [public good]."[43]

The question of determining which goods shall be public goods leads into the broad issue of justifying government intervention in a market economy. An early criticism of Samuelson's public goods approach is that it failed to shed light on this important question. Samuelson's reply was that it was not intended to provide criteria for government action; his public goods model was designed to deal with the issue of allocation of expenditures once the goods were determined. He did, however, elaborate on several criteria which he thought would justify government action:

---

[41] An example which has been used in the debate is television. Public broadcasts are picked up by anyone with a TV set. However, by "scrambling" the TV signal, the reception can be limited to only those sets with "descramblers." Now the TV signal is no longer a pure public good. The exclusion may be through other devices such as the size of the service. Thus, for example, the audience of a circus all share the service, yet as we move farther away from the center of the act we become increasingly excluded. For more on this point see Roland McKean, *Public Spending* (New York: McGraw-Hill, Inc. 1968), pp. 67-68.

[42] The best discussion of this is McKean, *Public Spending, op. cit.* J. M. Buchanan also devotes careful analysis to this issue in his book *The Demand and Supply of Public Goods* (Chicago: Rand-McNally & Company, 1968), chaps. 5 and 6. His discussion is nonmathematical, but highly abstract. Both of these authors argue that exclusion devices can eliminate the "publicness" of a good where the costs of exclusion are low.

[43] Samuelson, "Pure Theory . . . and Taxation," *op. cit.,* appendix, p. 5.

1. "Paternalistic" policies voted upon themselves by the electorate because they felt the market solution was not optimal.
2. Redistribution of income.
3. Regulation of industries which exhibit Marshallian "increasing returns."
4. A "myriad" of externality situations where public and private interests diverge.[44]

This list helps to point out the relation of public goods to the earlier framework of "externalities." Samuelson's emphasis is on a *consumption externality*, which arises from the government's offering of a good at no price to the public. Clearly the Pigovian externalities are also likely to be present in many of these goods.[45] In fact, this has caused some confusion in the debate over the theory of expenditure, for *conditions of supply* in the production of public goods may be the factor which caused them to be produced by the government sector. Externalities of the Pigovian type must be separated from the consumption externality arising in the public goods. Two situations of supply have received particular attention in the literature.

Almost every economist since Marshall has accepted the dictum that government regulation is required where *increasing returns* are present. Samuelson does not demur. A second aspect of supply is *joint production* of goods, a situation where more than one good or service is provided simultaneously. Here Samuelson concedes that the exclusion device is an appropriate means of achieving optimum conditions. *In both cases, however, the consumption externality is a distinct problem which is apart from conditions of supply.*[46]

Omniscient computers are useful devices of pure theory, and distinctions in classes of public goods may shed some light on the underlying issues of public expenditure. But where does this leave us? The theory of public goods does not provide ready answers even in a highly

---

[44] Samuelson, *Collected Papers, op. cit.*, pp. 1231-32.

[45] One of the best treatments of externalities and public goods is that of McKean, *Public Spending, op. cit.*, chap. 4. A more technical discussion of externalities and government can be found in F. Bator, "The Anatomy of Market Failure," *Quarterly Journal of Economics* (August 1958), 351-79. Bator distinguishes two additional externalities beyond the public goods case: technological relations which involve decreasing costs à la Marshall; and "ownership externalities" of the sort discussed by Frank Knight in the 1920's (see Chapter 12).

[46] On the questions surrounding supply, see the appendix to Samuelson, "Pure Theory . . . and Taxation," *op. cit.* Buchanan takes a somewhat critical position of Samuelson in his treatment of "Which Goods Should be Public?," in *The Demand and Supply of Public Goods, op. cit.*, pp. 171-90.

abstract environment—indeed as we noted above, it emphasizes the *absence* of such ready answers. Here, as in the case of index numbers, Samuelson's analysis points out the limits of our analytical abilities if we choose to avoid normative values in our proposals. So little is known of the manner in which governments measure the welfare implications of their actions that economists can add very little for the moment. But at least Samuelson feels that his model has conclusively demonstrated that the "easy formulas of classical economics no longer light our way."[47]

Samuelson and the New Economics

While the issues surrounding public goods and the role of the government in producing goods and services in our economy remain largely unsettled, the responsibility of the government in maintaining aggregate stability is virtually unchallenged today. This has been the dominating issue of the post-Keynesian world, and its focus has centered upon the effectiveness of the various policy alternatives before the government authorities.

To the neoclassicist of Marshall's time, the need to control aggregate demand was effectively served by appropriate *monetary policy* through the central bank. It was this position which the early—or extreme—Keynesians attacked. To them, *money did not matter*. Because of the weakness in the link between changes in the money stock and changes in aggregate demand, they contended monetary policy had little or no impact on the level of economic activity.

Such a view has been largely abandoned. Empirical research has shown rather clearly that *money does matter*; changes in the supply of money can have a significant effect on aggregate demand. A group of economists—whom Samuelson terms "monetary fanatics"—insists that *money alone matters*. These people view fiscal policy as just a complicated way of getting the banking system to create extra money. To them, the money stock is the single variable with which to regulate the level of economic activity.

Eclectic as always, Samuelson rejects extreme positions: "Personally, I prefer to stick to the middle-road of good, strong value."[48] His views

---

[47] Samuelson, *Collected Papers, op. cit.*, p. 1237. On the issues surrounding the difficulties of public choice, see also the cited material in McKean, *Public Spending, op. cit.*, and the views of Buchanan, *The Demand and Supply of Public Goods, op. cit.*, especially his concluding chapter.

[48] Paul A. Samuelson, "Money, Interest Rates and Economic Activity: Their Interrelationship in a Market Economy," in *Proceedings of a Symposium on Money,*

on monetary policy clearly reflect the influence of Hansen's "synthesis" of Keynes and neoclassical thought. The primary weapon of monetary policy—open market operations by the Federal Reserve—affects the economy:

> . . . *by lowering or raising the spectrum of interest rates,* thereby increasing or decreasing the flow of investment and durable-goods spending, which leads in turn to expansion or contraction in the aggregate of GNP flow.[49]

Though he accepts the role of money as being significant, Samuelson's views are not the same as those of the modern quantity theorists. They deny that the bulk of the adjustment process must be through interest rates, arguing that the influence of a change in the money stock will exert a pervasive effect throughout all markets.[50] It is a major difference in views, for the emphasis on interest rates as the means of adjustment in monetary policy is an important element in the "Keynesian" reluctance to rely on adjustments in money and credit as a means of achieving economic stability. Samuelson's reservations on monetary policy are representative of a large group of economists today. He sees several serious defects in a proposal to make monetary policy the principal focus of aggregate policy.

To begin with, Samuelson accepts the validity of what he terms a "depression-Keynes" model of the economy, where there is a *liquidity trap* which renders adjustment of aggregate demand through the money supply ineffective. Particularly in the short run, this model may be a reasonable approximation of the real world.[51]

More generally, Samuelson feels that monetary policy is *asymmetri-*

Interest Rates and Economic Activity (New York: American Bankers Association, 1967), p. 59. Hereinafter cited as *Symposium*. The discussion of this section is taken from this address to the American Bankers Association in April 1967. Another good source for his views on money is his testimony before the Canadian Commission on Banking and Finance. Paul A. Samuelson, "Reflections on Central Banking," in *Collected Papers, op. cit.,* pp. 1361-86.

49 Samuelson, *Symposium, op. cit.,* p. 55.

50 We explore this controversy further in the chapter on Milton Friedman (Chapter 14). Samuelson clearly does not feel his statement is unrepresentative of the neoclassical position; he has expressed the opinion that were Knut Wicksell—a noted monetary theorist of the Marshallian era—alive today, his analysis would be similar to Samuelson's. And, of course, Samuelson himself was a "classical" monetary theorist at the University of Chicago from 1932-36. To recall what that position involved, he has: "merely . . . to lie down on the couch and recall in tranquility upon that inward eye which is the bliss of solitude, what it was that I believed between the ages of 17 and 22." Paul A. Samuelson, "What Classical and Neoclassical Monetary Theory Really Was," *Canadian Journal of Economics,* vol. 1 (February 1968), 1.

51 Samuelson, *Collected Papers, op. cit.,* p. 1367.

cal in its impact on the economy. Extreme Keynesian writers often described monetary policy as a string which could be *pulled* to restrain excess demand, but could not be *pushed* to stimulate recovery. Samuelson points to a more general condition that monetary policy will be more effective both in *restraining and expanding credit* when interest rates are high, and less effective when they are low.[52]

Finally, there are limits on the usefulness of monetary policy in pursuing a spectrum of policy goals. Institutional constraints, such as the Federal Reserve's commitment to maintain "orderly markets," may inhibit vigorous policy.[53] Present international financial arrangements in the international market are another problem where the use of monetary policy to assist balance of payments may interfere with internal goals of full employment[54]

As might be expected from a man who did much to develop the Hansen synthesis of neoclassical and Keynesian thought, Samuelson insists on *a balance of monetary and fiscal policy.* The possibility of effecting such a balance is greatly increased by the fact that government now accounts for over a quarter of total output. Even relatively small shifts of expenditures will—through the leverage of the multiplier-accelerator—have a substantial effect on demand. Some of this effect can be made "automatic" through built-in fiscal stabilizers— such as the personal income tax—which counteract cyclical fluctuations in demand without any specific policy directives.[55] Samuelson favors such devices, but he argues that government must move well beyond these initial lines of defense against the business cycle. To him, the essential difference between the new economics and its predeces-

---

[52] This contention rests on the view that, when rates are high, borrowers will be "driven to the banks" as alternative sources of credit are gradually loaned out. Thus, the banking system's ability to lend funds carries greater leverage since they are now the principal source of additional funds. During periods of low interest rates, Samuelson argues that the leverage of the banks is reduced by the supply of other intermediaries who can lend funds to prospective borrowers. See *ibid.*

[53] As for example, the difficulties of the central bank policy and the savings and loan associations during the "money crunch" of 1967.

[54] For example, the use of high short-term interest rates to attract foreign capital eases the international payments problem, but it also tends to reduce investment at home. Like most theorists, Samuelson points out that such difficulties could best be removed by substantial changes in the mechanism for international adjustments.

[55] With a progressive income tax, as income increases, the tax revenues to the government increase more than proportionally, thus exerting a brake on aggregate demand. The reverse effect will stimulate demand when income falls. Unemployment insurance payments are an example of an automatic stabilizer on the expenditure side of the government ledger.

sor (s) is the former's *"activist attempts to stretch out the prosperity periods by explicit action."*[56] In supporting this view, one must be cognizant of the importance in assuring that the new economics *is a two-way street.* The policy maker must be willing to employ monetary-fiscal policy to both curtail and stimulate demand. Unfortunately, achieving such symmetry in fiscal policy is seldom easy in the political context of the United States today. Academic acceptance of the new economics postulates has not made Congressmen any more eager to impose taxes or spending cuts on their constituency.

Moreover, a new problem has appeared which has—at least in the eyes of many economists—further constrained the effectiveness of measures involving traditional monetary and fiscal policy. The specter of massive unemployment is gone; in its place is another worrisome problem: *inflation.* Inflation is an old phenomenon, quite familiar to the neoclassical writers. They explained it using the quantity theory. Increasing prices occurred whenever there was an excess demand for goods. The remedy for such a problem was simple: reduce the stock of money relative to the level of income and aggregate demand would be diminished. Although it involved a different perspective, the Keynesian analysis was equally straightforward. Inflation occurred whenever the sum of consumption, investment, and government expenditures exceeded the full employment capacity of production. The Keynesian prescription was again simple: employ fiscal and monetary policy to reduce aggregate demand.

Both of these explanations of inflation rely on an analysis where excess demand (or spending) bids up the general price level. Such a view has been challenged on the basis of empirical evidence since World War II, which indicates that inflation has been present at times, even though considerable excess capacity remained in the system. This would not be consistent with a view that predicted rising prices occur only after the point of full employment was reached. The result was to seek different theories of inflation which centered on the mechanisms through which price increases are generated in the market.[57]

---

[56] Arthur Burns and Paul Samuelson, *Full Employment, Guideposts and Economic Stability* (Washington, D.C.: American Enterprise Institute for Public Policy Research, 1967), p. 96. Hereinafter cited as *Full Employment.*

[57] We shall discuss one of these new approaches—Professor Lerner's "sellers' inflation"—in the next chapter. An excellent review of the inflation literature is in Harry Johnson, *Essays in Monetary Economics* (London: George Allen and Unwin Ltd., 1967), chap. III. On the large and growing literature of inflation, see F. Holzman and M. Bronfenbrenner, "Survey of Inflation Theory," *American Economic Review,* vol. LIII, no. 4 (September 1963), 593-61.

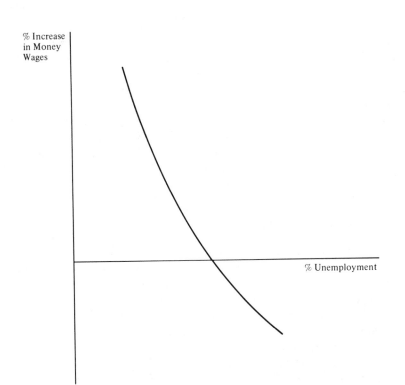

FIGURE 9.1

The principal aim of these new explanations was theoretically to show the way in which inflation and unemployment could be present concurrently. In 1958, a British economist attacked this problem empirically by presenting data on the relation between wages and employment in the United Kingdom from 1862 to 1957. He developed a graphical presentation which has become known as the Phillips Curve.[58] A hypothetical Phillips Curve is shown in Figure 9.1. The vertical axis measures the *percent change in money wages*; the horizontal axis measures the *percent of the labor force unemployed*. Thus, any point on the curve shows the level of unemployment which is associated

---

[58] A. W. Phillips, "The Relation Between Unemployment and the Rate of Change of Money Wage Rates in the United Kingdom, 1861-1957," *Economica* (1958), pp. 283-300.

with some level of increasing wages. It provides a measure, therefore, of the "trade-off" between employment and inflation. It is, we should immediately note, not a theory of inflation; rather it is an empirical relationship between the two variables expressed on the graph.

In 1960, Samuelson and Robert Solow brought the Phillips Curve analysis to the United States in a paper read to the American Economic Association.[59] In generalizing Phillips's analysis, they presented a Phillips Curve showing the relation of *increasing prices* (inflation) and the *unemployment rate*.[60]

Samuelson clearly regards the Phillips Curve as an important concept in the formulation of modern policy.[61] It is able to show the "menu" of alternatives which monetary and fiscal policy can achieve. Macroeconomic policy can, in Samuelson's view, *only move you along the Phillips Curve*. To see the significance of this, let us imagine two situations depicted by the Phillips Curves of Figure 9.2. Figure 9.2A shows the Phillips Curve which would be present in the "demand-pull" model. As long as aggregate demand is less than the full employment level, there is no pressure on prices. However, when the economy reaches full employment—which is assumed to be when unemployment is 3 percent in Figure 9.2A—idle resources have been employed and further expansion of demand will rapidly generate inflation without a reduction in the level of unemployment. The situation in Figure 9.2B is markedly different. Here it appears that inflationary pressures develop long before the level of unemployment has reached the 3 percent full employment level. If full employment is reached, prices will increase by 3 or 4 percent per year. Conversely, to maintain a stable level of prices would result in 5 1/2 percent of the labor force out of work.

The Phillips Curve analysis argues that to combat unemployment without inflation *requires a moving of the Phillips Curve*. That is, you must transform a curve such as that in Figure 9.2B into one such as that of Figure 9.2A. This is a marked departure from the anti-inflation

---

[59] Samuelson, *Collected Papers*, pp. 1336-53.

[60] Note that Samuelson and Solow have introduced an additional relationship in depicting the Phillips Curve as a relation between unemployment and rising prices. If wage increases are accompanied by rising productivity in labor, then the effect of some percentage increase in wages on prices is dependent on the behavior of productivity and prices. The simplest case is to assume that only increases in wages which exceed the rise in productivity generate inflationary pressures.

[61] See the comments in Burns and Samuelson, *Full Employment, op. cit.*, where Samuelson remarks that the Phillips Curve is "one of the most important concepts of our times." *Ibid.*, p. 54.

policies implied by the "demand pull" analysis. And, as we shall see, this shift is reflected in the policy recommendations of Samuelson.[62]

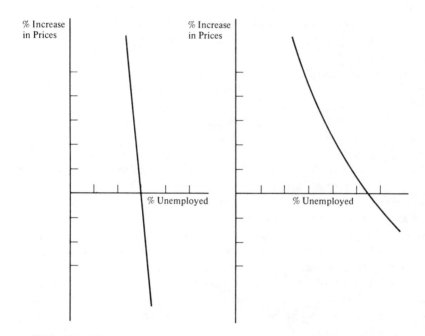

FIGURE 9.2 A   FIGURE 9.2 B

We have now traced the analytical tools with which Samuelson proposed to analyze modern policy. The tools have not remained idle, for with the election of John F. Kennedy in 1960, Samuelson became an active adviser. Even before Kennedy took office, the MIT professor

---

[62] Although the Phillips Curve analysis rests on the empirical determination of the relationship between inflation and unemployment, empirical verification of such a curve for the United States is imperfect at best. In their 1960 article, Samuelson and Solow conclude from limited data on wages and unemployment that: (1) to have wages increase by no more than the 2¼ percent increase in productivity each year (that is, to maintain stable prices) the U.S. would have to endure unemployment of from 5 to 6 percent of the labor force; (2) to maintain unemployment at the 3 percent level, the price index would have to rise by as much as 4 to 5 percent each year. This would imply a curve such as that in Figure 9.3B. See Samuelson, *Collected Papers, op. cit.,* p. 1351.

headed a "task force on the economy."[63] He was one of a handful of economists who helped to "educate" Mr. Kennedy on the new economics. Samuelson was Kennedy's initial choice as chairman of the Council of Economic Advisors. His views, therefore, provide a good guide to those of the new economics generally.[64]

We have already emphasized the extent to which Samuelson argues for a balance of monetary and fiscal policy and for "activism" in the use of discretionary policy to meet changes in activity in the private sector. The Federal Reserve System has always accepted a responsibility for aggregate policy, and it is at least nominally independent of the policies of the government.[65] Not surprisingly then, Samuelson has directed his attention largely to the encouragement of activist fiscal policy, for that is a relatively new concept of government expenditures. The Task Force for President Kennedy indicated just how radical a change was implied by activist fiscal policy when it reported its findings in 1962.[66] The report vigorously argued for *both* an expansion of government programs on a broad front *and* a sizable tax cut to further increase the stimulus to the economy. For the next four years, Samuelson continued vocal support of tax reduction as an appropriate cure for the presence of excess capacity in the economy. In 1964, the tax cut—amounting to about a 15 percent fall in income tax rates—became a reality. It was passed by Congress at a time when the federal government was already running at a sizable deficit. The proponents of the new economics had finally won a clear victory; fiscal policy was implemented on solely Keynesian grounds.[67] Moreover, the economy did respond with a pro-

---

[63] This report, ascribed solely to Samuelson, is in *Collected Papers, op. cit.*, pp. 1478-92.

[64] As Samuelson noted upon learning of his Nobel prize, "I'd like to think that it's a pat on the back for the 'New Economics' which I represent generally, as well as for my own efforts." He was characteristically brash about his own achievements and the prize: "It's nice to have hard work recognized." (Los Angeles *Times*, October 27, 1970).

[65] Samuelson minimizes possible problems of coordination which result from this independence, pointing out that:

. . . The Federal Reserve is like a constitutional monarch. He reigns as long as he does not rule. Within limits the Federal Reserve has an independence. It can delay matters.

Samuelson, *Symposium, op. cit.*, p. 132.

[66] Samuelson, *Collected Papers, op. cit.*, pp. 1478-92.

[67] This is not to say that Samuelson was the architect of the 1964 Bill, only that he was one of the more influential economists behind such a move. However, the economist most directly connected with the passage of the act was Walter Heller, then Chairman of the Council of Economic Advisors. Heller was a member of the Task Force on the Economy with Samuelson, and Samuelson supported Heller's appoint-

longed spurt of economic activity, although the long-run impact of the tax cut cannot be accurately discerned because of the escalation of the Viet Nam War in 1965-66. By 1966, the dominant issue before the government was no longer stimulating a sluggish economy; it was a question of the best way of restraining inflationary pressures.[68]

Although cautious at first, Samuelson increasingly became an advocate of a tax increase to stem inflationary pressures from government expenditures.[69] The passage of the surtax in 1968 was another triumph of the new economics, although once again the delay in gaining the victory was costly. The lowering and raising of tax rates in this fashion indicates some success in showing that fiscal policy is in fact a two-way street. Nevertheless, the deficiencies of discretionary policy in the form of political obstacles were made clear by the experience. The root of this is what Samuelson terms "upside-down" economics on the part of certain legislators. To an economist, higher taxes and lower expenditures are *substitutes* for fighting inflation. But, as Samuelson notes with regard to the congressional debates over the 1968 tax increase:

> Not so in politics. The more the President cuts spending the more will Wilbur Mills *reward* him with tax increases. This is upside-down economics with a vengeance.[70]

An earlier somewhat different example of "upside down" economic reasoning had hindered passage of the tax cut in 1964. At that time, the lowering of tax rates was urged on Keynesian grounds that aggregate demand was insufficient. Lower taxes would stimulate demand.

---

ment as CEA Chairman. It should also be noted that not all "liberal" economists supported the tax cut. Galbraith, whose ideas we examine in Chapter 11, disliked the notion of reducing government revenues at a time he felt the needs of the public sector were already largely going unmet. See Canterbery, *Economics on a New Frontier, op. cit.,* Chapter 18 for a discussion of the politics of the tax cut.

[68] Samuelson and his colleagues wanted the tax cut in 1961. By 1964, the situation was already changing; the economy was expanding even before the reduced taxes had their effect. Samuelson admits that the delay was costly, and that an accurate prediction of the situation after 1964 might have affected his judgment at that time: ". . . if I had had the foresight in 1964 to have known what Viet Nam would do, then I might have had a different opinion [on the tax cut]." Samuelson, *Symposium, op. cit.,* p. 113.

[69] See Paul A. Samuelson, "An Open Letter to Wilbur Mills," *Newsweek,* November 6, 1967, p. 81, for one of his strongest statements in support of a tax increase. By early 1967, he was a vigorous supporter of such a move.

[70] Paul A. Samuelson, "Upside-Down Economics," *Newsweek,* February 5, 1968, p. 71. Wilbur Mills was then chairman of the House Ways and Means Committee.

However, in order to get the bill passed, President Johnson had to promise *cuts in expenditures* to match the *cuts in taxes!* Again, we see the misunderstanding of the effects of fiscal policy. What was the price of such upside-down economics? Samuelson surmises that from 1962 to 1964 the delay of the tax cut by the House of Representatives cost the nation about $10 billion. This made Wilbur Mills "truly a valuable man."[71]

The surtax was an attempt to dampen excess demand and curb inflation. It failed to do this over the next 18 months. The battle against inflation apparently involved a Phillips Curve "trade-off" of unemployment or rising prices. Macroeconomic policy could not shift the curve; it only moved us along the curve. The Johnson Administration clearly accepted this analysis; in 1967, the President appointed a Committee on Price Stability whose principal duty was to study ways of shifting the Phillips Curve. The initial response of the administration had been to invoke voluntary *guideposts* as a means of "moral suasion" to discourage excessive demands from either business or labor.[72] Samuelson noted the use of such devices with approval. They cannot, however, be the foundation of anti-inflation policy; they can only supplement more basic measures.

But what other measures are at hand? The most obvious is having the government intervene through direct price controls. Samuelson explicitly rejects schemes of this sort—such as the proposals of Galbraith. Even the milder act of "freezing" wages and prices is ruled out as too severe a means of control.

While he clearly opposes measures of this sort, he is not so clear about how to solve the Phillips Curve dilemma. Samuelson sees a very diverse group of forces at work behind the Phillips Curve, and they are not always pushing in the same direction.[73] Thus, for example, one obvious factor in the Phillips Curve is wage rigidities. To counter this

---

[71] *Ibid.*

[72] The President's Council of Economic Advisors drew up estimates of the productivity increases in the economy for each period. On the basis of such average estimates, they released figures for wage increases which would not be considered inflationary. That is, the government hoped to "shift" the Phillips Curve by discouraging price increases beyond some prescribed limits. No enforcement mechanism was implemented to support the guideposts, although occassionally the government did try to bring indirect pressure on industries which exceeded the boundaries.

[73] This section draws heavily on views expressed in correspondence between the authors and Professor Samuelson. We wish to acknowledge our debt to him here. His most extensive published remarks can be found in Burns and Samuelson, *Full Employment, op. cit.*, pp. 53-57, 64-66, and 124-29.

problem, Samuelson argues for a vigorous policy of expansion. Over time, the effects of this sustained demand will cause the hard-core unemployed to "melt away" like a block of ice. This will be reflected by the Phillips Curve being more vertical and positioned nearer the level of full employment. On the other hand, the problem may stem from expectations of increasing prices which will strengthen demands for higher wages and prices. Added expansion of monetary or fiscal policy will not lower unemployment; it will simply generate rapid increases in prices. This "inflation psychology" is best broken—unfortunately, in Samuelson's view—by a slowing down of the economy.[74]

Is it contradictory to argue that vigorous expansion and an occasional recession will both bring about a better Phillips Curve? Samuelson insists it is not. The graphical description of the relationship between unemployment and inflation is highly simplified. Samuelson's comments are directed at two situations which relate to very different and *opposing* tendencies behind the Phillips Curve. The resultant of these forces cannot be determined by *a priori* reasoning. Samuelson is once again being pragmatic.

But his pragmatism also raises a possible contradiction of his contention that macroeconomic policy will only move us along the Phillips Curve. Clearly the "melting away" of unemployment in the face of expansionist fiscal policy is tantamount to saying that macroeconomic policy has *shifted* the Phillips Curve. Samuelson concedes that, in the longer run, the relation is more likely nearer that of Figure 9.2A— twisted toward the vertical—than that of Figure 9.2B. Yet he denies that it ever will be completely vertical.[75] His skepticism rests on the presence of what is called a *money illusion*, which exists when people respond to the *money values* of income, prices, and so on, rather than the *real values*.[76] During inflation, money values rise more rapidly than real values. Demand will be stimulated by the apparent rise in income,

---

[74] As Samuelson rather reluctantly put it:

I'm not the one to make the recommendation, but I think it might be argued that the optimal policy in a mixed economy like ours might be intermittent periods of letting a certain amount of slack develop, then getting the benefit of this slack in breaking inflationary expectations, and then going on strong.

Ibid., p. 163. This view of the business cycle as a "corrective mechanism" might reflect the attitude of his mentor at Harvard—Alvin Hansen.

[75] On the long run aspects of the Phillips Curve relation, see *Ibid.*, pp. 64-66.

[76] His belief in at least a slight money illusion over time is again a "Keynesian" heritage. Keynes insisted that the money illusion was present, and made it an integral part of the *General Theory*.

thus spurring the employment of any remaining idle resources. The trade off between increases in inflation and lower unemployment will not completely disappear.[77]

Samuelson's opinions on macroeconomics reflect the pragmatism of a great many American economists—not the least of whom was his teacher, Alvin Hansen. They insist on judging any situation within its own particular environment, rejecting acceptance of some formula—simple or complex—which might guarantee stability of the economy. In Samuelson's case, such pragmatism is reinforced by a healthy dose of skepticism regarding the ability of economic models to forecast the future accurately. He appreciates the fact that economic relationships are seldom as simple as the diagrams—or equations—would lead us to believe. The fact that our present state of the art does not allow the derivation of some unequivocal results, which imply firm policy rules, does not vitiate the vigorous exercise of discretionary policy. There will be times when "we simply have to use our best judgement and guess, realizing that sometimes we cannot have much confidence in our best guesses."[78]

Samuelson's willingness to favor activism in fiscal policy in the face of uncertainty reflects his concern that hesitancy would be an even greater error. His position is that government has a clear responsibility to *actively* ensure full employment and economic stability. And this is not the likely outcome of the market system by itself.

He is not unappreciative of the arguments of Adam Smith and the older schools of economic thought; he simply feels they must be considered in their own environment—not the twentieth century:

> . . . Smith gave two resounding cheers for individualism; but for state interference of the pre-nineteenth century type, he could muster up only a Bronx Cheer.
>
> And make no mistake about it: Smith was right. Most of the interventions into economic life by the State were then harmful both to prosperity and freedom. . . . In fact, much of what Smith said still needs to be said: good intentions by government are not enough; acts do have consequences that had better be taken into account if good is to follow.[79]

---

[77] In the absence of a money illusion, inflation would not affect the decisions regarding employment, since all prices would change proportionally. See the discussion in Chapter 14 for elaboration on this point.

[78] Personal correspondence with the authors, April 11, 1969.

[79] Samuelson, *Collected Papers, op. cit.*, p. 1409.

Scarcity of resources is an economic fact in every part of the world, past and present, rich and poor. The market, with all its impersonal efficiency, can bring about a solution to the problem of allocating these scarce resources. And, barring monopoly and other distortions, this solution will be both efficient and fair. Yet, in a sense, Samuelson argues, this allocation is effected through a form of coercion—prices control the distribution of goods through a system of "rationing by the purse."

Economists defend such forms of rationing, but they have to do so primarily in terms of its efficiency and fairness. Where it is not efficient—as in the case of monopoly, externality, and avoidable uncertainty—it comes under attack. Where it is deemed unfair by ethical observers, its evil is weighed pragmatically against its advantages, and modifications of its structure are introduced.[80]

When asked for a weighing of these problems "pragmatically" on the basis of his own preferences, Samuelson is not hesitant to see many areas of useful government actions. In the Task Force Report to President Kennedy, he covered a wide range of possible projects in education, urban renewal, health and welfare, and resource development.[81] He does not see such programs as "interference"; they are *public goods* where government action is necessary to correct deficiencies in the private market.

Few things elicit a statement of philosophy more forcefully than a presidential election. Samuelson, as we noted, supported Kennedy in 1960, and in 1964 he supported Lyndon Johnson. At the outset of his campaign, the Republican candidate, Barry Goldwater had commented on the size of government by saying:

Today you work from January through April just to provide the government with the money it spends.[82]

Rightly or wrongly, Samuelson read into the statement an implicit value judgment regarding the returns from government spending. Note how this reply brings out his own values regarding the benefits of public goods:

---

[80] *Ibid.*, p. 1415.

[81] *Ibid.*, pp. 1485-86. Compare Samuelson's list of areas where government expansion would be beneficial with the even longer list by Milton Friedman of areas of government activity where removal would be beneficial. See Chapter 14.

[82] Paul A. Samuelson, "The Case Against Goldwater's Economics," *New York Times*, October 25, 1964, p. 132.

What a way of putting the matter! It prejudges the whole question that ought to be subject to careful weighing and debate. Suppose somebody tells me: The first two hours of every day you toil by the sweat of your brow for the food you eat. Another hour is wasted on mere clothing.

The National income statistician knows better. He does not treat government expenditure on goods and resources as a *subtraction* from nation's product, any more than he treats expenditure on bread or movies as a subtraction. They are ways of using the national income.[83]

His annoyance, at what he felt was a pejorative sense in which Goldwater presented the government accounts, reflects his own belief that, if you carefully weigh the issues of government spending, you find that many areas return very handsome dividends on the tax dollar. Moreover, he rejects any implication that these goods or services are imposed upon an unwilling group of consumers:

At the margin in a well-running democracy a judgment has been made on the equal balance of advantages of another dollar spent privately as against publicly.[84]

It would not be unfair to say that Paul Samuelson mirrors the political views of most American economists today. He stops short of embracing the broad intervention of government advocated by Alvin Hansen or John Kenneth Galbraith, just as he balks at the more laissez-faire suggestions of Milton Friedman. As his analysis of public goods clearly showed, he is not certain that we really have the theoretical tools to deal adequately with the complexities of collective choice. For himself, he will accept the judgment of the electorate regarding the sphere of government action, since:

Democracy is not an evil, as the Economic Libertarians fear. In E. B. White's words, it is
'The recurrent suspicion that more than half the people will turn out to be right more than half the time.'[85]

---

83 *Ibid.*

84 *Ibid.*

85 *Ibid.*, p. 134. As we shall see in Chapter 14, those economists who call themselves Economic Libertarians would reject the assertion that democracy is an evil.

CHAPTER 10

ABBA P. LERNER—The Artist as Economist

*The nearest thing to a systematic philoso-
phy is my feeling that it is only a concern for
improving the condition of man which justi-
fies work in economics. This, in spite of the
keen enjoyment I have always felt, and still
do, in the mental exercise involved and in the
achievement of elegant proofs and diagrams.
However I have always felt that this could
have been obtained in a higher degree if I
had gone in for mathematics or chess, which
I refrained from doing for the very same
reason, namely that I found economics about
equally enjoyable and much more useful.*

ABBA P. LERNER

Although the *General Theory* is often thought of as revolution-
izing popular attitudes toward the desirability of government intervention to stabilize the economy, the book itself is devoted almost entirely
to pure theory. The reader of the *General Theory* will search in vain
for the tools associated with fiscal policy that the beginning student is
taught in the macroeconomics portion of the Principles course.[1] For

---

[1] Axel Leijonhufvud, *On Keynesian Economics and the Economics of
Keynes* (New York: Oxford University Press, 1968), pp. 401-4.

the truth is that the systematic treatment of fiscal policy and the concepts associated with it were due not to Keynes, but to his brilliant disciples, and principally in America. Thus, for example, it was Alvin Hansen and his student, Paul Samuelson, who incorporated the accelerator into the Keynesian system. This device seemed to show that only ever increasing government expenditures can maintain full employment. Furthermore, it was Samuelson who worked out the arithmetic of the income-expenditure models and of the balanced budget multipliers. And as we saw in Chapter 9, he invented the simple "Keynesian Cross" or 45 degree line diagram, with which the student is taught how fiscal policy, working through the multiplier, can close the "deflationary gap." In this diagram there is no role for money to play and no mention of interest rates, so that fiscal policy seems to be the Keynesian message for achieving full employment.

But perhaps the most important development in bringing about the economic policy revolution associated with the new economics is the notion that government fiscal policy can be used to fine-tune the economy so that full employment without inflation is always possible.

The logic of this argument was worked out by one of Keynes's earliest converts, Abba Ptachya Lerner. He deserves much of the credit for having secured the fetters of the new fiscal orthodoxy that had been welded by Keynes, and put in place by Hansen and Samuelson. This work, along with his other ingenious contributions to economic theory written in the clearest of prose, have made him one of the most influential academic scribblers of our time.

Abba P. Lerner was born in Bessarabia, Russia in 1903 and grew up in London, England. There he had a remarkably checkered career: Hebrew teacher, college dropout and business failure. He eventually matriculated, at the age of 26, as a student at the London School of Economics, having acceded to his friends' insistence that he was a bright fellow who should enter an academic environment. When he found himself indifferent to the choice between economics or psychology, he settled the matter by a toss of a coin.

The collection of students and teachers at the London School of Economics at that time included John R. Hicks, R.G.D. Allen, Victor Edelberg, Nicholas Kaldor, Paul Rosenstein-Rodan, Friedrich Hayek, and Lionel C. Robbins.[2] Seldom has such an impressive array of talent been assembled together in one place at one time. In this stimulating

---

[2] According to Lerner, it was Lionel Robbins who is "responsible for having made me into an economist." A. P. Lerner, *Essays in Economic Analysis* (London: Macmillan & Co., Ltd., 1953), p. v. Hereinafter cited as *Essays*.

environment, Lerner flourished. Within two years of entering the study of economics as an undergraduate, Lerner published his first paper, "The Diagrammatical Representation of Cost Conditions in International Trade."[3] This article was the first to make use of community indifference curves to illustrate a two-country equilibrium of international trade. It was a virtuoso performance, followed in two years by its sequel, "The Diagrammatical Representation of Demand Conditions in International Trade."[4]

Between the publication of these two important papers, Lerner read a paper titled, "Factor Prices and International Trade," before a seminar at the London School. In this essay, Lerner showed that even when factors are immobile, free trade will equalize their international prices. After the seminar, the paper was placed in the files of Lionel Robbins and was soon forgotten by everyone, including Lerner. In 1948, Paul Samuelson independently worked out the same proof which he published in the *Economic Journal*.[5] When Lionel Robbins saw it, he remembered Lerner's paper, exhumed it from his files, and it eventually was printed in *Economica* in 1952.[6]

On the occasion of Lerner's 60th birthday, Samuelson added a "further amazing parallel." As he told it:

> When my 1948 *Economic Journal* paper appeared, Joan Robinson wrote to point out that if both goods have identical production functions, there will generally not be equalisation. This is a just observation, which points up the crucial need for factor intensity assumptions. Now recall that everyone had forgotten the existence of the 1933 Lerner paper, including Joan Robinson and its author. So you can imagine my surprise when, after Robbins sent me a copy of the paper, I found the footnote [p. 73 of *Essays*] where Lerner acknowledges this suggestion 'by Mrs. J. Robinson of Cambridge.' The French must have a saying for this sort of thing.[7]

---

[3] A. P. Lerner, "The Diagrammatical Representation of Cost Conditions in International Trade," *Economica* (August 1932). Reprinted in *Essays, op. cit.*, pp. 85-100.

[4] A. P. Lerner, "The Diagrammatical Representation of Demand Conditions in International Trade, *Economica* (August 1934). Reprinted in *Essays, op. cit.*, pp. 101-22.

[5] Paul A. Samuelson, "International Trade and the Equalisation of Factor Prices," *The Economic Journal* (June 1948), 164-84.

[6] A. P. Lerner, "Factor Prices and International Trade," *Economica* (February 1952). Reprinted in *Essays, op. cit.*, pp. 67-100.

[7] Paul A. Samuelson, "A. P. Lerner at Sixty," *Review of Economic Studies* (June 1964), 172.

During Lerner's LSE days, he helped found *The Review of Economic Studies* and was its managing editor from 1933 to 1937. During this time he was turning out papers that were to become classics in their fields. In them, Lerner demonstrated his keen grasp of the elements of scientific prose and used his mastery of the tools of plane geometry to extend our understanding of economic theory. Lerner's name in economics soon became identified with lucidity of exposition.

During this period at the London School, Lerner was a confirmed neoclassicist. His main debts were to his teachers Robbins and Hayek, and his main efforts were devoted to extending the analysis of Marshall whom he greatly admired. Indeed it was Marshall's *Principles* which had greatest influence on him, especially during the third year of studying for his bachelor's degree. The year consisted very largely of violent discussions with a group of students, getting what seemed to be original ideas, and then finding that they were to be found in Marshall, after having argued the matters with his fellow students and then having brought them for adjudication to the teachers at the London School.

During his last undergraduate year, Lerner attempted to teach the then new ideas of Chamberlin and Robinson to his fellow students. Like most cub instructors, Lerner was apprehensive over the prospect of giving his first lecture, and so wrote it out in full. As he began to read each sentence, he found himself thinking of alternative possibilities and coming up with novel ideas. To his surprise, the notes he had so carefully prepared for his first lecture lasted him the whole semester. But Lerner has long felt that he learned more from his students than from fellow economists. As he put it, "It was in the course of trying to simplify and clarify my ideas to what seemed like stupid students that most of my ideas got refined."[8]

Among the many significant contributions of this early period in his career were his rediscovery of the notion of Pareto-optimality and a clear statement of the reason why welfare is maximized when price equals marginal cost. In this article, Lerner, for the first time anywhere, made use of consumer indifference curves and production possibility curves to show the importance of the tangency point between them. This diagram has become standard equipment in the microeconomics sections of textbooks. He then went on to show that an optimum is reached where no one can be made any better off without making someone else worse off. He also demonstrated that the loss involved in monopoly is the divergence between price and marginal cost.[9]

---

[8] Personal Correspondence, August 21, 1967.

[9] A. P. Lerner, "The Concept of Monopoly and the Measurement of Monopoly Power," *Review of Economic Studies* (1934). Reprinted in *Essays, op. cit.*, pp.

During this period, Lerner also refined Marshall's analysis of the elasticity of demand and showed how to derive it geometrically.[10] Other geometric exercises on the subjects of the elasticity of substitution, spatial duopoly, and the theory of price index numbers followed.[11]

In 1935, Lerner received a fellowship to spend a semester at Cambridge. There he met John Maynard Keynes and heard firsthand the new ideas on employment theory that Keynes was developing. A first draft of the *General Theory* had already been completed, and it was in process of being criticized by Keynes's colleagues and students. Lerner joined the enterprise. But he resisted mightily the new arguments. Eventually, however, Keynes and Mrs. Joan Robinson were successful in changing the "Hayekian Saul into the Keynesian Paul."[12]

With this conversion, Lerner turned his fine talent for clarifying exposition to the task of elucidating Keynes's new theory. In 1936, Lerner was invited by the International Labor Organization to summarize Keynes's new book in terms intelligible to the nonspecialist. Lerner wrote the article and showed it to Keynes who gave it his blessing. The essay is noteworthy for the early understanding and insight it revealed.[13] In particular, it once again demonstrated Lerner's uncanny ability to state the most difficult ideas in the clearest possible language, an ability that has survived throughout his career.

In 1939, Lerner moved to the United States where he began a peripatetic existence, moving from one university to another: Columbia, Virginia, Kansas City, Amherst, The New School for Social Research, Roosevelt, Johns Hopkins, Michigan State, and finally, the University of California at Berkeley. During this time he established his reputation as a brilliant theorist, publishing over 100 articles and five books.

3-37. In referring to this contribution of Lerner, Samuelson has said, "Today this may seem simple, but I can testify that no one at Chicago or Harvard could tell me in 1935 exactly why $P = MC$ was a good thing, and I was a persistent Diogenes." Samuelson, "A. P. Lerner at Sixty," *op. cit.*, p. 173.

[10] Lerner suggested that elasticity should be measured as the relationship between *proportional* rather than *percentage* changes in price and quantity demanded. The usual formulation using percentages—the difference between two numbers divided by the first one mentioned—gives a different answer according to whether we are considering a price increase or decrease. This ambiguity is avoided if elasticity is measured as the difference between two numbers divided by either the smallest *or* largest—just so you are consistent. See A. P. Lerner, "The Diagrammatical Representation of Elasticity of Demand," *Review of Economic Studies* (October 1933). Reprinted in *Essays, op. cit.*, pp. 137-46.

[11] All reprinted in Lerner, *Essays, op. cit.*, pp. 147-212.

[12] Samuelson, "A. P. Lerner at Sixty," *op. cit.*, p. 176.

[13] A. P. Lerner, "The General Theory," *The International Labour Review*, reprinted in Seymour E. Harris, ed., *The New Economics* (London: Dennis Dobson, Ltd., 1947), pp. 113-32.

But his life-style also helped establish his reputation as an eccentric. In appearance, he is a cross between David Ben-Gurion and Groucho Marx. With his bald pate surrounded by tufts of hair that jut out straight on the sides, he gives the impression of a man with his finger perpetually stuck in an electric socket. Indeed he looks like nothing so much as George Stigler's caricature of the popular notion of the wild economist whispering absurd schemes into Franklin D. Roosevelt's ear. Lerner shuns neckties, wears open-toed sandals and speaks with an inflection that combines an English accent with the singsong chant of a man reading from the Torah. There are few economists in the fold who can match him for color, wit, or pure shock effect.

Lerner the artist has left his imprint on any economics department he has inhabited. Hanging from the ceiling of the department office is often a wire mobile of a cat or whale or other creature, whose graceful lines have captured his imagination and challenged his ingenuity. Lerner's wire sculpture has been exhibited at various meetings of the American Economic Association. In style it is typically Lernerian: the distinguishing feature is its striving for simplicity. This is a task that Lerner takes with the same seriousness that he does the elucidation of his most abstruse arguments on economic theory.[14]

Functional Finance

The most important contribution Lerner has made to the acceptance of Keynesian ideas and the establishment of a policy-structured new economics is his theory of "functional finance." These ideas were printed originally in 1941 in a relatively obscure journal published at the University of Kansas City when Lerner was on the faculty.[15]

---

[14] "While many people make the regular remark that my sculpture must be a nice relaxation from my work, I have to say that it is not that nature at all. It involves very strenuous concentration and is extremely similar to what I try to do in my economic theory, namely to get at the simplest possible presentation of an idea." Personal correspondence, August 21, 1967.

[15] The term functional finance was not used in Lerner's article in Kansas City's *University Review*, but first made its way into print in an article which he published in 1943 in *Social Research*. But the ideas in the earlier article were virtually the same as those he spelled out later. See A. P. Lerner, "The Economic Steering Wheel," *The University Review* (June 1941). Reprinted as Chapter One in his *The Economics of Employment* (New York: McGraw-Hill, Inc., 1951). See also A. P. Lerner, "Functional Finance and the Federal Debt," *Social Research* (February 1943), 38-51. The fullest development of functional finance is to be found in A. P. Lerner, *The Economics of Control* (New York: The Macmillan Company, 1944), chaps. 23-24, pp. 285-322.

In this article, Lerner fashioned an approach to Keynesian economics that clarified the policy tools needed to implement full employment programs and put discussion of them on a fruitful basis. Again, the outstanding characteristic of his approach is its simplicity.

Lerner's point is that governmental financial activities should not be judged by the principles of "sound finance" (budget-balancing), but by considering the effects of each act and deciding whether these effects are desirable. Thus, for example, the effects of any tax payment are two: the government has more money and the taxpayer less. The fact that the government has more money is an unimportant effect, since the government can print money if it wishes. But the effect on the taxpayer is important, since the individual cannot legally resort to the printing press. It follows, therefore, that the government should impose taxes only if there is a good reason for wanting the taxpayer to have less money. The government should tax only if it is desired to make tax-payers poorer to discourage spending because of inflation, or because there are certain transactions it wished to discourage.[16] If it wishes people to have debt instead of cash, then the government should borrow. If it is desirable that people have more cash so as to encourage spending, the government should cut taxes, or buy goods, or repay debt, or a combination of all three. In this way, Lerner was able to reduce everything that government can do in the macroeconomic field to one or more of six basic elements. The six elements form three pairs, with one of each pair being the reverse of its partner: (1) buying and selling; (2) giving and taking (that is, subsidizing and taxing); (3) lending and borrowing.

As Keynes had pointed out, the level of employment depends on the level of aggregate demand. But it was left for Lerner to show how the level of spending might be regulated by policy makers to keep the total rate of spending from going too high or too low. If the rate of spending is deficient to maintain full employment, then the government can buy goods and services. Selling goods that the government has acquired in the past has the opposite effect, and is appropriate when the rate of spending is so high as to be inflationary.

---

16 Of course today it is recognized that this view is oversimplified. Since, as Samuelson notes, a major purpose of the fiscal structure is to provide certain collective goods and services, decisions regarding the appropriate amount of such goods and services must be made on considerations that have nothing to do with inflation or depression. Much of modern public finance theory is concerned with the question of which goods should be provided collectively. Once this is decided, taxes might be the appropriate method for financing them. See James M. Buchanan, *The Public Finances*, rev. ed. (Homewood, Ill.: Richard D. Irwin, Inc., 1965), pp. 130-32.

Government giving (or subsidizing) will increase the total rate of spending, because it diminishes the price of the subsidized commodities or because it increases the money that the receivers of the subsidy can spend. A subsidy is in essence a negative tax, since taxing works in the opposite direction.

The function of *lending* is to make it easier for potential spenders to borrow for either consumption or investment. Of course, government debt repayment has the same effect. The opposite effect is achieved by government borrowing which makes it harder for others to obtain loans and lowers the total rate of spending.

These instruments thus provide the government with six ways to increase the total rate of spending and six ways to reduce it. This is true because, if the total rate of spending is deficient and there is unemployment, the government can increase its *buying* or its *giving* or its *lending*, and at the same time reduce its *selling* or its *taxing* or its *borrowing*. And if the level of aggregate demand is too great, the process can be reversed.

But Lerner is careful to point out that functional finance is not a policy, since it does not tell us how to choose between this wealth of instruments. Moreover, it tells us nothing about the objectives of society other than that of avoiding depression and inflation.[17]

This set of analytical instruments was a *tour de force*, stripping economic policy to its elements. Of these ideas, Samuelson was moved to remark, ". . . certainly no economist can be the same after reading Lerner's *Functional Finance*."[18]

There is an important difference between Lerner's *Functional Finance* and Hansen's *Compensatory Fiscal Policy* that has been generally overlooked in the literature. Indeed, the two conceptions are so hopelessly confused that it seems fruitful to spend some time noting the chief characteristics of Lerner's approach.

Although "functional finance" is often referred to as fiscal policy, it could more accurately be interpreted as containing elements of both

---

[17] Lerner later attempted to show how functional finance can be applied to achieve various social objectives which have nothing to do with the problem of full employment. See Abba P. Lerner, "An Integrated Full Employment Policy," in *Planning and Paying for Full Employment*, eds. Abba P. Lerner and Frank D. Graham (Princeton, N.J.: Princeton University Press, 1946), pp. 163-220.

[18] Samuelson, "A. P. Lerner at Sixty," *op. cit.*, p. 177. Samuelson was so impressed by the originality of Lerner's conception that he asked him why he didn't call it Lernerism. As Samuelson tells the story, "He answered, rather seriously, that some of his students at Kansas City had urged this, but he feared it might limit the popularity of the doctrines." *Ibid.*, p. 177.

monetary and fiscal policy. For Lerner puts his discussion mainly in terms of what happens to the money supply as a result of various government activities, both monetary and fiscal. In Lerner's schema, buying, giving, and lending are mainly effective because they increase the stock of money and, therefore, spending. Selling, taxing, and borrowing are contractionary because they reduce the supply of cash which reduces aggregate demand. To see clearly the difference between Lerner's approach and that of Hansen, note the following statements of Hansen in regard to compensatory fiscal policy:

> It is amazing how many people, otherwise well informed, have not yet learned that compensatory fiscal policy is not a one-way program. Properly managed, it is always on the job, prepared to fight *inflation*, no less than *deflation*. Responsible management of compensatory fiscal policy means the control of expenditures, taxes and borrowing so as to promote *stability*.[19]

So far the discussion sounds precisely like Lerner's functional finance. But in the next sentence, Hansen presents what he considers the specific tools required to do the job. In so doing, the key difference between Hansen and Lerner on these issues is brought out: "To fight inflation, a budget surplus and debt reduction are in order."[20] Note that Hansen had juxtaposed two basic elements of Lerner's functional finance that in fact have reverse effects. Lerner's analysis indicates that to fight inflation a budget surplus and a debt increase would be in order, not a debt reduction. For government borrowing has the effect of removing money from the economy, while debt reduction increases the money stock. In an inflation, therefore, the government should be increasing its borrowing, not reducing it. (Assuming, of course, that the proceeds are not spent.) For borrowing has the same effect as any open market sale of government securities, and *in itself* is contractionary. Debt reduction is, by itself, an open market purchase which clearly is expansionary. That Hansen would suggest debt reduction as an anti-inflationary tool indicates that he sees the budget itself as the key to economic stability with no regard for the supply of money. It is this emphasis on budgetary deficits and surpluses which characterizes compensatory fiscal policy and has led to a widespread belief that "money doesn't matter" among those Keynesians influenced by Hansen. But

---

[19] Alvin Hansen, *Economic Policy and Full Employment* (New York: McGraw-Hill, Inc., 1947), p. 11. The italics are Hansen's.

[20] *Ibid.*, p. 11.

Lerner always is careful to recognize the importance of what is happening to the money stock as governmental buying, selling, subsidizing, taxing, lending, and borrowing take place.

Lerner's Keynesianism is much truer to the intent of Keynes. For his interpretation of Keynes is essentially the view that to cure a depression the quantity of money in real terms must increase—that is, money relative to prices. To Lerner, the Keynesian approach differs from the neoclassical approach only in the way by which this ratio is increased. In Lerner's view, Keynes believed that instead of trying to reduce the denominator P in the fraction M/P, we should increase M, the nominal quantity of money, since there are tremendous difficulties in waiting for P to fall.[21]

To Lerner, it is wrong to interpret Keynes as having played down the importance of money. But readers of Hansen, one of Keynes's most influential disciples, can be forgiven this misinterpretation.[22]

Lerner is also a disciple of Keynes in the sense that he believes, along with Hansen and Samuelson, that monetary policy is ineffective in a severe depression. He accepts the ideas of a liquidity trap and a highly inelastic investment demand schedule under such circumstances. As he puts it:

> In such cases monetary policy, with which the greater part of Keynesian analysis is concerned, does not work and something else is needed to cure the depression. This is where fiscal policy comes in. Fiscal policy can cure the depression by increasing expenditure and incomes *directly* instead of by way of an increase in the stock of money in real terms. The government can increase its own expenditure or it can reduce taxes, leaving more money for the taxpayers to spend.[23]

Thus, it is Lerner's view that monetary policy is ineffective only in the very special case of a severe depression, when there has been a

---

[21] As we shall see in the chapter on Milton Friedman (Chapter 14), the modern neoclassical economist is Keynesian in the sense that he prefers increases in the real quantity of money not by waiting for P to fall, but by having a rule that would increase the nominal quantity of money. The real issue between Lerner and his critics on this point is not over the economic analysis of the importance of money, but rather over the question of whether we should use discretionary policy rather than policy based on rules. See Chapters 13 and 14 for further discussion of this point.

[22] That Keynes recognized the importance of monetary policy is well brought out by Leijonhufvud, *On Keynesian Economics and the Economics of Keynes, op. cit.*, pp. 401-16.

[23] Abba P. Lerner, "A Program for Monetary Stability," in *Proceedings*, Conference on Savings and Residential Financing, Chicago, Illinois, 1962, pp. 37-38.

collapse of confidence, so that investment does not look profitable at any rate of interest, however low it might be, and the demand for cash to hold in idle balances is infinite.[24]

Because Lerner accepts the possibility of a highly inelastic investment demand schedule, he recognizes the importance of an unbalanced budget to fight depression. The point is that the government may find that increasing the money supply either to the public or the commercial banks through the purchase of securities on the open market will only result in excess reserves or idle cash balances. On the other hand, if the government *borrows* money from the public and spends the proceeds, the money supply remains unchanged. But, in addition to the same stock of money, the public now has a near-money—a highly liquid asset that it did not possess before the transaction. Of course, the issuing of the government securities might have some effect on interest rates, causing them to go higher, since the government would now be competing with private enterprise for funds. However, assuming a highly inelastic investment demand schedule, the effect would not be very great. If the government then spends the funds directly by purchasing goods and services, it will directly employ people who were formerly unemployed. Money would then flow from what were idle balances to active balances. Thus, with the same stock of money, velocity would be greater and income would rise. Or, to put it in more Keynesian terms, government investment would generate a multiplier effect (the magnitude of which would depend on the marginal propensity to consume), and income would rise by some multiple of the government investment. At higher incomes, the public would now wish to hold the same stock of money at the new higher interest rate. The net effect of such an operation, therefore, is to increase income and employment and the rate of interest, while leaving the money supply unchanged.

Furthermore, there are other effects that are expansionary. The public now holds a greater supply of liquid assets than it held before and therefore is wealthier (as implied by the assumption that in the depression, private enterprise would not be issuing bonds or other assets to the public which would have substituted for the government bonds). So we have the possibility of an unbalanced budget increasing society's wealth. The greater is society's private wealth in the form of government debt, the greater is the incentive to consume (or the less is the

---

[24] Doubtless Lerner and others were influenced by their interpretation of the events of the Great Depression of the thirties in believing that monetary policy is ineffective. In Chapter 14 we shall see that this interpretation has been seriously challenged by Milton Friedman.

incentive to save out of current income). So the average propensity to consume rises, generating a multiplier effect which increases income. So long as there is any unemployment, the government can continue to deficit finance by issuing bonds which would continue to increase private wealth and encourage further spending. Eventually full employment would be reached and there would be no further need for deficit financing. Eventually the budget would be automatically balanced. The effect on spending of a growing volume of outstanding government debt is one of Lerner's most original contribtions and has become known as the "Lerner effect." But note that the balanced budget that eventuates automatically from the effects of the growing debt is a *result of applying the principles* of functional finance and *is not a principle* of functional finance.

Of course Lerner recognized that full employment could be achieved by directly printing money to finance the government projects rather than by issuing debt. This could be done by borrowing from the central bank and spending the proceeds directly on some government project or distributing it to the poor. But Lerner feels that "it is probably advisable . . . to allow debt and money to increase together in a certain balance, as long as one or the other has to increase."[25]

It is clear that if government projects were financed by printing money, rather than by issuing interest-bearing debt, the wealth effect identified by Lerner would be even stronger, since money is more liquid than government bonds and should stimulate greater spending. But to Lerner the issuance of near-money, rather than money, would eventually produce full employment. In a sense, the "Lerner effect" is a quantity theory of near-money. As such it has a distinctly Keynesian tone.[26]

---

[25] Lerner, "Functional Finance and the Federal Debt," *op. cit.*, p. 48.

[26] Note that the belief in the efficacy of the "Lerner effect" rests on the assumption that: (1) Private enterprise would not have been issuing assets in the absence of the new government securities (which is probable in a deep depression). (2) The loss in capital value of previously issued assets (when the interest rate rises) does not offset the wealth effect of the increasing government debt. (We are indebted to Roland McKean for this observation.) However, it seems likely that the wealth effect of ever-increasing government debt would eventually swamp the capital loss effect. This is so because the rise in interest rates when the debt is issued (assuming no liquidity trap) would be a once and for all occurrence with new debt being issued at the same rate in subsequent periods. (We are indebted to Pat Culbertson and Joseph Camp for pointing this out to us.) (3) It is assumed that the tax liabilities inherent in debt issue are not discounted by individuals who will eventually pay these taxes. Since Lerner assumes that interest payments are to be paid for by issuing more debt, this is not a problem in his analysis.

The Burden of Public Debt

In order to support his argument for functional finance, Lerner recognized that he would have to overcome long-standing objections to the existence of a large amount of government debt and unbalanced budgets. The prejudice against unbalanced budgets is an old one, cutting across all lines of the political spectrum. For example, both President Hoover and President Roosevelt campaigned on a promise to balance the budget.[27] Lerner recognized that he would have to show that government debt was not a burden on the nation, if functional finance were ever to become an instrument for achieving full employment and price level stability.

Lerner's clearest views on this were presented in 1948 and were quickly received into the Keynesian-oriented textbooks of the time. The argument was lucid and persuasive and can be easily compressed.[28]

The declaration that public debt puts an unfair burden on our children, who are therefore made to pay for our profligacy, is a result of reasoning from false analogy. Since the internally held national debt is a debt which the citizens of the country owe, through the government, to the holders of the government bonds who happen to be the people in the country, we, as a nation, owe the national debt to ourselves. Thus, there is no analogy between the national debt and a private debt. The payment of private debt implies consuming and enjoying less than one would otherwise be able to. But if the national debt is repaid, some money is taken from some of the inhabitants of the country and is given to others. The nation as a whole does not have to consume any less than before. The converse is also true. When a personal debt is incurred, the borrowed funds enable the borrower to consume more than he earns himself. But this is not true for the national debt. For the lenders are also inhabitants of the country, and the borrowing only involves a transfer among consumers and investors within the country.

---

[27] However, as Herbert Stein points out, Roosevelt's budget balancing proclivities were not so strong that he was willing to sacrifice much for it. See Herbert Stein, *The Fiscal Revolution in America* (Chicago: University of Chicago Press, 1969), p. 43.

[28] Abba P. Lerner, "The Burden of the National Debt," in Lloyd A. Metzler *et al.*, eds., *Income, Employment, and Public Policy: Essays in Honor of Alvin H. Hansen* (New York: W. W. Norton & Company, Inc., 1948), pp. 255-75. Excerpts from Lerner's article, as well as from other articles and books on the question of debt burden, have been collected into one volume. See James M. Ferguson, *Public Debt and Future Generations* (Chapel Hill: University of North Carolina Press, 1964).

Clearly, the issuance of government securities does not enable the country to consume more than it produces. Since a nation does not have to loosen its belt when debt is issued, it does not have to tighten it again when debt is repaid.

It is a simple step from this reasoning to Lerner's contention that the national debt cannot be a burden on future generations. If the debt should be repaid by taxpayers in the future, the bondholders, who are members of that generation, would be receiving the repayment. Our grandchildren *qua* taxpayers are worse off since they can consume less; but our grandchildren *qua* bondholders are better off since they can consume more. The two effects precisely cancel. Lerner's conclusion is that the burden of public debt rests squarely on the generation alive at the time the debt is issued. For by parting with money, the bond purchasers are giving the government claims on real resources which would have been used to satisfy the desires of private individuals. Thus resources are transferred from the private to the public sector. The burden of debt is measured by the loss of satisfaction incurred at the time the resources are shifted to the government. Since a project that uses up resources needs them immediately, the debt burden cannot be postponed or shifted.[29]

Lerner on Sellers' Inflation

In the latter part of the 1950's, Lerner changed his mind about the ability of functional finance simultaneously to provide full employment and price level stability. He delivered a paper to the Johns Hopkins Political Economy Seminar in late 1957 in which he discussed the problem of the coexistence of inflation with depression, or unemployment.

In this paper, he developed a third alternative to the neoclassical versus the Keynesian approach to inflation. To the quantity theorist, the price level rises because the money supply is too great. A reduction in the supply of money will, other things being equal, reduce the price level. If the price level falls so low that it increases the real wage above the full employment level, money wages will fall and restore equilibrium at full employment. The result would simply be a lower price level, a lower money wage with the real wage and employment remaining the same. So the cure for inflation was a reduction in the rate of

---

[29] For an opposing view, see James M. Buchanan, *Public Principles of Public Debt* (Homewood, Ill.: Richard D. Irwin, Inc., 1958).

increase in the money supply, with full employment being guaranteed by price and wage flexibility.

To Keynes, classical and neoclassical economics "came into its own" in a period of inflation. Although increases in employment and output would be accompanied by rising prices, as monetary and fiscal policy was used to bring the economy out of a depression, "true inflation" could not set in until relatively full employment was reached. After full employment, any increase in aggregate demand would lead to rising prices because the demand for real output would outstrip the ability of the economy to satisfy it. The Keynesian prescription for eliminating inflation would not have shocked any quantity theorist: monetary and fiscal policy should be used to choke off the excessive aggregate demand to a position consistent with full employment. Neither Keynes nor the neoclassical economists discussed the possibility of inflationary depression.

After 1955, however, economists witnessed an upward creep of prices despite the unprepossessing phenomenon of unemployment. Such a situation did not rest well on the foundation of either neoclassical or Keynesian theory. Both recognized inflation as occurring as a result of excessive demand, as a "demand pull" phenomenon. In the 1950's, a whole spate of literature was forthcoming in an attempt to explain the evidence of a coexistence of inflation with unemployment. The first attempts stressed the mechanics of "cost-push" inflation, that is, price level increases resulting from strong unions administering wages without considering demand. Emphasis shifted from the "demand side" to the "supply side" of the inflation process. But this explanation seemed rather unsatisfactory, since it stressed only the unilateral actions of trade union leaders and typically neglected the question of profits and the monetary and fiscal policy of the government.

Lerner, in his paper to the Johns Hopkins Political Economy Club, and in a number of further papers and in testimony before the Joint Economic Committee of Congress, urged the more precise idea that inflation can be understood as a resultant of increased wages and profit margins, made in anticipation that they will be validated by permissive monetary and fiscal policy. This type of inflation, stressing both the demand-pull and cost-push aspects, was designated "sellers' inflation" by Lerner.[30] This discussion provided the theoretical underpinnings

---

[30] Abba P. Lerner, "Inflationary Depression and the Regulation of Administered Prices," *The Relationship of Prices to Economic Stability and Growth*, Joint Economic Committee Compendium of Papers, 1958, pp. 257-68. See also, his, "On Generalizing the General Theory," *American Economic Review*, vol. L (March 1960),

for the "Phillips Curve" analysis that we discussed in Chapter 9, and which Samuelson and Solow introduced into the United States.

Lerner's argument was essentially that monopolies, trade unions, government controls, and other institutions can circumvent the market in the determination of wages and prices. These institutions not only prevent wages and prices from falling in the event of unemployment, but can make wages and prices rise even in the face of a deficiency of demand. Any attempt to cure the inflation by restrictive monetary and fiscal measures simply increases the unemployment. The attempt to cure the unemployment by expansive monetary and fiscal policy aggravates the inflation. So, as the Phillips curve showed, there is some amount of unemployment that is necessary to maintain price level stability. Lerner developed his "sellers' inflation" theory to explain this. In order to make Lerner's analysis clear, it will be helpful to utilize the same diagram used in Chapter 7 to discuss Keynes's notion of unemployment equilibrium.

In Figure 10.1, we depict the Keynesian labor supply curve, S, which is a function of the money wage rate and the value of the marginal product curve VMP_0, intersecting the labor supply curve at N_1 with unemployment in the amount N_1N_2. With a money wage of W_0 and demand curve VMP_0, there is equilibrium unemployment in the amount N_1N_2. In order to eliminate this unemployment, the Keynesian prescription would be to increase aggregate demand through appropriate expansionary monetary and fiscal policies under the rules of functional finance.

As aggregate demand increases however, prices begin to rise (under the Keynesian assumption of increasing marginal costs) and the value of the marginal product rises. This is represented by a movement to the right of the VMP curve which is associated with a fall in the real wage, since the money wage remains constant. The ideal situation would be for functional finance to be employed until the new VMP curve cuts the labor supply function at N_2, so that full employment is reached. In this case we would have full employment and stable prices. If inflation set in, the tools of functional finance would simply be put into reverse gear.

121-43; "Sellers' Inflation and Administered Depression: An Analysis and a Suggestion for Dealing with Inflationary Depression," in *Administered Prices: A Compendium on Public Policy*, Subcommittee on Antitrust and Monopoly of the Committee on the Judiciary, U.S. Senate, 1963; and *Everybody's Business* (East Lansing: Michigan State University Press, 1961), chapter XI, pp. 81-92.

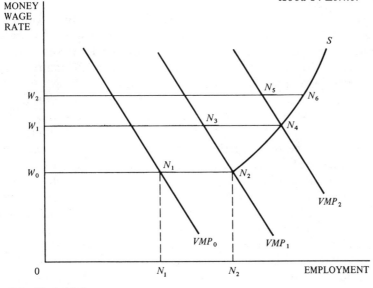

FIGURE 10.1

But in this "Keynesian World," in which full employment is guaranteed by proper use of functional finance *and* in which there are strong labor unions and business monopolies, it is impossible to have full employment with price stability. For these groups may attempt to get more than 100 percent of the available product, since they have market power to raise prices and wages. Profit-push as well as wage-push can occur in the absence of full employment. Assume, for example, that strong labor unions demand higher wages as the slack in the labor force is removed. These wage increases might not be very fiercely resisted since price increases will be validated by permissive monetary and fiscal policy. So the money wage rate moves up to W_1, even before the VMP curve cuts the labor supply curve at N_2. At this new wage rate, there may be no increase in employment (in the extreme case), or the effect could be split between increases in employment and increases in wage rates. With wage rate W_1 and demand curve VMP_1, there is unemployment N_3N_4. If the government decides to use Lerner's functional finance to cure the unemployment, the VMP curve shifts to the right in an effort to cut the labor supply function at N_4. But once again, there is a round of wage increases, and a new money wage of W_2 results, associated with unemployment N_5N_6. Any attempt to increase aggregate demand to N_6 will continue the inflationary depression process.

This administered depression has great costs. In 1962, Lerner estimated that we needed roughly 6 percent or 7 percent unemployment in order to maintain price stability. Since prices rise unless there is a certain minimum level of depression, it is argued by Lerner that the price mechanism is not working. If we are unwilling to tamper with the automatic price mechanism, the choice before us is *either* full employment *or* price stability, and we are therefore in the position of trading inflation against unemployment. To Lerner, we can have either no inflation with roughly 7 percent unemployment, or full employment with roughly 5 percent inflation. Lerner then attempted to use the tools of marginal analysis to calculate the optimum trade-off, that is, he calculated the marginal cost of extra bits of inflation and depression. For equal percentage rises, inflation appears less damaging than depression. A 5 percent inflation, for example, redistributes less than 5 percent of the output from creditors to debtors, since the economy is not strictly divided into pure debtors and pure creditors, but there are people on both sides of the account causing a cancelling out of some of the redistribution. He estimated that 2 percent unemployment was necessary for the economy to operate efficiently (Keynes's frictional unemployment) but that each additional 1 percent unemployment cuts national output by roughly 2 percent. Since price level stability is consistent with 7 percent unemployment, Lerner argues "Our choice is between 10% depression [2 x (7-2)] and 5% inflation. It would therefore seem rational to choose full employment (i.e., 2% unemployment) with 5% inflation or at most, say, 2% depression (i.e., 3% unemployment) with 4% inflation."[31]

Lerner then attempted to answer the question of what we can do to avoid the unhappy choice between depression and inflation. His answer is price regulation. Lerner distinguishes this kind of price regulation from price control. Wages could rise according to increases in productivity. In industries where labor is scarcer than in general, the increase could be greater, and in industries where there is an excess supply of labor greater than the economy as a whole, wages could not rise as fast. Prices could not rise unless there was a shortage of the particular commodity in question, but shortages could not be claimed if the firm were operating at less than capacity; if the firm were operating at substantially below capacity, prices would be forced down.

Since this chapter is concerned with the contributions of Lerner to the new economics, it will not discuss his many pivotal ideas unrelated to his attack on neoclassical economic policy. His writings have covered

---

[31] Lerner, "A Program for Monetary Stability," *op. cit.*, p. 44.

a catholic range of issues from the question of the rational calculation of prices in the absence of a price system[32] to the prevention of nuclear annihilation by applying principles of economic reasoning to foreign policy.[33]

In his attack on both Marxist planners and extreme laissez-faire free enterprisers, Lerner attempted to show that a decentralized system of bureaucratic firms could be compelled to follow rules that would result in an optimum in accordance with Paretian efficiency. Lerner advocated the use of market socialism, in which the rule of setting price equal to marginal cost would be followed in every nook and cranny of the economy.

Abba Lerner's contributions to the new economics have been enormously significant. By making Keynes intelligible to the rest of the economics profession and by his contribution of functional finance, he seemed to have provided the "tool-box" which administrators could use to achieve full employment and price level stability. Furthermore, his "Sellers' Inflation" theory helped explain the new inflation of the late 1950's and provided a rationale for the wage and price guideposts that were presented in the 1962 *Economic Report* of President Kennedy.[34]

Lerner has never been one to underestimate the power of academic economists to change the world. He has well-stated the importance of his own contributions to economic literacy:

> When I say that we may be witnessing in our lifetime the failure of the free world to withstand the totalitarian onslaught, it is not my language but the objective situation that is melodramatic. We may fail because we are unprepared to make the effort needed and because we are using the superstition of the primacy of a balanced

---

[32] Abba P. Lerner, "Economic Theory and Socialist Economy," *Review of Economic Studies* (October 1934), 51-61; "Statics and Dynamics in Socialist Economics," *Economic Journal* (June 1937), 253-70; and *The Economics of Control, op. cit.*

[33] Abba P. Lerner, "Nuclear Symmetry as a Framework for Coexistence," *Social Research*, vol. 31 (Summer 1964), 141-54. Lerner also invented a proof that equality of income distribution would maximize probable satisfactions, in his *Economics of Control, op. cit.*, chapter 3. For a critical evaluation and restatement, see William Breit and William P. Culbertson, Jr., "Distributional Equality and Aggregate Utility," *American Economic Review*, vol. LX (June 1970) 435-441.

[34] These guideposts became increasingly explicit with the 1965 and 1966 economic reports in which average productivity was to be related to wage settlements, much as Lerner had recommended. See George P. Schultz and Robert Z. Aliber, eds., *Guidelines, Informal Controls, and the Market Place* (Chicago: University of Chicago Press, 1966), pp. 2-4.

budget to excuse the failure to make the effort. Economic knowledge, by re-exploding this reincarnation of an old fallacy, and by showing how the authorities can avoid sellers' inflation, can set us free to apply our vast resources for the defense of the free world and the economic development of the poor world in our fight with the totalitarian world. This is the task and this is the case for political economy.[35]

A true student of Keynes, Lerner has never disparaged the power of ideas "for good or evil."

---

[35] Lerner, *Everybody's Business, op. cit.*, p. 134.

CHAPTER 11

JOHN KENNETH

GALBRAITH—Economist as

Social Critic

*I believe that a good phrase is better than a
Great Truth—which is usually buncombe.*

H. L. MENCKEN

Despite the increasing interest which the field of economics has generated in recent decades, few, if any, of the really important tracts in economic thought are ever read by a wide audience. Keynes's *General Theory* or Samuelson's *Foundations of Economic Analysis* are rarely found on the household bookshelves. Few laymen have ever heard of E. H. Chamberlin, A. C. Pigou, Alvin Hansen, Abba Lerner, or Alfred Marshall. Indeed, of the men considered thus far in the present volume, only Thorstein Veblen achieved a very wide audience for his views on the science of economics—and he was depressed that his work was considered so "popular." To be sure, economists such as Paul Samuelson and Milton Friedman are reaching an increasingly diverse group of readers through their columns in *Newsweek*, periodic pieces in the *New York Times* and *Washington Post*, and similar elements of the "popular press." Yet their collective audience—and those of most other eminent economists as well—could be matched by that of a single man: John Kenneth Galbraith. Galbraith's success in bringing the "dismal science" to the interest of the average reader is so great that he was even invited to be one of the celebrated interviewees for *Playboy* magazine. Naturally, he accepted.[1]

---

[1] *Playboy*, vol. 5, no. 6 (June 1968).

At a time when the economics profession is increasingly turning towards greater division of labor within the various "fields" of economics, Galbraith has been remarkably successful in swimming against the tide. Eschewing the gains from specialization in a narrow field, he has chosen to comment on the entire range of economic and social problems confronting society today. His approach is simple: "I've never thought for a moment that I had popularized economics. . . . All I've done is sought to write economics, however difficult, in clear English."[2]

Although his wide range of interests harkens back to the views which Smith, Ricardo, and Mill had of the domain of "Political Economy," Galbraith is still a very long way philosophically from the classical writers. For he is the epitome of the twentieth century liberal.[3] He assails at every turn the social and economic values of modern society and the institutions which reinforce them. He argues for change; and he is not hesitant in choosing the State as the vehicle to accomplish the necessary reforms. To those who warn that intervention of the State in the economy will impair individual freedom, Galbraith replies in very much the same vein as Paul Samuelson:

> The instinct which warns of danger in this association of economic and public power is sound. . . . But conservatives have looked in the wrong direction for the danger. They have feared that the state might reach out and destroy the vigorous, money-making entrepreneur. They have not noticed that, all the while, the successors to the entrepreneur were uniting themselves ever more closely with the state and rejoicing in the result.
>
> The danger to liberty lies in the subordination of belief to the needs of the industrial system.[4]

During the past decade and a half, Galbraith has emerged as a leading social critic in American life. His name may never be placed alongside those men credited with engineering new and pathbreaking analytical contributions to the economic science. Nevertheless, he is probably the most widely read economist of this or any other time. Two of his books —*The Affluent Society* and *The New Industrial State*—remained on the

---

[2] *Ibid.*, p. 138.

[3] Queried as to whom he might nominate as the "head" of the Establishment, Galbraith replied that "some people believe that I am studying hard for the job." *Ibid.*, p. 78.

[4] John K. Galbraith, *The New Industrial State* (Boston: Houghton Mifflin Company, 1967), pp. 397-98.

best seller list for prolonged periods after their publication.[5] Unlike Veblen, Galbraith was not upset at this turn of events; he seeks a large audience for his views. His books are not confined to economics; they cover politics (*The Liberal Hour*), memoirs (*The Scotch*), polemical arguments on foreign affairs (*How to Get Out of Viet Nam*), and most recently, a novel (*The Triumph*).

His success in communicating economics to a large group of readers has not been a cause for joy among economists generally. For of all the targets he chooses to attack, Galbraith reserves his most blistering remarks for the "conventional wisdom" governing economic thought today. Not since Veblen's attack 50 years earlier has economics been subjected to such withering fire. Many a student has been made uneasy over the assumptions underlying the logic of contemporary economic theory. Galbraith's books are assigned in a wide variety of courses in over 100 colleges.

Unlike his fellow New Frontierman, Paul Samuelson, Galbraith relishes political involvement. As early as 1952, he was a leading figure in the Democratic Party as an advisor to Adlai Stevenson. As chairman of the Americans for Democratic Action in 1968, he vigorously supported Eugene McCarthy, thus exacerbating a bitter split in that organization. Galbraith remained undaunted; he had been a leading spokesman against the Viet Nam involvement since the early period of the Kennedy Administration. He was fairly close to President Kennedy; an association which dated back to Galbraith's tutoring at Winthrop House when the future president was at Harvard. The two men corresponded frequently while Galbraith was ambassador to India, and the economist probably played a large role in convincing Kennedy of the efficacy of the new economics.[6] He brought Paul Samuelson and the President-

---

[5] In 1969, in responding to one of his critics who had accused him of lack of concern for the problems of the poor because of his personal affluence, Galbraith decided to make a "full disclosure" of the returns which he has made from his writing. In the nine years from the publication of *The Affluent Society* (Boston: Houghton Mifflin Company, 1958), to the publication of *The New Industrial State*, *op. cit.*, the average return was $17,500 a year. Approximately half was allocated to secretarial and other assistance. Galbraith's conclusion was that "all who want effortless wealth are strongly advised to have invested some years ago in IBM." See John Kenneth Galbraith, "Professor Gordon on 'The Close of the Galbraithian System,'" *Journal of Political Economy*, vol. 77 (July-August 1969), 497n.

[6] He cites Kennedy's espousal of the new economics in policy as the single most impressive accomplishment of the President's tenure of office. *Playboy*, *op. cit.*, p. 70. For reminiscences of his years as ambassador to India and of his relationship to President John F. Kennedy, see John Kenneth Galbraith, *Ambassador's Journal* (Boston: Houghton Mifflin Company, 1969).

elect together in 1960 and advised Kennedy to name the MIT professor as chairman of the Council of Economic Advisors. (The advice was taken, but Samuelson refused the offer.)

As a leading spokesman for the liberal wing of the Democratic Party, Galbraith has offered considerable amounts of advice over the past decade. It may be, as he notes, that people have mistaken the quantity of advice offered for that which was actually taken. Nevertheless, it can hardly be said that his voice has been ignored in recent years. Apart from his personal influences on government officials, his books have occasionally caused official reaction as well. The appearance of *The New Industrial State* prompted the Senate Subcommittee on Monopoly to hold hearings and gather testimony on the implications of the Galbraithian system. Few other economists have seen such rapid response to their work. Galbraith could by this time take such a compliment in stride; it was not the first time his comments had caused a flurry on Capitol Hill. In 1954, he appeared before the Senate Subcommittee on Banking and Finance to testify on the stock market. Drawing heavily from his forthcoming book *The Great Crash*, Galbraith told the senators that the 1929 experience could be repeated. While he was speaking, the New York Stock Market experienced a sharp decline in prices. There were some who went so far as to draw a causal connection.[7]

Galbraith began his career as an observer of social life in the Scotch community along the northern edge of Lake Erie where he was born.[8] He worked his way through Ontario Agricultural College and eventually went on to a doctorate in agricultural economics at the University of California, Berkeley in 1936 where he steeped himself in Veblen and Marx. The following year he went to Harvard as an instructor, then traveled to Cambridge (England) for a year as a Social Science Research Fellow. He did not meet Keynes then, although the ideas of the *General Theory* were quickly accepted by the young Galbraith. He

---

[7] In fact, Senator Homer Capehart of Indiana was sufficiently upset over Galbraith's statements (and a few other remarks which the economist had made regarding the strength of the Communist world) to suggest that Galbraith should be called before another Senate committee to account for his views. Nothing came of it, although Capehart and Galbraith exchanged statements in the press. Galbraith's principal regret about the incident is that it failed to stimulate the sales of *The Great Crash* when the book appeared. John K. Galbraith, *The Great Crash 1929* (Boston: Houghton Mifflin Company, Sentry ed., 1961). See his account of the episode in the preface, pp. xii-xix.

[8] For a highly entertaining look at his childhood society, Galbraith's account of *The Scotch* provides a delightful glance at the community on the Ontario Peninsula. John K. Galbraith, *The Scotch* (Boston: Houghton Mifflin Company, 1964).

returned to the United States and taught at a variety of schools prior to the war and his appointment as Deputy Director of the Office of Price Administration in 1941.[9] Before returning to Harvard permanently, he paused briefly to serve as an editor of *Fortune*.[10] He is currently Paul Warburg Professor of Economics at Harvard.

His physical appearance adds effect to his professional credentials, towering over most adversaries from a height of six feet eight inches: "I am the tallest man in the world," he once replied when questioned about his height.[11] He savors his size by noting that other people appear to be abnormally short. Of course, not all adversaries are intimidated; William Buckley once commented that Galbraith behaves as one who ". . . is on very short leave from Olympus, where he holds classes on the maintenance of divine standards."[12] Galbraith's own observation on the tactics to be employed in argument is very straightforward:

> Like most other liberal academicians, I had been a thoughtful observer of the methods of the Wisconsin Titus Oakes. Two had always seemed worth adopting by anyone attacked. The first was to avoid defense of one's self and instead assault the accuser. The second was to avoid any suspicion, however remote, of personal modesty.[13]

As many a critic has discovered, Galbraith is not hesitant to put this policy into effect.

The Notion of the "Conventional Wisdom"

Our concern is primarily with Galbraith's economics, and his basic contribution here is contained in two major works: *The Affluent Society* and *The New Industrial State*.[14] The two books are, as the

---

9 He later became Director of the U.S. Strategic Bombing Survey, and head of the Office of Economic Security Policy in the State Department. President Truman awarded him the Medal of Freedom for his work.

10 According to *Time* Magazine, Galbraith credits Henry Luce with teaching him how to write while serving with *Fortune*. *Time*, February 16, 1968, p. 28.

11 *Ibid.*, p. 27.

12 *Ibid.*, p. 28.

13 Galbraith, *The Great Crash*, *op. cit.*, p. xviii.

14 The other work which deals with economic theory is his *American Capitalism*. John K. Galbraith, *American Capitalism* (Boston: Houghton Mifflin Company, 1952). His *Economic Development* is a broad treatment of that subject. John K. Galbraith, *Economic Development* (Cambridge: Harvard University Press, 1962).

author points out, really a single argument; the second volume was delayed by his visit to India as ambassador from the United States under the Kennedy Administration.

To Galbraith, the ideas behind policy today—and indeed at any time—are governed by what he terms the *conventional wisdom*. The basis on which these ideas are accepted is their *familiarity*, which:

> . . . may breed contempt in some areas of human behavior, but in the field of social ideas it is the touchstone of acceptability.
>
> Because familiarity is such an important test of acceptability, the acceptable ideas have great stability. They are highly predictable. It will be convenient to have a name for the ideas which are esteemed at any time for their acceptability and it should be a term that emphasizes this predictability. I shall refer to these ideas henceforth as the conventional wisdom.[15]

The power of the conventional wisdom is in its control over men's action. Galbraith cites Keynes's famous dictum on the power of ideas with approval, and then adds:

> . . . the rule of ideas is only powerful in a world that does not change. Ideas are inherently conservative. They yield not to the attack of other ideas but to the massive onslaught of circumstance with which they cannot contend.[16]

To Galbraith, it is apparent that they do not change nearly fast enough. Commenting on that bastion of the conventional wisdom—the United States Senate—Galbraith remarked that: "Tourists visiting Washington, D.C. should not miss the nineteenth century museum pieces in the Senate."[17]

In no area of society has the "massive onslaught of circumstances" been greater than in the transformation into an industrial economy. This perhaps explains the vigor with which Galbraith attacks contemporary economic theory. It is, he insists, imperative that the ideas now widely held give way to new approaches to the problems of a changing

---

[15] Galbraith, *The Affluent Society, op. cit.*, p. 9.

[16] *Ibid.*, p. 20.

[17] Nor is there any sign that—like Samuelson—Galbraith is mellowing with age. The remark about the Senate was attributed to him by *Time* Magazine on his 60th birthday.

economy and society. Like Veblen, he attacks the foundations of *all* the accepted paradigms of modern economics.

The Conventional Wisdom in Economics Today

Galbraith does encounter a major problem: defining those economic propositions which are widely held by everyone. Keynes, faced with a similar problem, chose the work of A. C. Pigou as representative of the "classical system" which he was attacking. Critics accused him of setting up a "straw man." Galbraith avoids Keynes's error of choosing a single work, but as a result his interpretation of the conventional wisdom in economics is rather vague. He appears to feel that the best example is provided by the content of Samuelson's introductory text. The "accepted" explanation of consumer demand is essentially that of the neoclassical school, and on the supply side, Marshall's theory of the firm seems to have undergone slight modification. In macroeconomics, Galbraith notes that the conventional wisdom has been altered over the past three decades with the Keynesian attack. But the overthrow was incomplete; although the Keynesians succeeded in modifying the analysis of aggregate demand in the neoclassical model, they did not press their attack to the faults in microeconomics.[18]

Galbraith's generality on the specifics of accepted theory today is understandable. And he does focus his main attack on two points which do appear to be widely accepted among economists. The first is the assertion that the consumer's tastes or preferences are derived outside the economic system and thus must be taken for granted by the economist, who then proceeds to use the theory of marginal utility to derive the consumer's equilibrium. In the modern industrial economy, claims Galbraith, wants are a result of the economic process itself; they are not independent of the system. His second objection concerns the assumption of profit maximization on the part of the producers. This is simply not so in an economy dominated by huge corporations and run by people who do not receive the profits generated by the firm.

As is often the case with criticism on a broad scale, Galbraith has collected a large number of ideas and welded them together into a set of propositions regarding the analysis of the modern economy. His general approach to the entire setting of the economic problem is highly reminiscent of Thorstein Veblen—particularly his attack on the theory

---

18 This interpretation of Galbraith's views is, of course, our own. It rests on his general remarks towards economic theory in Chapters III through V of *The Affluent Society* and his treatment of specific points throughout his analysis.

of demand and his view of technology in the modern economy. Although Veblen receives very little explicit credit in Galbraith's work, his presence appears to be always in the background.[19] The two men center their attacks on the assumptions behind the elegant logic of economic theory. They reject the notion of consumer rationality by questioning the values which are produced in an industrial society, and they argue for a revision of these social values.

Galbraith's literary skill is sufficiently refreshing in a profession such as economics that one ought not to complain.[20] Nevertheless, his style at times makes it difficult to distill the basic elements of his attack into propositions which can be carefully evaluated. His system involves two basic arguments: one on the irrelevancy of utility in demand, the other on the distortions of production from the "industrial system."

We begin with the attack on the theory of demand.

The Affluent Society

It is an indisputable fact that the United States has become an affluent society relative to the time of Adam Smith. Scarcity of resources may still govern the allocative mechanism, but such grim specters as the "necessities of life" and the "subsistence level of wages" which dominated nineteenth century tracts in political economy no longer haunt the industrial society of mid-twentieth century America. The science of economics has been made correspondingly less "dismal" as the success of the production process finally removed the constraints holding output to meager levels. The problem, Galbraith points out, is that the conventional wisdom has not kept pace; it continues to act as though we were analyzing consumers living in an economy of nineteenth century poverty. There are, he claims, two basic propositions underlying the theory of demand: (1) the law of diminishing marginal

---

[19] Galbraith clearly is indebted to Veblen's work—see his comments in *The Affluent Society, op. cit.,* pp. 54-55. Moreover, he concedes Veblen's work influenced the development of his own thought. Personal correspondence, June 12, 1967.

[20] To those who do complain that he "popularizes" economics, Galbraith replies:

> Economics, like all sciences has its crotchets, its petty jealousies, and its minor feuds. I have no doubt that a certain number of people have said from time to time, "Galbraith is unfair by not making use of the normal tendencies to obscurity: he's as guilty as a doctor who writes prescriptions in clear English instead of illegible Latin." But these are the attitudes of inconsequential people, and I've always successfully ignored them.

Playboy, op. cit., p. 138.

utility; and (2) the assertion that wants are generated from within the individual (that is, that "tastes" are determined outside the economic system). Today, neither of these propositions seems tenable.

Marginal Utility and Affluence

We have already seen that, in the neoclassical analysis of the consumer, the concept of diminishing marginal utility implied that as the stock of a good increased, the additional satisfaction to the purchaser from successive units would decline. Galbraith wonders why, with rising income, this would not also be true for all goods taken as a group:

> With increasing per capita real income, men are able to satisfy additional wants. These are of a lower order of urgency. This being so, the production that provides the goods that satisfy these less urgent wants must also be of a smaller (and declining) importance. . . . So it must be assumed that the importance of marginal increments of all production is low and declining. The effect of increasing affluence is to minimize the importance of economic goals. Production and productivity become less and less important.[21]

He is aware, of course, that the earlier theorists attempted to come to grips with this problem. For it is the utility of *each good* which declines as the stock *of that good* increases. This is the crucial relationship which explains the decline in desire to pay and the corresponding fall in satisfaction from each good. Since purchases of separate goods are made *over time*, not all at once, the level of wants will be sustained. Moreover, the range of new goods confronting the consumer will ensure that he will not find declining levels of satisfaction as he collects more goods. Galbraith demurs:

> This position ignores the obvious fact that some things are acquired before others and that, presumably, the more important things come first. This, as observed previously, implies a declining urgency of need.[22]

Neoclassical—and modern—theorists did not deny the possibility of such a phenomenon. Indeed, this very point caused considerable problems in Marshall's analysis of utility and demand. Did the marginal utility of *money* (that is, income) fall as the level of income rose? As

---

[21] Galbraith, *The Affluent Society, op. cit.,* pp. 145-46.
[22] *Ibid.,* 148.

Galbraith rather contemptuously points out, the economist bounded by the notion of utility theory can "have nothing to say" on this point. He must fall back on the rather lame fact that:

> There is room . . . for the broad assumption—given the large and ever growing variety of goods awaiting the consumer's attention— that wants have a sustained urgency.[23]

To Galbraith, this neutrality on the issue of whether or not the marginal utility of money falls as income rises is a necessary part of the theory of demand. Despite his own feeling that it obviously decreases with higher income, he concedes that this point can no more be proven than the opposite view. The conventional wisdom is invulnerable to attack as long as consumers' tastes are determined by noneconomic forces.

The Dependence Effect

Since marginal utility is a very convenient tool to explain the allocation of expenditures on various goods, there is little incentive for economists to explore the issue further. If they did, they might find out that:

> . . . there is a flaw in the case. If an individual's wants are to be urgent they must be original with himself. They cannot be urgent if they must be contrived for him. And above all they must not be contrived by the process of production by which they are satisfied. For this means that the whole case for urgency of production, based on urgency of wants, falls to the ground. One cannot defend production as satisfying wants if that production creates the wants.[24]

We have come to one of the cornerstones of the Galbraithian critique: the assertion that "contrived wants"—since they are clearly less "urgent" than "original wants"—cannot be used as a basis for evaluating the need for production. The defense of production is weakened still further, when the wants are contrived by the production process itself. It is a sufficiently important point that it is worthwhile to quote Galbraith at some length:

> As a society becomes increasingly affluent, wants are increasingly created by the process by which they are satisfied. This may oper-

---

[23] *Ibid.*, p. 150.
[24] *Ibid.*, pp. 152-53.

ate passively. Increases in consumption, the counterpart of increases in production, act by suggestion or emulation to create wants. Or producers may proceed to actively create wants through advertising and salesmanship. Wants thus come to depend on output. In technical terms it can no longer be assumed that welfare is greater at an all-round higher level of production than at a lower one. It may be the same. The higher level of production has, merely, a higher level of want creation necessitating a higher level of want satisfaction. There will be frequent occasion to refer to the way wants depend on the process by which they are satisfied. It will be convenient to call it the Dependence Effect.[25]

This *dependence effect* is probably the most controversial aspect of Galbraith's analysis, and both Galbraith and his critics agree that it is crucial to his later conclusions.

It has been met with some skepticism by economists. Few would deny that the vast bulk of our "wants" are in fact "contrived" (determined might be a better term) by our social environment. And many would admit that the aggregate level of wants in a country such as the United States is not independent of the efforts by producers to influence consumers' tastes through advertising. But is there some meaningful way in which we can say that these contrived wants are much less "urgent" than the necessities? Is it in fact the case—as Galbraith argues —that the level of welfare may remain constant as production increases because wants increase proportionately? The conclusion is hardly obvious, for the line between those demands based on "necessities" and those which are contrived by production is not distinct. The most vehement of Galbraith's critics would agree with Professor Hayek that the notion of a dependence effect is a *non sequitur* since virtually *all* wants are acquired.[26] Others might content themselves with simply pointing out that the application of the dependence effect will necessarily require some implicit set of values by which we rank the "urgency" of any wants expressed by the consumer. As in Veblen, this involves a value judgment of considerable importance. Unfortunately, it is a subjective issue which is central to the Galbraithian scheme of things, for much of what Galbraith subsequently argues—both in the

---

[25] *Ibid.*, p. 158.

[26] F. A. Hayek, "The Non Sequitur of the 'Dependence Effect,'" *Southern Economic Journal* (April 1961), 346-48. Reprinted in E. Phelps, ed., *Private Wants and Public Needs* (New York: W. W. Norton & Company, Inc., 1965), pp. 38-39. Hayek contends that aside from "food, shelter and sex" every want is culturally determined. To discuss degrees of "urgency" between such wants is, in his view, nonsense.

Affluent Society and *The New Industrial State*—turns on acceptance of *his* interpretation of the dependence effect. If one denies the introduction of value judgments in economic analysis, then the strength of these later arguments is greatly reduced. We shall leave it to the reader to judge the merits of the dependence effect as an analytical tool. One should note, however, the implications of acceptance of Galbraith's view on the existing body of economic theory.

The Dependence Effect and Economic Theory

Once the dependence effect is granted, we can easily dispose of the notion of consumer sovereignty. The consumer is not viewed as "sovereign"; he is manipulated by producers into inventing new and artificial wants to suit the aims of producers. The idea of a "rational consumer" thus loses meaning. This being so, only "social nostalgia" leads us to insist that the market is a reasonable allocator of resources according to social need. Two brief examples will suffice to illustrate the impact of such a conclusion on economic policy.

We noted in our discussion of Samuelson that in the modern economy, control of inflation through conventional monetary-fiscal policy tools may involve an expensive trade-off between inflation and unemployment. The menu offered by the "Phillips Curve" is the best that we can achieve short of changing the structural relations in the market. Samuelson—in Galbraith's view an example of the conventional wisdom par excellence—hesitated in recommending direct price controls to achieve this aim. But why shrink from such measures if the dependence effect leads us to insist that the market prices are not a meaningful index of welfare? Galbraith insists that price control is a reasonable alternative. Moreover, he argues that it is quite feasible today. Here he draws on his experience as the Deputy Director of the Office of Price Administration during World War II. The wartime experience shows the success in such policies where the social aims are served by such controls. Prices can be efficiently regulated in a modern economy, and the dependence effect removes the conflict between such regulation and the "economic ethos" of the conventional wisdom.[27]

---

[27] The issues brought up in this section are dealt with in Chapters XV-XVII of *The Affluent Society*. He also takes up a more general debate on inflation in *The New Industrial State*, Chapter XXII. For an exposition of Galbraith's faith in the ability of government to manage a problem so complex, see his short monograph, *A Theory of Price Control* (Harvard University, 1952). Galbraith considers this book to be his best theoretical piece.

The greatest impact of the dependence effect is as a basis for the argument of social imbalance. The operation of the dependence effect generates a very sizable bias in demand by consumers toward the production of private goods—with low levels of urgency—thus denying the possible gains from more urgently needed public goods. The result is an imbalance in the collective choice of goods. Again, the assertion that private goods have "low urgency" removes any need for hesitation by the policy maker in sweeping aside the pattern of production observed in the market. Extension of government goods and services is justified by the overvaluation of private production and the undervaluation of public goods.[28]

These examples serve to demonstrate the power of the dependence effect when applied to economic reasoning. In his typically sardonic vein, Galbraith charges that:

> It is easy to see why the conventional wisdom resists so stoutly such a change. It is a far, far better thing to have a firm anchor in nonsense than to put out on the troubled seas of thought.[29]

After nearly a decade of reflection on the conditions of the sea, there remains a large body of economists still unwilling to weigh anchor. And this was only the introduction to Galbraith's attack on modern economics. We now turn to his second avenue of assault: the theory of production.

The New Industrial State

For Galbraith, the means by which we have gained affluence presents a serious threat to our social system. Our educational system, our relations of government, and our social values are all affected by the changes of an industrial revolution. At the center of the forces for change in the United States is the area of the economy which Galbraith calls the *"industrial system."* He develops a series of hypotheses, which we shall summarize in three basic propositions, which hold for this sector:

1. The technological revolution in the past century has generated a pervasive force leading to ever-increasing size of industrial organization. Many important markets today are dominated by a few giant firms.

---

[28] The picture we leave here is incomplete. We shall return to the question of social imbalance and the role of the state.

[29] Galbraith, *The Affluent Society, op. cit.*, p. 160.

2. The complexities of modern technology require a group of skilled engineer-managers to run the firm. Because this group does not own any part of the firm, they will not be governed by the traditional assumption that firm managers will maximize the firm's profits.

3. Size greatly increases the cost of failure. The firm will seek to minimize this risk by controlling its markets through planning. This results in a determination of price and output which is not dependent upon market supply and demand.

These are bold assertions which many economists would question. We shall, however, reserve comment until we have added substance to the outline.

The Role of the Large Firm

As early as the 1890's the emergence of large firms in the United States was a statistical fact which no one could deny. Today, about 500-600 large firms dominate markets in communications, transportation, and many areas of manufacturing production and retail trade.[30] While Galbraith is quite aware that not all markets are dominated by these few firms, it is the study of this world of the giant corporation which will provide us with the insights necessary to explain economic change today. He argues that:

This is the part of the economy which, automatically, we identify with the modern industrial society. To understand it is to understand that part which is most subject to change and which, accordingly, is most changing our lives. . . . to understand the rest of the economy is to understand only that part which is diminishing in relative extent and which is most nearly static. It is to understand very little.[31]

Hence his virtual exclusion of the rest of the economy in his analysis.

---

[30] Although concentration in industry is clearly evident today, it would be rash to assert that the level of this concentration has increased significantly since the merger movements just before the turn of the century. The list of firms which dominated the markets 75 years ago is not the same today; the *average level of concentration* for all industry remains approximately the same; the level for individual industries may change substantially over time. See G. Warren Nutter and H. A. Einhorn, *Enterprise Monopoly in the United States, 1899-1958* (New York: Columbia University Press, 1969); and R. Nelson, *Concentration in Manufacturing Industries in the United States* (New Haven: Yale University Press, 1963), for statistical evidence relating to this point.

[31] Galbraith, *The New Industrial State, op. cit.,* p. 9.

The most important element in the behavior of these giant firms is the role of modern technology. Technology exerts a continuous and pervasive pressure forcing ". . . the division and subdivision of any task into its component parts." It provides the necessary element which enables us to apply knowledge to the development of better means of production. The result has been to alter greatly the structure of the firm. The impact of technology can be seen in a wide variety of areas: capital needs are greatly enlarged by the scale of enterprise necessitated by modern techniques. Organization within the firm becomes more and more geared to the decentralized decision-making required by an increasing division of labor within the management of the firm. Changes in specialization of the labor force result in a different demand for labor; higher levels of skills and education will be necessary to master changing technology. Most important of all, there will develop a greatly enlarged pressure for comprehensive planning within the firm to cover the entire range of the production process—from inputs to the sale of the output.[32]

The Technostructure and the Quest for Profits

In the face of this massive change, the decision apparatus of the firm has undergone considerable transformation. The "entrepreneur," whom economic theory pictures as controlling the capital and organizing the other factors of production, is buried under the task facing the firm's management. Group decision making replaces the old chain of command from the "captain of industry" to his subordinates. "Management" ostensibly runs the firm, but in fact they depend on others to make the decisions which actually determine the operation of the firm.[33] Galbraith's description of this group is worth careful notice:

> This is a collective and imperfectly defined entity; in the large corporation it embraces chairman, president, those vice presidents with important staff or other departmental responsibility, occupants of other major staff positions, and perhaps, division or department heads not included above. It includes, however, only a small proportion of those who, as participants, contribute informa-

---

[32] This summary is derived from the comments in *ibid.*, pp. 12-21. Galbraith's emphasis on technology as the driving force behind the economic system is another of the aspects of his work which makes him closely associated with Veblen, who held a similar position.

[33] Here again, Galbraith sounds very much like Veblen—a point noted by many critics. Galbraith insists that the similarity is only superficial. See his remarks in "A Review of a Review," *Public Interest* (Fall 1967), 109-18.

tion to group decisions. This latter group is very large; it extends from the most senior officials of the corporation to where it meets, at the outer perimeter, the white and blue collar workers whose function is to conform more or less mechanically to instruction or routine. It embraces all who bring specialized knowledge, talent or experience to group decision-making. This, not the management, is the guiding intelligence—the brain—of the enterprise. There is no name for all who participate in group decision-making or the organization which they form. I propose to call this organization the Technostructure.[34]

The gains from having such specialization in management are clearly rather large; however, the division of labor introduces a complication into the accepted explanation of the firm's behavior. The theory of the firm insists that whoever is in control of the firm will be motivated by a desire to maximize his own profits. How can we be sure that the division between ownership (the stockholders as represented by their managers) and the control (by the technostructure) will not produce a different set of goals for the corporation? The drive for personal gain— when properly restrained by Adam Smith's invisible hand—is a necessary assumption to the proposition that the firm operates efficiently. For it is this pressure to maximize profits which leads the entrepreneur to seek the most efficient mix of resources in determining his level of output. To demonstrate that such incentives *do not* exert their influence is to undermine seriously the conventional explanation.

And, Galbraith insists, this is precisely the problem which emerges with the technostructure. They will be motivated to increase their *own* utility, whether or not this results in maximizing the profits of the owners. Galbraith is rather eloquent in pressing this point home to the reader:

> The members of the technostructure do not get the profits that they maximize. They must eschew personal profit-making. Accordingly, if the traditional commitment to profit maximization is to be upheld, they must be willing to do for others, specifically the stockholders, what they are forbidden to do for themselves. It is on such grounds that the doctrine of maximization in the mature corporation now rests. It holds that the will to make profits is, like the will to sexual expression, a fundamental urge. But it holds that this urge operates not in the first person but the third. . . . In

---

[34] Galbraith, *The New Industrial State, op. cit.,* p. 71.

further analogy to sex, one must imagine that a man of vigorous, lusty and reassuringly heterosexual inclination eschews the lovely, available and even naked women by whom he is intimately surrounded in order to maximize the opportunities of other men whose existence he knows of only by hearsay. Such are the foundations of the maximization doctrine when there is full separation of power from reward.[35]

Of course, deprivation of women is not the only basis on which Galbraith builds his case for the "divorce of ownership and control." In fact, the existing literature in this area abounds with assertions that firms do not maximize profits in a modern industrial society.[36]

If the profit motive is not the driving force behind the firm's behavior, then what is? Galbraith's response is in two parts. First he argues that the most plausible set of goals for an individual member of the technostructure will be *identification* with a successful organization. The second step is to construct a set of goals which the technostructure can apply to the operation of the firm itself to make it "successful." Galbraith emerges with the following list of goals—in order of descending importance:

1. The primary aim of the corporation must be *survival*. To ensure this, the technostructure will act to maintain some *minimum rate of earnings*. Such behavior will guarantee the position of the technostructure in the firm, and it will also reduce the possibility of outside interference.

2. Given some level of minimum earnings, the technostructure will then act to *maximize the growth of the corporation*. This is more than a matter of prestige. A major problem confronting the large firm is its dependence on capital to finance large investments necessary in modern markets. Ideally, this capital will be supplied by earnings retained in the firm. The higher the rate of growth, the lesser the dependence on

---

[35] *Ibid.*, p. 117.

[36] Galbraith cites a number of references to substantiate the degree of separation between owners of capital and operators of the firm. The most notable include: A. Berle and G. Means, *The Modern Corporation and Private Property* (New York: The Macmillan Company, 1934), which is the pathbreaking study in this area; R. A. Gordon, *Business Leadership in the Large Corporation* (Washington, D.C.: Brookings Institution, 1952); and E. Cheit, *The Business Establishment* (New York: John Wiley & Sons., Inc., 1964). For a penetrating analysis of an opposing view, see Gordon Tullock, "The New Theory of Corporations," in *Roads to Freedom: Essays in Honour of Friedrich A. von Hayek*, ed. Erich Streissler, *et al.* (London: Routledge & Kegan Paul Ltd., 1969), pp. 287-307.

outside financing. Again, the technostructure is preoccupied with the threat of outside interference.

3. In the event that both of these primary goals are met, a set of subsidiary goals then may exert an influence. Technical virtuosity on the part of the firm would be such a goal. Support of education and other community affairs may also enter. But only insofar as the initial goals of minimum earnings and growth are satisfied.

So we have Galbraith's view of the industrial system. Huge firms, run by a technostructure which is not tempted by profit maximization, dominate markets for goods and services. But how will such firms behave differently from the traditional firms described by Marshall and his followers?

Planning, the Dependence Effect, and Prices

As it normally appears in the textbooks, the conventional wisdom argues that the firm's price and output are determined through an equilibrium process in the market. Generally, the situation would be such that the firm—however great its monopoly control over supply may be—must still accept the constraint of limited demand in the market. It must trade off between increases in prices and increases in quantity sold along a falling demand curve. Galbraith envisages a revision of that process. Rather than the *firm adjusting to the market demand*, he maintains that the *market will adjust to the firm*. The key to this lies in the firm's use of planning to implement the dependence effect.

The greatest threat to the stability of the firm is uncertainty. Thus, the technostructure will attempt to minimize risk. The greatest risk is in market uncertainty. With large capital investments at stake, it is imperative that unexpected shifts in these markets be prevented. The firm must be able to carefully plan its operation from beginning to end —from the acquisition of inputs to the demand for final output. And therein lies the role of the dependence effect. The large corporation will not be so docile as to take consumer tastes as given; it will act to create those wants which are necessary for the sale of its output. This is the logic of the dependence effect on a microeconomic scale. From the viewpoint of Chamberlin's analysis, Galbraith is asserting that the firm can, through an adjustment of selling costs, infinitely increase the demand for its product. The details of this mechanism are not spelled out. Galbraith only says that the task of the firm is made much easier by the affluence of consumers:

The further a man is removed from physical need the more open he is to persuasion—or management—as to what he buys. This is, perhaps, the most important consequence for economics of increasing affluence.[37]

Galbraith's analysis does not press into the question of interdependence between firms; a point which was an integral part of Chamberlin's exposition of oligopoly. Under what he calls the "revised sequence" of price determination, the firm can apparently offset any effects of interdependence through planning and manipulation of demand. The result is that the firm is no longer bound by the constraint of the market. This is only true, of course, in the industrial system; elsewhere in the economy the market may serve to determine prices through the conventional sequences of demand and supply. This will be of little consequence in the industrial system.

The management of consumer demand in the interests of producers is only the most obvious result of the changes which created the industrial system. There are others. The technostructure's behavior is very strongly influenced by *risk avoidance*. The need to reduce uncertainty in the firm's environment requires that the technostructure become involved in many areas of economic policy. Four such areas are discussed below.[38]

1. *The Control of Aggregate Demand.* The firm can control its own demand, but it cannot do so for the system as a whole. Yet economic stability is an "organic requirement" for the industrial system. Small fluctuations in aggregate demand could impose heavy losses by presenting the firm with unexpected shifts in markets. As a result, Galbraith argues, leaders of the industrial system have gradually come to embrace the tenets of the Keynesian doctrine as being in their own interest. They support stability of prices and employment.[39]

2. *Employment and Labor.* While labor clearly gains from the reduction of toil brought about by the efficiency of production, certain con-

---

[37] Galbraith, *The New Industrial State, op. cit.*, p. 202. He refers here to *The Affluent Society* and *American Capitalism* for more detailed discussion.

[38] The points are drawn from Galbraith, *The New Industrial State*, chaps. XX-XXV.

[39] The acknowledged hostility of the business community toward deficit spending policies to achieve full employment does pose a difficulty in this endorsement of the new economics by the industrial system. Galbraith argues that such resistance comes from businessmen *outside* the industrial system. Stability is less of a requirement for these firms. This point is unclear; most economists would argue that the small businesses were less able to withstand the pressures of a recession.

flicts may develop between labor and the industrial system. The technostructure will have a strong bias toward replacing labor with capital. This is due to the greater certainty which the purchase of capital equipment affords. The firm has its own resources with which to plan investment; it has no such guarantee of available labor in the factor market. Moreover, although it favors high levels of employment in the aggregate, a problem develops with regard to the demand for labor from the industrial system, for the technology requires an ever-rising level of skills. Education becomes an important requirement for employment. The result is a decline in importance of blue collar workers within the industrial system. There is a large (and growing) pool of labor which is *rejected* by the system and will *never* be employed. Galbraith sees no incentive to the firm to aid these people. Finally, of course, there is the question of unions and the industrial system. Here Galbraith concedes no clear pattern can be predicted. But he points out that the technostructure is not inimically opposed to unions. Unions serve to regulate the supply of labor; they reduce the uncertainty in the labor market. Moreover, they ensure uniform pricing throughout industry. Nor are their wage demands a threat to the firm's position. With rising productivity through technological change, and the revised sequence of pricing to manage demand, the firm will be in a position to grant wage increases regularly.

3. *Education.* The demand for increasing skills to cope with changing technology naturally leads the industrial system to support education. Thus, the rise of industry coincides with the emergence of a new and powerful group in society: the "educational and scientific estate." As the importance of technology and science in production increases, the power of this group grows commensurately. For the technostructure depends on them to provide the skilled manpower required by the industrial system. Historically, the intellectuals have remained aloof and often rather hostile to the aims of industry. But with the decline of the acquisitive monetary goals of the technostructure, much of the friction between these two groups vanishes. Education finds an important ally in the industrial system. And, despite occasional reluctance over the goals they express, the educational and scientific estate acts to reinforce the aims of the technostructure. In economics, this is particularly true. Consider the emphasis on "economic growth" in recent years. This is exactly what the industrial system requires for its ever expanding production of goods.

4. *National Security and the Industrial System.* The dominance of technological pressures in the large firm generates a large demand for investment in basic research. Continued expansion of technological progress depends on a steady flow of new ideas. But investment in this

area is far too risky a venture for the firm to support alone. The government must fill the void. And it does. A substantial share of basic research both in industry and the educational system is supported by government funds. Unfortunately, the impetus for this intervention stems from the Cold War. With its steady demand for newer and more sophisticated weapons, the arms race provides an ideal rationale for developing new technology in the name of "national security." Such projects are seldom questioned. Galbraith does not wish to argue that the industrial system inherently supports war; its reliance on defense expenditures to develop technology arose by accident. Any program which provided funds for basic research—such as NASA's Apollo project—would serve equally well. But it appears as though the arms race is the only stimulus which is sufficiently great to satisfy the needs of the industrial system. Lacking an alternative source, we depend on the cold war to generate our technological improvement.

The State and the Industrial System

Galbraith has cleverly tied the diverse interests of various groups to those of the industrial system. Labor is rewarded for its cooperation by reaping the gains of rising productivity. The educational and scientific estate is content to reinforce the aims of a system in which its role is becoming increasingly important.

And so we come to the role of the state. The involvement of the state in the industrial process is obvious from the analysis above. Not surprisingly, Galbraith sees control of the state falling into the groups supporting the aims of the industrial system:

> Only the innocent reformer and the obtuse conservative imagine the state to be an instrument of change apart from the interests and aspirations of those who comprise it. The interests or needs of the industrial system are advanced with subtlety and power. Since they are made to seem coordinate with the purposes of society, government action serving the needs of the industrial system has a strong aspect of social purpose. And, as we have seen, the line between the industrial system and the state becomes increasingly artificial and indistinct.[40]

Social Imbalance and the Industrial State

And so we have the *Industrial State*. It is dominated by the interests and goals of the few powerful firms comprising the industrial system.

---

[40] Galbraith, *The New Industrial State, op. cit.,* p. 307.

Other groups, despite their potential power, have allowed this sector to replace gradually the social objectives of the society with those of the technostructure and the industrial system. Therein lies the threat to our society in the mind of Galbraith. For these goals are essentially *economic* objectives: increasing levels of production, income, and employment which must be satisfied through the dependence effect. As social goals such aims are inadequate, for

> Allowing for numerous exceptions, they will be prone to identify economic goals with all of life. They are not, accordingly, the best proponents of the public, aesthetic, and intellectual priorities on which the quality and safety of life increasingly depend. They are, in the main, the natural allies of the industrial system.[41]

The bias against expenditures on important social investment will generate an imbalance which will not be redressed by the market system. Galbraith is not alone in this conclusion. Alvin Hansen reached much the same result reasoning from the Keynesian and Chamberlinian economic theory. Paul Samuelson approached the same problem in a technical way with his discussion of public goods and the theory of expenditure by the public sector.

But Galbraith arrived at this point from another direction: he attacked the basic premises upon which economic theory was constructed. Moreover, his broader view of the problem allows him to push on to the issue of social imbalance with a more general exposition than either Hansen or Samuelson. For, as we have seen, the state will *not* automatically provide the public goods if the choice is left to the consumer; the state is essentially an arm of the industrial system itself. Like Hansen, Galbraith insists that *values* in the society must be changed.

To effect this change Galbraith nominates the intellectual community. This group has considerable power through its control over an essential input of the productive process. More important, Galbraith feels the educational and scientific estate is the only group which is able to affect substantially the attitudes of the community.

> If the educational system serves generally the beliefs of the industrial system, the influence and monolithic character of the latter will be enhanced. By the same token, should it be superior to and independent of the industrial system, it can be the necessary force for skepticism, emancipation, and pluralism.[42]

---

41 *Ibid.*, p. 384.
42 *Ibid.*, p. 370.

The task will not be an easy one, but it is an essential job. Only a revision of political power which allows policies divergent from the aims of the industrial system will allow us to deal with the social problems of an affluent society. As he states at the outset of his inquiry: it is time that we reassess our values to take cognizance that perhaps "what counts is not the quantity of our goods but the quality of life."[43]

The Affluent Industrial State *vs.* the Conventional Wisdom

Galbraith is unquestionably one of the most literate of the present generation of economists. No other leading member of the profession can claim to be a Fellow—in literature—of the National Institute of Arts and Letters. His books draw a large audience on their literary merits alone. Large audiences do not guarantee that the work will leave a lasting impression on the discipline. Yet Galbraith's thought—both now and in the longer view of history—may turn out to be more profound than his critics concede at the moment. Veblen's attacks on the neoclassical system failed to have any appreciable impact when they first appeared. Most economists agreed with Frank Knight that Veblen's observations were not relevant to the structure of economic theory. And the theory remained unshaken. Much the same response has greeted Galbraith's work, as we shall see. But there are important differences. Veblen wrote in a period when the progressive movement had made little headway against the orthodoxy of nineteenth century liberalism. Few took his proposals seriously in the first decade of this century. It is less clear that the same could be said of Galbraith. Set in a far more conducive atmosphere for recommendations for government action, Galbraith's policy oriented observations have attracted wide attention. And his attacks have not been ignored by economists. As he appraises it:

> I've never been disposed to sacrifice truth to modesty. I think that there are certain ideas from my own books that slightly modify the way people think about economic life.[44]

Or, again in his terminology, the ideas of *The Affluent Society* are now part of the conventional wisdom.

In spite of—indeed some would say because of—his success as an

---

43 *Ibid.*, p. 80.
44 *Playboy, op. cit.*, p. 78.

author, Galbraith's work has not been well received by the academic economists. His flamboyant personality and popularity with the Establishment have done little to endear him to his academic colleagues. His sneering attitude towards the conventional wisdom and his superficial treatment of some important points in his analysis have added a certain degree of irritation. But the hostility with which his work has been reviewed involves more than mere jealousy over his success as a writer. Wounded professional pride is supported by objections which appear to show some serious shortcomings of the Galbraithian system. Without intending a detailed critique of that system, we shall look at some of the more frequent complaints lodged against it by critics.[45]

As we have already noted, Galbraith does not state his hypothesis in a fashion which allows easy evaluation. We summarized the foundations

---

[45] To avoid frequent—and repetitious—citations in support of the arguments in this section, we refer the reader to several reviews which present the case against Galbraith. None of them are at all technical. We have already discussed the reaction to the Dependence Effect when it appeared in *The Affluent Society, op. cit.* Most of the reviews cited here refer specifically to *The New Industrial State, op. cit.* However, the interrelation between the two works makes it virtually impossible to comment on one without the other.

Perhaps the best summary of the argument is Robert Solow's "Son of Affluence," *Public Interest* (Fall 1967), 100-108. Galbraith chose to answer Solow's comments with his "Review of a Review," *op. cit.*, 109-18. The exchange illustrates very well the schism between Galbraith and the economics profession.

Another, slightly more sophisticated, statement of the usual objections to Galbraith's work can be found in the testimony by Walter Adams and Willard Mueller before the Senate Subcommittee on Monopoly. Walter Adams and Willard Mueller, Testimony before Senate Subcommittee on Monopoly in *Hearings of Senate Subcommittee on Monopoly*, June 29, 1967 (Washington, D.C.: U.S. Government Printing Office). A penetrating critique of the entire Galbraithian system—from the viewpoint of a staunch advocate of the marketplace—is the review by Scott Gordon, "The Close of the Galbraithian System," *The Journal of Political Economy*, vol. 76, no. 4 (July-August 1968), 635-44. George Stigler presents a similar viewpoint more concisely in the *Wall Street Journal*, June 26, 1967, p. 16. Gordon's review brought on a heated reply from Galbraith, *Journal of Political Economy*, vol. 77, no. 4, pt. 1 (July-August 1969). Gordon promptly issued a rejoinder in a similar tone, *Journal of Political Economy*, vol. 77, no. 6 (November-December 1969), which again illustrates the emotions raised by both sides of the debate.

More friendly reviews are illustrated by those of Kenneth Boulding, Book Week, *Washington Post*, July 18, 1967, p. 2, and Irving Kristol, *Fortune*, July 1967, pp. 90-91 and 194-95.

To date, we know of no really careful empirical study of the Galbraithian system. George Trivoli, "A Critical Examination of Galbraith's Industrial System Hypothesis" (Ph.D. Dissertation, University of Virginia, 1970), has been useful in summarizing some of the empirical evidence relating to the Industrial System Hypothesis.

of his argument in three major propositions. Each has come under fire by critics.

Technology and the Large Firm

Economists readily concede the presence of large firms. Less obvious is the extent to which they comprise a "system" which has as its apparent stereotype General Motors. Nor would all agree that these large firms are the *only* producers in the economy of interest to the economist. More economic activity takes place outside Galbraith's industrial system than within it. Indeed, only about one-fourth of total output is produced in industries which would generally be considered "oligopolistic." Since Galbraith does not analyze this sector at all, it requires a major act of faith to accept his dismissal of it as a barren wasteland devoid of economic change.

Even granting the dominance of large firms in some areas of manufacturing, the role of technology in this industrial complex is open to considerable question. Galbraith takes his views on the influence of technology in the large firms largely for granted; little evidence in support of his contentions is offered. Empirical work on the issue of firm size and technology has not, in general, been able to substantiate either: (1) the proposition that innovation and technology provide the basis for large size; or (2) the proposition that large firms lead the way in developing and introducing new innovation in the market. Galbraith subscribes to both of these views. The weight of evidence does not appear to be in his favor.[46]

The Technostructure and Profits

Critics have pointed out at some length that in his analysis of a technostructure operating the firm without maximizing profits, Galbraith is merely taking sides in a very old theoretical controversy. Although Galbraith supports his argument by citing numerous studies showing divorce of ownership and control, empirical research on firm management has failed to turn up any group which would seem to be Galbraith's "technostructure." Given the nature of such a group, this is not surprising; the point is that the question of who *really* runs the firm, and their incentives for dong so, remains a moot point. To proponents of Marshallian price theory, the entire debate is beside the

---

[46] See K. Elzinga, "Oligopoly, The Sherman Act, and the New Industrial State," *Social Science Quarterly* (June 1968), 49-57, on this point.

point. All that is needed is that firms behave *as if* they desire to maximize profits.[47] Again, the evidence on rates of return is hardly conclusive, but Galbraith's technostructure seems to be doing well enough in making their firms profitable.

The "Revised Sequence of Pricing"

Galbraith has postulated a set of objectives for his technostructure. Are the results better than that derived from the profit maximizing assumption? Many economists remain unconvinced. They point to a number of serious weaknesses in the analysis of the "revised sequence."

First is the empirical question regarding the firm's ability to shape demand to suit its particular needs. The firm must be able to derive a relationship between selling effort, and the resulting shifts in demand for its product, which is accurate enough to allow the planner to consider market demand as a variable under his control. This appears to be a rather bold assertion of the effectiveness of advertising and marketing. Galbraith cleverly anticipates the experience of Ford Motor Company and the Edsel. This, he says, is the exception which proves the rule. A more likely claim would be that it was simply one of the most spectacular failures of the revised sequence. In fact, why does the firm risk introduction of new products at all? If it can control demand, it need not incur the enormous costs of developing new products; it need only convince buyers to continue to purchase existing models.[48] Much more evidence needs to be presented before we can conclude that the firm's control over demand is sufficiently great that it can evade the market altogether. As one critic (Scott Gordon) put it, Galbraith's analysis fails to perceive the distinction between planning in a *market oriented firm* and that of a *nonmarket situation*. Planning under conditions of market constraint does not necessarily ensure the removal or evasion of those constraints. Galbraith exaggerates the firm's control over its market environment.

Even if the firm *could* manipulate its demand without any checks, Galbraith's analysis is still incomplete. The revised sequence fails to take account of the interaction involved in the determination of a *general equilibrium among all firms* in the system. What of the interdependence between oligopolistic firms which was prominent in the Chamberlin approach? Nowhere does Galbraith deal with such interde-

---

[47] This point was not developed by Marshall himself; it was explored at some length by Milton Friedman. See Chapter 14.

[48] We are indebted to Roland McKean for this observation.

pendence. He is carrying the Chamberlinian emphasis on the equilibrium of the *firm* to its extreme by completely ignoring the equilibrium of the *industry* (or "group" of interdependent firms). Galbraithian oligopolists apparently behave on the assumption that they can offset any reaction on the part of other firms. Such a situation would seem to be rare. Even in that epitome of the industrial system—the automobile industry—the largest firm is not entirely free from effects of price-quantity decisions of the rivals in the market. In his earlier work, Galbraith had employed the notion of a countervailing power among firms which would deal with the issue of interdependence.[49] This concept does not return in his analysis of the firm in the industrial system, and indeed is inconsistent with it.

Perhaps the most glaring weakness in the failure to consider a more general market analysis is Galbraith's treatment of allocation of capital. Here his omission of the nonindustrial sector is particularly puzzling, for large flows of saving and investment take place outside the world of large corporations. Galbraith insists the firm can ignore the capital market because it will generate internal funds for investment. But this would require a rate of saving sufficient to cover all contingencies; what if internal savings were insufficient? Or, in the event of a surplus, would the firm accumulate liquid balances waiting for some future need regardless of the alternative rate of return in the market for funds? Even large firms do not seem to ignore the market rate. Finally, Galbraith offers no insight as to the manner in which savings are allocated within the firm.

Proponents of the conventional wisdom center their objections on the inadequacies of the Galbraithian alternative. Neither his theory of prices in the industrial system nor his approach to the question of social imbalance adds new insight to the problem. So much for the prosecution.

The Galbraithian Reply

Whether his observations are right or wrong; whether his theory is useful to economists or not; Galbraith has a large body of noneconomist followers. This is not surprising. Economists may attack his work for its inadequacies in offering solutions to the questions raised, but even his bitterest critic is forced to concede that he raises pertinent issues. And he has done so in a very provocative form. The influence of giant

---

[49] See Galbraith, *American Capitalism, op. cit.* He does refer briefly to this idea in the determination of equilibrium between the technostructure and unions.

corporations *is* a reality; rising levels of affluence *do* pose problems beyond the scope of most economic analysis today.

And the tools of economics may not be the ones to solve these problems. Galbraith's complaint against the conventional wisdom is not so much that it is *wrong*; the problem is that it is *irrelevant*. The theory was developed within a completely different setting from the one which exists today. Economics is clinging to an approach geared to the situation of the last quarter of the nineteenth century. Thus, on the question of consumer equilibrium,

> The problem of economics here . . . is not one of original error, but of obsolescence. . . . The model of consumer behavior, devised for these conditions, was not wrong. The error was in taking it over without change into the age of the industrial system. There, not surprisingly, it did not fit.[50]

Economic thinking must be updated to face contemporary problems.

In Galbraith's analysis, the central problem of the affluent society is *not* allocation: "[one of the marks] of an affluent society is the opportunity for the existence of a considerable margin for error on such matters."[51] The issue at hand is the *normative implications* of a society where consumer wants are a *result* of the economic process. To throw out the dependence effect, because it requires a subjective evaluation of wants by the analyst, does not solve the problem; it merely places it outside the area of study of economics. And this is precisely what Galbraith objects to. Economics must broaden its perspective to include the issue of affluence. To his way of thinking, the criticism of his work by the profession has completely missed the point of what he wants to accomplish with his analysis. The attention of economics must move away from the dogmatic, unrealistic premises of the conventional wisdom to a broader framework of analysis. Failure to respond to the forces will, in Galbraith's view, doom economics to sterile logical arguments over irrelevant issues. As he argues:

> To enhance the well-being of the individual has, in the past, seemed a sound social purpose. To assist the individual in his subordination to General Motors will not be so regarded. The sanctity of economic purpose will also be questioned if well-being as conventionally measured continues to improve and leaves unsolved the problems associated with collective need—those of the cities

---

50 Galbraith, *The New Industrial State, op. cit.,* p. 215.
51 Galbraith, *The Affluent Society, op. cit.,* p. 321.

and their ghettoes and the by-passed rural areas—or if this progress involves an unacceptable commitment to the technology of war. And the doubts so engendered will be especially acute if concentration on narrow economic priority appears to be a cause of other social shortcomings.[52]

Why, one might ask, has the discipline of economics not adjusted to deal with contemporary problems? To some extent it has. The "conventional wisdom" is a far more flexible system of analysis than Galbraith's attack indicates. For example, the theory of public goods is a development dealing with the issues of interdependence in a society. And economists are reluctant to abandon their present "scientific" approach for a "normative" one. Galbraith has deployed a set of values to show what appears to be wrong with the present economic system. He can—and does—persuasively argue that his values are superior to those of others. But he can never show this absolutely; his system will always rest on the interpretation which one places on the "dependence effect."

Perhaps the problem is that, as Robert Solow points out, "economists are determined 'little thinkers,' " whereas Galbraith is a "big thinker." To illustrate his point he refers to:

> . . . the old story of the couple who had achieved an agreeable division of labor. She made the unimportant decisions: what job he should take, where they should live, how to bring up the children. He made the important decisions: what to do about Jerusalem, whether China should be admitted to the United Nations, how to deal with crime on the streets.[53]

Undaunted by his detractors, Galbraith continues on in his role as all-purpose critic. Perhaps his work will survive largely as a curiosity for future scholars interested in the intellectual debates of our time. But then, that might be all that Galbraith asks. In the decade after the publication of the *Affluent Society*, he already feels that his writing has had a small effect in shifting attention to the problems of modern society. As he warned in the conclusion of that book:

> To have failed to have solved the problem of producing goods would have been to continue man in his oldest and most grievous

---

[52] Galbraith, "A Review of a Review," *op. cit.*, pp. 117-18.

[53] Solow, "Son of Affluence," *op. cit.*, p. 100. Galbraith, it might be added, was not at all amused by the analysis. See his reply, "A Review of a Review," *op. cit.*, pp. 109-18.

misfortune. But to fail to see that we have solved it and to fail to proceed thence to the next task, would be fully as tragic.[54]

Ten years later he proceeded toward the next task with the *New Industrial State*. There is little sign that he proposes to relent in his efforts to alter the conventional wisdom in the future.

---

[54] Galbraith, *The Affluent Society, op. cit.*, p. 356.

PART IV

THE NEW
NEOCLASSICISM

CHAPTER 12

FRANK H. KNIGHT—
Philosopher of the Counter-
revolution in Economics

So far as I can make out, I believe in only one thing: liberty. But I do not believe in even liberty enough to want to force it upon anyone. That is, I am nothing of the reformer, however much I may rant against this or that curse or malaise. In the ranting there is usually far more delight than indignation.

H. L. MENCKEN

In 1924, four years after A. C. Pigou fired his lethal salvo at the policy prescriptions of neoclassicism, an economist at the University of Iowa published a rather technical paper in the prestigious *Quarterly Journal of Economics*. The author, Frank Hyneman Knight, already had some slight reputation in economics. Eight years earlier he had submitted a dissertation to the faculty of Cornell University which was accorded a second prize in a competition sponsored by Hart, Schaffner and Marx.[1] The dissertation was published under the title of *Risk, Uncertainty and Profit*.[2] It won for its young author a considerable

---

[1] The name of the winner of the first prize in this contest seems to have been lost in the mists of antiquity.

[2] Frank Knight, *Risk, Uncertainly and Profit* (New York: Hart, Schaffner and Marx, 1921).

amount of fame as a skillful analyst of one of the more difficult, unsettled questions in economic theory, namely, the nature and determination of profits in the competitive economy. In his 1924 article, Knight believed he had detected a major fallacy in the Pigovian argument for taxing increasing cost industries and subsidizing decreasing cost industries.

Pigou on Market Failure

The reader will recall that Pigou had contended that the laissez-faire market mechanism necessarily failed to achieve efficient resource allocation. One example was that of road congestion, and it will be instructive to review his reasoning at this point.

Pigou attempted to demonstrate that profit maximizing entrepreneurs will invest excessively in industries of increasing cost and underinvest in industries of constant or decreasing cost. His concrete example was that of two roads connecting two cities. The first road is wide enough to easily accommodate all the traffic that cares to use it, but is badly surfaced and graded (the decreasing cost industry). The second highway is well graded and superior in every way except that it is quite narrow and limited in capacity (the increasing cost industry). Pigou demonstrated that if operators of road vehicles were free to choose either of the two routes, they would tend to distribute themselves in such a way that the average cost of transportation would be the same for each unit of traffic on both roads. But, as we know, it is the equating of marginal costs that guarantees efficiency.

As more vehicles use the better but narrower road, traffic congestion would develop to the point where it would become equally advantageous or profitable to use the poorly graded but wider route. But in equilibrium, where marginal private costs are equal, there are too many vehicles on the well-surfaced road and too few on the wider road. The reason for this surprising result lies in the Pigovian distinction between private costs and social costs. Each individual road user would select the highway that is *privately* most beneficial to him, but would have no reason to calculate the costs of the congestion he imposes on others using the same route. The congestion resulting from the addition of any particular vehicle to the traffic on the good road would affect in the same way the cost of all the vehicles using that road. Thus, the addition to total costs from adding one more automobile to the narrow road (the marginal social cost) is necessarily greater than the additional cost borne by that car alone (the marginal private cost). The latter cost would be the *average* cost of all vehicles using the road up to that point. But the true marginal cost for all vehicles as a result of adding the additional vehicle would be higher than the average cost for all vehicles. In equilibrium, the average costs on the two roads would be equal, but it is clear that the marginal costs would differ. For if we could transfer a vehicle to the broad road, after this equilibrium is reached, the decrease in costs to those units remaining on the good road would be a pure gain to *all* traffic. The traffic that had been re-routed would incur no loss since the marginal private costs on both roads are the same in equilibrium. Any individual unit of traffic has an incentive to use the narrow road, as long as there is a difference in costs to him of using the two roads; but because of the externality of congestion, the advantage is reduced to zero for all the vehicles together. So Pigou was able to conclude that individual freedom results in misallocation of resources between increasing and decreasing cost industries.

Some simple numbers will help enlighten us at this point. The figures in Table 12.1 show the various cost schedules for alternative units of traffic on the narrow road.

TABLE 12-1

Cost Schedules for Alternative Units of Traffic

Vehicles	Total (Private) Cost I	Marginal (Private) Cost II	Total (Social) Cost III	Marginal (Social) Cost IV	Average (Social) Cost V
1	5	5	5	5	5
2	15	10	20	15	10
3	35	20	60	40	20
4	75	40	160	100	40
5	175	100	500	340	100

The marginal private cost to the first vehicle using the narrow road is $5, to the second $10, to the third $20, to the fourth $40, and so on. The rapidly increasing cost is due, of course, to the increased congestion. Vehicles will enter the flow of traffic on this road up to the point where the marginal private cost on the narrow road is exactly equal to the marginal private cost of his using the bad road. But the crucial point to note is that the individual, in making this private adjustment, does not calculate the costs he imposes on all other vehicles using the road. These costs can be seen in a glance at columns III and IV. In column III, we have calculated the *total* social costs of using the good road. It is computed by multiplying the number of vehicles on the road by the marginal private cost of each vehicle. Column IV shows the marginal social cost, which is simply the addition to total social cost of adding an additional vehicle to the road. Note that this cost is greater than the marginal private cost at some point. (In our example, that point is reached after more than one vehicle enters the traffic flow.) But this column reflects the true marginal costs when all costs, including that caused by the traffic congestion, are taken into account. It is important to note, further, that the average social cost (column V) is the total social cost divided by the number of units of traffic. This is precisely equal to the marginal private cost for each vehicle. Thus, the individual under freedom of choice conditions, in equating his marginal private cost on the good road to the bad road to reach equilibrium, is in actuality equating the *average* social costs to each other. The marginal social costs are above the average, as we can see when we compare columns IV and V. But efficient allocation requires, as we have noted before, that marginal costs be equated. Hence, an inefficient allocation of resources occurs under a laissez-faire scheme of production.

From this subtle reasoning, Pigou contended that government interference is justified. The proper prescription, of course, as with most of Pigou's welfare-increasing recommendations, was to levy a tax on each vehicle using the narrow road. The owner of the vehicle would now take this tax into his calculations when trying to determine which route was most advantageous to him. The flow of traffic would then be reduced to the point where the marginal cost on the narrow road, taking all social costs into account, would be equal to the marginal cost on the broad road. The tax would simply be the difference between the average cost and marginal cost of an additional unit of traffic on the well-surfaced road. Since the total amount of tax proceeds is precisely equal to the total costs of congestion, no individual vehicle would incur higher costs than if no tax had been imposed. Hence, welfare is increased by the tax policy.

Knight's Response to Pigou

Knight's devastating critique of this Pigovian argument caused Pigou to drop his road example from subsequent editions of his *Economics of Welfare*. But it is doubtful whether Pigou understood the full implications of Knight's argument. For encompassed in its relatively few pages is an approach to economic problems that ran counter to the anti-neoclassical trend of economic thought. Those who accepted Knight's message and followed through on his reasoning became counterrevolutionaries who were to form a major part of a school of thought that, for descriptive convenience, we call the "new neoclassicism."

For Knight's article, in effect, rehabilitated the neoclassical view that under competitive conditions, efficient allocation of resources would prevail. The results that Pigou discovered were only valid if private property rights were not clearly established. This can be demonstrated if we assume private ownership of Pigou's good but narrow road. Assuming competitive conditions, so that the traffic could use the wide, unsurfaced road for free, how would the profit maximizing entrepreneur set his toll for use of the narrow road? He could always charge a price which was precisely equal to the difference between the value to the vehicle owner of using the narrow road and the wide road. But this difference is exactly equal to the difference between the marginal cost and the average cost of an additional vehicle using the good road.[3] This, in effect, means that private owners of the road would be induced to charge a toll which would be exactly equal to the ideal tax that Pigou recommended. So traffic will flow to the superior road, up to the point where the marginal cost to the vehicle (which now includes the vehicles' toll) is equal to the marginal cost to him of using the alternative road. At that point, the vehicle owner would be indifferent between the two roads. In Knight's words, "The toll or rent will be so adjusted that *added* product of the last truck which uses the narrow road is just equal to what it could produce on the broad road. No truck will pay a higher charge, and it is not to the interest of the owner of the road to accept a lower fee. And this adjustment is exactly that which maximizes the total product of both roads."[4] The full implications of this technicality in economic theory are far-reaching. The market failure which Pigou and his disciples thought they had demonstrated was precisely the opposite of market failure. It was the failure of government to establish property rights in scarce resources that caused the congestion. To Knight, the market order is efficient if property rights are clearly identified. One of the basic functions of government—the identification of property rights—has not been carried out. After all, the establishment and enforcement of property rights had always been accepted as a function of government by both classical and neoclassical

---

[3] The reader familiar with the history of economic thought will perhaps have noted that Knight is applying Ricardo's differential rent theory to the problem of optimal pricing in the case of two roads of differing productivity. The analogy between Ricardo's land of differing fertility and Pigou's roads of differing productivity should be evident. The difference between the value of the product on the good road and the bad road is Ricardo's definition of "rent."

[4] Frank H. Knight, "Fallacies in the Interpretation of Social Cost," *Quarterly Journal of Economics* 38 (May 1924), 582-606. Reprinted in Frank H. Knight, *The Ethics of Competition and Other Essays* (New York: Harper and Row, Publishers, 1935), pp. 221-22.

economists. Now Knight showed that the failure of government to carry out its clearly delegated function had misled Pigou and other economists to call for government intervention into the economy.

The keen insight revealed by Knight in this article was to form the basis for much research into the study of property rights and externality problems at the hands of his disciples. In particular, the labors of Armen A. Alchian, James M. Buchanan, and Ronald Coase were to be an intensive tilling of the ground broken by Knight in this pioneering essay.[5]

The Philosophy of Skepticism

That Frank Knight should have paved the way for the counterrevolution of the new neoclassicism is perhaps not surprising. Born in McLean County, Illinois, in 1885, and brought up in the religious orthodoxy of prairie evangelism, he studied at Milligan College in Tennessee and the University of Tennessee. Eventually he moved to Cornell and studied economics under Allyn Young, the same man who so influenced E. H. Chamberlin. But in every sense Knight was a product of the midwest, and in the words of one of his students, "it is difficult to imagine that he could have emerged from the more sophisticated culture of the eastern seaboard."[6] After receiving his Ph.D. in 1916, Knight taught at the University of Iowa, but it was after he joined the faculty of the University of Chicago in 1927 that he began to have his greatest impact on students.

Knight was to the students of economics at Chicago in the 1930's what Alvin Hansen was to their counterparts at Harvard, namely, the father image and social philosopher, whose seminars and classrooms were attended with reverence and who awakened within some of the best young minds of a generation the excitement of the intellectual quest. He was a critic of orthodoxy, including what he considered the new dogma of the new economics. As Buchanan has put it, "His reaction against religious orthodoxy was perhaps an essential ingredient

---

[5] Armen A. Alchian, "Pricing and Society," Occasional Paper # 17 (London: Institute of Economic Affairs, 1967); James M. Buchanan, "Congestion on the Common: A Case for Government Intervention," *Il Politico*, vol. 33, no. 4 (1968), 776-86; Ronald Coase, "The Problem of Social Cost," *The Journal of Law and Economics* (October 1960), 1-44. Reprinted in Breit and Hochman, *Readings in Microeconomics* (New York: Holt, Rinehart and Winston, Inc., 1968), pp. 423-56.

[6] James M. Buchanan, "Frank H. Knight," *International Encyclopedia of Social Sciences*, ed. D. L. Sills (New York: The Macmillan Company and The Free Press, 1968), p. 424.

in his intellectual development: having rejected it, the less rigid dogma encountered in the world of scholarship became easy prey to the mid-western skeptic." Skepticism is perhaps the best single word summary of his philosophic approach. For Knight was in the tradition of the classical liberals of the late eighteenth century. Like David Hume, he rejected the view that the solution of social problems is to be found by the direct approach to them. And like Adam Smith, he had little hope that social reformers or "do-gooders" would solve problems and he thus was willing to allow the market to solve them.

His presidential address to the American Economic Association in 1950 contains the best succinct statement of Knight's philosophical view of social reform, a view that is dominant in the thinking of those who followed Knight's lead and whom we regard as members of the new neoclassicism.

> Time was, no doubt when society needed to be awakened to the possibility of remedying evils, and stirred to action, mostly negative action, establishing freedom, but some positive action too. Now, we have found not only that mere individual freedom is not enough, but that its excess can have disastrous consequences. And a reaction has set in, so that people have too much faith in positive action, of the nature of passing laws and employing police-men, and the opposite warning is needed. At least so I hold; per-haps it is a prejudice—how can one tell?—I mistrust reformers. When a man or group asks for power to do good, my impulse is to say, "Oh, yeah, who ever wanted power for any other reason? And what have they done when they got it?" So, I instinctively want to cancel the last three words, leaving simply "I want power;" that is easy to believe. And, a further confession: I am reluctant to believe in doing good with power anyhow. With William James, I incline to the side of "the slow and silent forces," slow as though in all conscience they are—and though time is fleeting.[7]

It is asserted that to understand Frank Knight completely, one had to have been his student attending his courses. Otherwise, his writings remain somewhat obscure. A rather bombastic personality, his approach to life is similar to David Hume's and, perhaps surprisingly, H. L. Mencken. Although he has the healthy skepticism of both, and the bombast of Mencken, his writing style falls woefully short of the latter's lucidity. Perhaps the best place to get the flavor of the man is in his

---

[7] Frank H. Knight, "The Role of Principles in Economics and Politics," *American Economic Review*, 41 (March 1951), 29.

last work, *Intelligence and Democratic Action*,[8] since these essays were delivered orally at the University of Virginia and edited from tapes made during his lectures.

Some of Knight's contributions have become so central to the core of economics that they are standard fare, included in the beginning texts. For example, he was the first economist to spell out, in a clear and unequivocal form, the functions of an economic system, into which the beginning student usually is initiated on the very first day of class. Another device adopted by textbook writers is Knight's concept of the wheel of wealth or circular flow model of the economy. Moreover, he must be credited with having spelled out the most complete formulation of the assumptions of the perfectly competitive model.[9]

But it was not Knight's shaping of the teaching of economics with which we are concerned, but rather with his shaping of economic policy. Here the impact is not direct; rather it was to be felt through his social philosophy as depicted in the typically Knightian prose noted above.

Knight's Rehabilitation of Economic Man

One of Knight's most important contributions to the revival of neoclassicism was his original and refreshing approach to the concept of economic man. Knight's objection to Veblen and his followers was not that the economic man of neoclassical thought was in any way realistic. Indeed, Knight repeatedly emphasized that economic man was not the actual man of the world. The criticisms of Veblen and his disciples were really wide of the mark. To Knight, the "man" of economic theory must be an unrealistic replica of his actual counterpart in order to abstract from reality and build a rigorous and useful science of economics. Knight pointed out that man is indeed multi-dimensional as Veblen argued: he has a physical, biological, and social dimension. But the economist makes use of one aspect of men's social dimension: his actions which are deliberately purposive, in which he consciously uses means to attain his ends in some predefined manner. Economic theory takes it that man maximizes his ends in his role as consumer (utility maximizer) and producer (profit maximizer). Consumers and producers are seen in a constant process of maximizing the attainment of their

---

[8] Frank H. Knight, *Intelligence and Democratic Action* (Cambridge, Mass.: Harvard University Press, 1960).

[9] Frank H. Knight, "The Ethics of Competition," *Quarterly Journal of Economics*, 37 (August 1923), 579-624. Reprinted in Knight, *Ethics of Competition, op. cit.*, pp. 41-75. See George J. Stigler, "Perfect Competition, Historically Contemplated," *Journal of Political Economy*, vol. 45 (February 1957), 1-17.

ends. This view of man is analogous to that of the frictionless machine or the perfect vacuum of physics and is just as essential to the analysis. But, avers Knight, once such an assumption is made, economic theory loses its behavioral content, since the rational calculator is truly predetermined. He has no real choice. For this reason Knight has always cautioned against the overzealous application of economic theory to noneconomic problems.

> "It is . . . one of the errors, not to say vices, of an age in which the progress of natural science and the triumphs of its application to life have engrossed men's attention, to look upon life too exclusively under this aspect of scientific rationality. It is requisite to a proper orientation to economic science itself as well as necessary to a sound philosophy of life, to see clearly that life must be more than economics, or rational conduct, or the intelligent manipulation of materials and use of power in achieving results . . . Living intelligently includes more than intelligent use of means in realizing ends; it is fully as important to select the ends intelligently, for intelligent action directed toward wrong ends only makes evil greater and more certain.[10]

Knight's restatement of the economic man became the basis of the methodological approach of his followers who accepted his view that the assumptions of economics cannot be "realistic," just as the assumptions of the natural sciences are abstractions from reality. But they often paid little heed to his caveat that theories constructed on the basis of the rationally calculating man must not be pushed too far into other social sciences, since the noneconomic behavior of man may be better analyzed using assumptions more directly relevant to those fields. For economic theory is simply a representation of idealized behavior and can have relevance for real-world behavior, only to the degree that man in fact acts in conformity with these assumptions. Economic theory is a logical system for analysis and understanding—but not for prediction. For this reason, Knight rejects the view that economic theory can "be operational in the modern methodological sense."[11]

In sum, then, Knight accepts the view that economic theory must proceed on the basis of unrealistic assumptions, but must not be used to

---

[10] Frank H. Knight, "Social Economic Organization," *Readings in Microeconomics, op. cit.,* p. 4. Reprinted from Frank H. Knight, *The Economic Organization* (New York: Harper and Row, Publishers, c. 1933, 1951), pp. 3-30.

[11] See Buchanan, "Frank H. Knight," *op. cit.,* p. 426. See also Frank H. Knight, "Social Science," *On the History and Method of Economics* (Chicago: University of Chicago Press, 1956), pp. 121-34.

exceed the "common sense" limits of applicability. It is the clarification of the nature and significance of economic man that Knight considers his major contribution to economic methodology.

Knight's Response to Veblen

Having rehabilitated economic man by pointing out his usefulness as well as limitations in social science, Knight took up the question of the Veblenian dichotomy between industrial and pecuniary employments. He notes that the simplest view of Veblen's antithesis is that industrial or technological values are those of which he disapproves. But Knight argued that all such distinctions ultimately resolve into value judgments, and at that point, argument must cease. When Veblen sarcastically described the conspicuous consumption of the business culture, he meant to disapprove of consumption devoted to keeping up appearances. But all consumption above the level of brute material existence smacks of such emulative behavior. And it is doubtful if Veblen would want to abolish such gratifications. Hence, Veblen's attack on the consumer sovereignty criterion of welfare in essence comes down to disapproving of "improper" consumption, which, as Knight points out, is consumption "of which he (Veblen) disapproves. If he (Veblen) has an objective test for distinguishing between valid and false aesthetic values . . . he does the world grievous wrong in withholding it from publication."[12] Knight also pointed out that in a democracy it is extremely difficult to apply the distinction between Veblen's "real value and trumpery." These remarks by Knight have been repeated in one form or another by almost all critics of those who followed Veblen in attempting to castigate consumer sovereignty. And to the diehard advocate of free enterprise and political democracy, they have never been successfully answered.

Risk and Consumer Sovereignty

Any summary statement of Frank Knight's influence on economic thought and policy would be inexcusably incomplete if no mention

---

12 Frank H. Knight, "Review of the Place of Science in Modern Civilization," *Journal of Political Economy* (June 1920), 520. Notwithstanding his reservations about Veblen's dichotomy, Knight was appreciative of some aspects of Veblen's economics and he was one of those who insisted that the American Economic Association select him as President in 1925. J. Dorfman, "The Source and Impact of Veblen's Thought," *Thorstein Veblen: A Critical Reappraisal*, ed. D. Dowd (Ithaca, New York: Cornell University Press, 1958).

were made of his key ideas in his first book, *Risk, Uncertainty and Profit*.[13] For this book contains his chief contribution to the body of contemporary economic thought—Knight's theory of the nature and role of profits in the competitive model. Here Knight adumbrated a sketch of a theory of the firm which has been accepted by his students, and which contains their answer to the Veblen-Galbraith notion of the manipulation of consumer preferences by corporations. The basic contribution is Knight's distinction between risk and uncertainty. The perfectly competitive model assumed perfect knowledge on the part of consumers and producers. But, under such an assumption, profit would be nonexistent. If every entrepreneur had complete knowledge of future demand and cost conditions, each would immediately move into areas of highest return and profit would disappear. And there would exist no residual income after all costs of production, including the wages of management, were paid.

But Knight insists that a slight relaxation of the extreme assumptions of perfect competition would permit an explanation of the existence of profit. By eliminating the assumption of perfect knowledge, the element of "uncertainty" becomes a part of the economic game. And it is from this uncertainty that profit arises. The real world can be characterized by a probability calculus, by which we can infer from events what the future will be like with certain degrees of confidence. The degree of confidence with which we predict a future event is a measure of how likely it is that this past event will recur. If this can be done with complete accuracy, then there is no uncertainty. Uncertainty exists only when we cannot accurately determine the probability of an event. This is a concept to be contrasted with "risk." The latter exists if we can attach some accurate probability distribution to its occurrence. Thus, risk is a measurable uncertainty and can be insured against. In Knight's words:

> The practical difference between the two categories, risk and uncertainty, is that in the former the distribution of the outcome in a group of instances is known (either through calculation *a priori* or from statistics or past experience), while in the case of uncertainty this is not true, the reason being in general that it is impossible to form a group of instances, because the situation dealt with is in a high degree unique.[14]

---

13 Knight, *Risk, Uncertainty and Profit, op. cit.*
14 *Ibid.*, p. 233.

In order to clarify Knight's meaning, an example will perhaps prove instructive. Let us assume the existence of an individual who prefers to bear risk and decides to enter the women's fashion industry. By one who prefers risk, we mean that he is willing to take the consequences of a decision involving an uncertain outcome. Since the occurrence is uncertain, others with a similar willingness to bear risks may not have the same belief regarding the outcome of the individual's prediction. Indeed, since the outcome is uncertain, many possible eventualities would in fact be predicted.

Let us further assume that the uncertain event involves the question of hemlines. Specifically, how many inches above the knee will women prefer their hemlines next season? Since the women's fashion industry is highly competitive and women's future fashions are difficult to predict with accuracy, there can be expected many different guesses regarding women's preferences next year. But the prediction regarding future tastes must be made today since the productive process is time-consuming and an order with a manufacturer must be made at least a season in advance. While our risk bearing entrepreneur makes the prediction that the fashion to be preferred next season is a hemline four inches above the knee, it can be expected that other risk takers predict varying degrees of hemline lengths. But if our individual is right and his prediction is borne out, his inventories will be in great demand in comparison with those of other fashion entrepreneurs. After paying his contractual obligations—wages, rent, and interest—he will have a residual. Now what is the nature of this residual? It is a return that he gets on the basis of no advance contract, but is the difference between his total contractuable costs and his total revenues.[15] It is this difference that Knight calls *profit*.

Note that our individual had this return because the predictions of his competitors proved incorrect regarding consumer preferences. Had they all made the same prediction as had our successful entrepreneur (that is, had no uncertainty existed), there would be no profit. In our example, however, in which at least one entrepreneur turned out to be a correct predictor, those who predicted wrongly have negative profits, also arising from uncertainty. Profit is thus a return—both positive and negative—for bearing uncertainty.[16]

---

[15] The reason it is the difference between the total *contractuable* costs and total revenues is because the entrepreneur could have hired himself out to a competitor for some contracted salary. This is a cost in the sense that it is an opportunity foregone at the time of decision making and it must be added to his wages, rent, and interest actually contracted to get the total costs in the economist's sense.

[16] It should be noted that if our entrepreneur were able to repeat his feat of accurate prediction season after season, it would become evident to his competitors

Thus, as we have seen, the entrepreneur such as our individual above must determine both the quality and quantity of his final output. But the decision in regard to these matters is made on the basis of imperfect knowledge regarding consumers' tastes, incomes, and alternatives. This knowledge is imperfect because the productive process is time-consuming, and the longer the period of time involved, the greater the amount of uncertainty. The consumer cannot help him out, since he does not himself know precisely his future tastes. He does not know what he will want nor how badly he will want it. Furthermore, the consumer is not willing to bear the uncertainty and cost of predicting his own tastes. This problem of prediction is left to the producer. Thus, consumers willingly allow the manufacturer to bear the uncertainty of future demand. The entrepreneur is the uncertainty bearer because he is a decision maker in a situation where the outcome is unknown and unpredictable.

It is here that Knight anticipates the answer to Galbraith's main attack on consumer sovereignty, the answer to Galbraith's contention that consumer demand is manipulated by producers in the sense that wants are "created" which producers then proceed to satisfy. Knight's analysis in *Risk, Uncertainty and Profit* casts a different light on the problem. For the producer is the uncertainty bearer—the decision maker—and this role is assigned to him by the uncertainty averting consumer. The consumer merely maintains a veto power if the resulting product fails to meet his preferences at the time.

In sum, through his writings and, probably more important, through his teaching, Frank Knight contributed to the contemporary revival of interest in neoclassical economics. In attempting to answer some of the main critics of neoclassicism, specifically Veblen and Pigou, he was led to restate in solid analytical form the basic premises of that model and indicate its vitality for dealing with significant issues. In his magnum opus, *Risk, Uncertainty and Profit*, he completed the neoclassical system by examining the nature of profit and the role of the entrepreneur in economic life. This reexamination of the neoclassical economics contains an alternative interpretation to that of Veblen and Galbraith of the activities of producers in influencing consumer tastes. More important,

---

that he had a unique skill to forecast accurately. Under these conditions, he would doubtless find that he could contract his talent out for a salary equal to some average of his previous profits. If he is offered a contract that he can accept at any time, but refuses the offer, he no longer receives Knightian profits (except for the amount that he receives over and above the amount for which he could sell his services). Uncertainty for him no longer exists and what previously was calculated as profit—which he is now able to contract for—would be a rent.

his social philosophy was attractive enough to some of the brightest young men studying economics at Chicago in the thirties and forties, that they made it their own. But it should be noted that Knight's counterrevolutionary influence was in the realm of philosophy and microeconomics. It was left to one of his colleagues at Chicago, Henry Simons, to question the validity of the macroeconomics of the Keynes-Hansen variety and, thus, help to complete the building of the new neoclassicism.

CHAPTER 13

HENRY C. SIMONS—
Radical Proponent of
Laissez-faire

Torturing straw men and raping straw women is eloquently sanctioned by your favorite oracle, precedent . . . [But] your audience may be credited with suspecting . . . that the blood-assay of straw is like that of turnips.

> LETTER FROM HENRY
> C. SIMONS TO HAROLD
> GROVES, OCTOBER 26,
> 1943.

At the time of his death in April of 1946, John Maynard Keynes was unquestionably the best known economist in the world. Not surprisingly, his death merited front page attention in the United States. In a lengthy obituary, the *New York Times* praised Keynes's substantial contributions to economic thought and policy.[1] Two months later, the

---

[1] *New York Times*, April 22, 1946. Ironically, the same issue of the *Times* provided evidence that at least one major group still was reluctant to accept the arguments of the *General Theory*. In a two column story immediately over the report of Keynes's death was a story beginning:

> Endorsing the principle that a balanced budget is essential to national solvency, 26 Republican and Democratic governors issued statements yesterday criticizing deficit spending and continued borrowing as an "unsound fiscal practice" and calling on Congress to provide a balanced budget beginning July 1.

death of another economist received far less attention; buried far inside the June 20, 1946 issue of the *Times* was a story noting the death of "Henry Simons, forty-six, associate professor of Law and Economics at the University of Chicago." After commenting on the immediate circumstances of his death—an apparent overdose of sleeping tablets—the *Times* provided the following summary of Simons' career:

> Born on October 19, 1899 in Virden, Illinois, Professor Simons was educated at the University of Michigan. He became an instructor and member of the faculty at the University of Iowa, remaining there until 1927 when he received his appointment at the University of Chicago.[2]

The *Times*, and the rest of the public, may be excused for paying so little heed to the passing of a relatively unheralded academic. Henry Calvert Simons wrote no major opus in economics to compare with Keynes's *General Theory*, nor was he a prolific writer in the style of Keynes or Alvin Hansen. His work was cut short by his early death; virtually all his important contributions to economics appeared in the short span of years between the onslaught of the Depression and the end of World War II. They have been collected into a single 300 page volume appropriately titled, *Economic Policy for a Free Society*.[3]

His obscurity as a public figure belied the influence which Henry Simons exerted on the shaping of economic thought in the turbulent years of the Roosevelt era. While the students at Cambridge—and increasingly elsewhere in the United States—were pondering the advantages of the Keynesian doctrine, a generation of students at the University of Chicago listened to Simons's articulate defense of the laissez-faire philosophy and neoclassical economic theory. Not surprisingly, Simons was a great admirer of another influential teacher at the University of Chicago—Frank Knight. They had been on the faculty at the University of Iowa, and when Knight moved to Chicago in 1927, Simons came with him. Their interests complemented each other well: Simons concerned himself with policy; Knight with theoretical issues.

---

[2] *New York Times*, June 20, 1946. Obituary.

[3] Henry C. Simons, *Economic Policy for a Free Society* (Chicago: University of Chicago Press, 1948). Hereinafter cited as *Economic Policy*. Although we shall indicate the particular article concerned, the page references in this chapter will refer to this book except where noted. Two other books by Simons involved taxation. Henry C. Simons, *Personal Income Taxation* (Chicago: University of Chicago Press, 1938), and *Federal Tax Reform* (Chicago: University of Chicago Press, 1950). The latter was published posthumously in 1950. Neither of these works had the impact of the essays in *Economic Policy for a Free Society*.

A social philosophy which insisted that the preservation of individual freedom was a goal far more important than the achievement of narrow economic objectives made each of them less interested in the technical details of economic logic than in the broader implications of economic reasoning for the free market society. Each was branded a "conservative" (and in Simons case, a "radical conservative") as a result of their reluctance to favor government over private actions in a market economy. Such views ran counter to the prevailing atmosphere in Washington. Doubtless this reluctance to support the New Deal stemmed in large part from their midwesterner mistrust of bureaucratic power; neither Simons nor Knight could see substantial gains from placing power in the hands of the few—whether it be government or any other group.

Simons *versus* Keynes and Hansen

Curiously, Simons also had a great deal in common with the leader of the new economics—John Maynard Keynes. Each was primarily concerned with issues of policy. Both recognized the catastrophic dimensions of the Depression, and sought ways to effect recovery. Moreover, their economic analysis of the collapse was strikingly similar. Keynes placed considerable blame on the uncertainty of the investment markets; Simons concurred. The sudden shift in liquidity which Keynes explained through his "liquidity preference" schedule is reflected by Simons's emphasis on what he viewed as the "perverse" behavior of velocity.[4] But there the similarities ended, for when they turned to the question of appropriate policies to combat the Depression, the two economists drew very different conclusions from their common empirical judgments. Keynes's outlook was on the short run; one of his more celebrated comments pointed out that "in the long run we are all dead." Accordingly, his proposals centered on programs to effect immediate recovery—stimulation of investment by direct government spending. Simons thought that this emphasis on the short view was dangerous; he felt the government intervention suggested by Keynes would result in an encroachment of freedom which far outweighted its monetary bene-

---

[4] Simons, of course, wrote within the framework of the Quantity Theory. Thus, the increase in liquidity of Keynes is a sharp fall in velocity to Simons. For an interesting interpretation of Keynes and Simons in the 1930's, see the remarks of one of Simons's more illustrious students: Milton Friedman. Milton Friedman, "The Monetary Theory and Policy of Henry Simons," *Journal of Law and Economics*, vol. X (October 1967), 1-13. As it happens, Friedman later gathered substantial evidence which tended to refute Simons's interpretation of the demand for money during the depression.

fits. He was highly skeptical of the implications of the Keynesian assault on economic orthodoxy:

> Not content to point out the shortcomings of traditional views, Mr. Keynes proceeds to espouse the cause of an army of cranks and heretics simply on the grounds that their schemes or ideas would incidently have involved or suggested mitigation of the deflationary tendencies in the economy.
>
> . . .
>
> Attempting mischievious and salutory irritation of his peers . . . he may only succeed in becoming the academic idol of our worst cranks and charlatans—not to mention the possibilities of the book as the economic bible of a fascist movement.[5]

Keynes, of course, was himself aware of the appeal of his policy recommendations to totalitarian regimes. Writing a preface for the German edition of the *General Theory*, he commented:

> The theory of aggregate production, which is the point of this following book, nevertheless can be much easier adapted to the conditions of a totalitarian state (*eines totalen saats*) than the theory of production and distribution of a given product put forth under conditions of free competition and a large degree of laissez faire.[6]

Simons would certainly concur. He was firmly convinced that the proposals which in fact emerged from the implications of the *General Theory* would undermine the essential prerequisites of a free market. This made him an implacable foe of the new economics; he became a virulent critic of the various schemes for postwar economic programs. His style at times produced caustic remarks on the implications of government intervention. Commenting on one such proposal by Lord Beveridge in Great Britain (from what he admitted was an "unsympathetic view"), Simons noted:

> So a sporting old Englishman urges England to take over the German Game, not diffidently as in the thirties but zealously, and to show the world how it should be played. England's commercial power is to be mobilized and concentrated, to improve her terms of trade, to recruit satellites for a tight sterling bloc, and to insulate

---

[5] Henry C. Simons, "Keynes' Comments on Money," *Christian Century*, July 22, 1936, pp. 1016-17.

[6] John Maynard Keynes, *The General Theory of Employment Interest and Money*, German Edition (Berlin and Munich: Duncker and Humblot, 1936), pp. 39-41.

herself and them from unstable, unplanned, economies, that is, from the United States.[7]

His salvos at the government policies were generally made from afar, for Simons's intense distaste for bureaucratic affairs made him assiduously avoid appearances in Washington, D.C. Yet his attacks were not unnoticed by those he singled out for comment. And his favorite target was the leading academic Keynesian—Alvin Hansen. Simons appreciated the appeal of Hansen's writing. Reviewing *Fiscal Policy and Business Cycles*,[8] he commended the book's "clarity of statement and excellence of style." But, he went on:

> I come to bury Hansen—albeit respectfully and despairingly. Praise he will receive elsewhere, for learning and assiduous inquiry which merit all praise and because he accepts and applauds the powerful political trends of the day. . . . So, as an unreconstructed, old fashioned liberal, I must counterattack as best I can, hoping thereby to diminish slightly that impetus which the book must give to trends of thought and action which to me seem wholly dangerous.[9]

Simons made no apologies for his "old fashioned liberalism." He insisted that philosophical beliefs are necessarily the foundations of any economist's policy conclusions. He scoffed at those who tried to practice economics as a "science" devoid of any set of values:

> It has become conventional among students of fiscal policy . . . to dissemble any underlying social philosophy and to maintain a pretense of rigorous, objective analysis untinctured by mere ethical considerations. The emptiness of this pretense among economists is notorious. . . . Having been told that sentiments are contraband in the realm of science, they religiously eschew a few proscribed phrases, clutter up title pages and introductory chapters with pious references to the science of public finance and then write monumental discourses on their own prejudices and preconceptions.[10]

The opening paragraph of his "Positive Program for Laissez Faire"[11]

---

[7] Simons, *Economic Policy, op. cit.*, p. 278.

[8] Alvin Hansen, *Fiscal Policy and Business Cycles* (New York: W. W. Norton & Company, Inc., 1941).

[9] Simons, *Economic Policy, op. cit.*, p. 185.

[10] Simons, *Personal Income Taxation, op. cit.*, pp. 1-2.

[11] Henry C. Simons, "A Positive Program for Laissez Faire," in *Economic Policy, op. cit.*, pp. 40-77.

provides a typical example of his own frankness regarding underlying philosophies:

> This is frankly a propagandist tract—a defense of the thesis that traditional liberalism offers, at once, the best escape from the moral confusion of current (1945) political and economic thought and the best basis or rationale for a program of economic reconstruction.[12]

His defenses of this position—and his "counterattacks" against Keynesians such as Hansen—provide some of the most articulate statements of the laissez-faire position to be found anywhere in the literature of economics. Defenses of laissez-faire were hardly uncommon in the 1930's; what singles out Simons was his insistence on recognizing the *positive* actions which were required of a government to maintain a free market. His overriding concern was with policy, and his approach to the issues was invariably that of a "radical." He did not propose new monetary *policies*; he insisted on a thorough reform of the *entire financial system*. His aim was not to *regulate* private monopoly, but to *eliminate its sources*. It is in connection with these radical proposals that Simons is best known.

Simons seldom dwelled on the intricacies of economic theory—more often than not such points were relegated to lengthy footnotes. Using the neoclassical approach to allocation and money as the foundation, Simons tried to explore the institutional arrangements which would best suit the operation of a free market in the modern world. His academic post reflected this interest in institutional arrangements; he was the first of several eminent economists to become members of the Law Faculty at the University of Chicago.[13] The relevance of law to economics was apparent in Simons' approach to the "economic problem." A market can only operate effectively in the context of a stable environment. It is the responsibility of the government to seek actively to create such an environment. In what is perhaps his most significant economic essay, Simons stated this responsibility very clearly:

> The liberal creed demands the organization of our economic life largely through individual participation in a game *with definite rules*. It calls upon that state to provide a stable framework of rules within which enterprise and competition may effectively control

---

[12] *Ibid.*, p. 40.

[13] He held a joint appointment from 1937 on. The continuing contact between the two disciplines ultimately produced the *Journal of Law and Economics* in 1957. One of Simons's students, Aaron Director, was the journal's initial editor.

and direct the production and distribution of goods. The essential conception is that of a genuine division of labor between competitive (market) and political controls—a division of labor within which competition has a major, or at least proximately primary, place.[14]

The need for establishing some rational set of rules to constrain the arbitrary authority of government is a dominating theme throughout all of Simons's writing. He did not favor the establishment of a *status quo*; nor did he advocate a government policy involving a complete absence of intervention. He called for a *positive* program of government action which would emphasize that delicate *division of labor* between government and the free market. In Simons's view this division of labor had seldom been optimal in the past. Government had intervened in many areas where it should have remained aloof; but more important, it had *ignored* several fundamental areas where forceful control was *essential to the operation of the market system*. In his discussion of positive action by the state, Simons spelled out five broad areas of concern:[15]

1. Elimination of all forms of private monopoly.
2. Reform of the monetary system and the establishment of "rules of the game" for monetary authorities to follow.
3. Reform of the tax system.
4. Removal of all tariff levies.
5. An effort to limit the "squandering of our resources" on merchandising and advertising practices.

Simons took great care to point out that the suggestions are presented in order of their importance as he viewed it. In particular, he noted the overriding importance of the first proposal, since:

> The case for a liberal-conservative policy must stand or fall on the first proposal, abolition of private monopoly; for it is the *sine qua non* of any such policy.[16]

While elimination of monopoly power is the cornerstone of Simons's approach to economic policy, it has been his views on monetary policy which received the widest audience. His ideas in this area show the rationale behind the establishment of "rules" to curb the exercise of

---

[14] Simons, *Economic Policy, op. cit.*, p. 160.

[15] This list was paraphrased from the proposals in "A Positive Program for Laissez Faire" in *Economic Policy, op. cit.*, pp. 40-77.

[16] Simons, *Economic Policy, op. cit.*, p. 57.

arbitrary "authority" in the economic system. Accordingly, we shall take up the issues of his monetary reform before tackling the broader aspects of his program for laissez-faire.[17]

Rules *vs.* Authorities

The most hotly debated issue at the time Simons wrote was, of course, the government policy and economic stability. He felt that the elimination of monopoly power—through greater price flexibility— would lessen the impact of economic cycles. Yet—quite apart from his own pessimism as to the possibility of actually reducing monopoly— Simons contended that this would not be sufficient to guarantee stability. Accordingly:

> The major responsibility for the severity of industrial fluctuations . . . falls directly upon the state. Tolerable functioning of a free- enterprise system presupposes effective performance of a funda- mental function of government, namely, regulation of the circulat- ing medium (money).[18]

The details of Simons's monetary policy are not always explicit in his writings. His basic framework of analysis was that of the neoclassical quantity theory.[19] Yet he was moving toward a more sophisticated treatment of that argument than appeared in the literature up to that time. He certainly agreed with the neoclassicists that the stock of money was an important element in the level of what he termed "aggregate turnover" (that is, Keynes's aggregate demand). Simons's emphasis on the aggregate turnover led him to concentrate his anal- ysis on the behavior of *velocity*—people's behavior in desiring and spending money. Velocity, he felt, was subject to sudden and very wide fluctuations in the short run. His interest in velocity stemmed from his puzzlement over the lethargic condition of the economy following the Great Crash:

---

[17] Two of Simons's articles contain the basic logic of his policy proposals on monetary policy: Henry C. Simons, "Rules vs. Authorities in Monetary Policy," *Journal of Political Economy*, vol. XLIV, no. 1 (February 1936), 1-30, reprinted in *Economic Policy, op. cit.*, pp. 160-83; and Henry C. Simons, "Hansen on Fiscal Policy," *Journal of Political Economy*, vol. L, no. 2 (April 1942), 161-96, reprinted in *Economic Policy, op. cit.*, pp. 184-219. The latter is his scathing review of Hansen, *Fiscal Policy and Business Cycles, op. cit.*

[18] Simons, *Economic Policy, op. cit.*, p. 54.

[19] See our discussion of the quantity theory of money in Chapter 2.

What we need now to understand and explain is why our economy of the thirties, though flooded with money, failed to revive adequately or to function effectively.[20]

In his work on monetary reform, Simons appears to be moving towards a formulation of the quantity equation of exchange which would envision the term velocity as some sort of behavioral variable depending on a large number of possible influences.[21] The variable which he particularly addressed himself to in the context of the 1930's was the influence of institutional arrangements. He insisted that the climate of uncertainty generated by the periodic collapse of financial markets led people to react sharply in their attitudes on holding money.

Simons was appalled by the "preposterous" rules under which the medium of exchange was controlled in the United States. A reluctance on the part of the federal government to provide a circulating media had resulted in this function being "usurped" by the private sector—that is, the commercial banks. The "money" of the United States economy was for the most part a huge mass of short term debt held in the form of demand deposits. Simons described the evolution of the "money" industry with characteristic candor:

> During the past century or more, a thriving economy, denied adequate proper media for liquid reserves, created and encouraged private agencies to provide what government itself blindly failed to provide. Thus, we evolved a fantastic financial structure and collections of enterprises for money-bootlegging, whose sanctimonious respectability and marble solidity only concealed a mass of current obligations and a shoestring of equity that would have been scandalous in any other type of business.[22]

He conceded that the arrangement had thus far been able to satisfy the secular demand for money in the system, but it did so at enormous cost, for it exposed the economy to frequent "precipitous, catastrophic deflations."

The core of the problem is the *fractional reserve banking*, which allows the commercial banks to hold liabilities in the form of demand

---

[20] Simons, *Economic Policy, op. cit.*, p. 186.

[21] For the more sophisticated version of the quantity equation, see Chapter 14. It is interesting to note that the leading proponent of the "modern" theory describes Simons's views on monetary theory as "highly sophisticated." Milton Friedman, "The Monetary Theory and Policy of Henry Simons," *op. cit.*

[22] Simons, *Economic Policy, op. cit.*, p. 198.

deposits up to some multiple of the "reserves" available in the bank. Simons was convinced that such an arrangement could *never* be truly secure from potential liquidity crises:

> No real stability of production and employment is possible when short term lenders are continuously in a position to demand conversion of their investments, amounting in the aggregate to a large multiple of the total available circulating media, into such media.[23]

He preferred an economy where all debt would be of a very long maturity—preferably "consols" issued in perpetuity. Recognizing the impossibility of achieving such a situation, Simons contented himself with a proposal which was less ambitious, but still highly radical: all commercial banks would be required to hold reserves behind 100 percent of the demand deposits on hand. This would remove much of the inherent instability of a fractional reserve system; the presence of a myriad of "near monies" created by financial institutions would be removed.[24]

An interesting postscript to the arguments put forward by Simons in his plan for monetary reform involves a subsequent debate among monetary economists in the early fifties, surrounding the proliferation of highly liquid assets issued by "non-bank financial intermediaries." These institutions—savings banks, insurance companies and the like—may affect velocity by their creation of liquid debt. This, in turn, could affect the efficacy of monetary policy in meeting a situation. Apart from this controversy, the issues raised by Simons in his banking scheme have been largely ignored in the postwar literature.[25]

The aspect of Simons' monetary proposals which does appear in contemporary policy discussion is his insistence that monetary authorities

---

[23] *Ibid.*, p. 166.

[24] Simons' plan for banking reform is summarized in his "A Positive Program for Laissez Faire," *op. cit.*, and spelled out in more detail in several mimeographed essays circulated at the University of Chicago. It proposed to set up two groups of financial institutions. The first would serve merely as warehouses for money, deriving income from the charges for deposits held. These deposits would be covered by 100 percent reserves. The second group would perform the lending function of commercial banks. They would obtain their capital through security issues and be sort of "investment trusts." Naturally, Simons recognized that restrictions on debt issue of other financial institutions might be necessary. Simons would regulate these functions through the terms of corporate charter.

[25] Economists such as Milton Friedman, however, continue to support quietly 100 percent reserve banking. See his comments in "The Monetary Theory and Policy of Henry Simons," *op. cit.*

should be curbed in their freedom to exercise discretionary power. To wit:

> . . . first, that monetary authorities must be bound by simple, definite rules (a price index) and, second, *that their only real powers should be those of conducting operations in the public debt.*[26]

This recommendation was in no way dependent upon acceptance of his banking reforms.[27] Restriction of the discretionary power of the monetary authority follows directly from his insistence that the government must establish some consistent and stable framework within which the market can operate. Monetary policy is not the domain of the central bank, for it depends essentially on the levels of expenditure and taxation, not the bank rate. Hence his insistence that the central bank be confined in its operations to debt management.

Simons was not really concerned over the nature of the rule which should be adopted; what was essential was the agreement that *some* rule must be followed. In his writing, Simons toyed with two possible alternatives, and was unable to really decide which rule was better:

1. Fix the money supply and maintain it at that level.
2. Establish a price index and instruct the central bank to maintain that index at a given level.

He recommended the second rule (constant prices) for the time in which he was writing; but he clearly preferred a situation where the first (fixed money supply) could be introduced. The impracticality of the fixed money rule was a result of the erratic (and sudden) shifts in velocity. Since he insisted that this stemmed in part from the instability of a fractional reserve banking system, adoption of this rule must await banking reform. Simons was also cognizant of the problems of a fixed supply of money with a rigid price structure. Here his monetary proposals dovetail into his general advice to remove monopoly. With more flexible prices, the establishment of a fixed money stock becomes feasible.

The price level guideline would, he thought, serve as a suitable substitute. Here again, he was aware of the practical problem such a

---

[26] Simons, *Economic Policy, op. cit.*, p. 205. (Italics in original.)

[27] See for example, his comment in reviewing Hansen's book where he notes that some would regard his monetary scheme as that of a "crank." He proceeds to present the rules versus authority argument independently of monetary reform. Simons, *Economic Policy, op. cit.*, pp. 184-219.

proposal would encounter. For the monetary authorities to carry out such a rule:

> . . . it must be accepted by the whole community, and obeyed by the legislatures, as the guiding principle of sound government finance—as the basic criterion of sound fiscal policy.[28]

Thus far our discussion of Simons's proposals has centered on his radical proposals for long-run reform. What of his suggestions for immediate response to the depression? Clearly, Simons felt his long run objectives would be a necessary part of any recovery. Yet he did comment on the appropriate fiscal-monetary policy for the early thirties. His prescription was simple and to the point: the money supply should be increased through government deficits. He was very clear in this proposal that the money financing this deficit must be *printed*, not *borrowed*.[29] The danger of borrowing on the part of the government was not an economic one—it stemmed from Simons's basic distrust of bureaucratic power. Assaulting (once again) the proposals of his adversary, Hansen, Simons wrote:

> Vulgar prejudice will support Hansen's implication that borrowing is less dangerous than issue. I am firmly convinced of the opposite. Injection of money, within limits, is like putting fuel in the furnace; borrowing, like accumulating dynamite in the basement, with the explosion risk growing as the pile accumulates.[30]

Advocating a government deficit through the use of a printing press in the basement of the treasury is—as Simons himself noted—a rather Keynesian approach to the problem of unemployment. It illustrates again the willingness of Simons to approve government intervention to correct imbalance *as long as a set of rules limits the arbitrary use of authority*. His attacks on Keynes's proposals reflect the fact that they did not, in his judgment, properly consider the need for constraint of government power.[31] It is his "political credo" which leads him to reject much of the policy proposed in the thirties.

---

[28] *Ibid.*, p. 176.

[29] Note the relationship between this proposal and Lerner's functional finance.

[30] Simons, *Economic Policy, op. cit.*, p. 196.

[31] See in particular his review of the *General Theory*. Simons, "Keynes' Comments on Money," *op. cit.* He sharply criticizes Keynes's failure to discuss the monetary institutions behind the problem of liquidity.

A Positive Program for Laissez-Faire

"The great enemy of democracy is monopoly, in all its forms" Simons wrote, and he went on to define broadly monopoly as *"any organization and concentration of power within functional classes."* His writing emphasized the need to remove the *sources* of such concentrations of economic power. He found two major flaws in the existing system: inadequate control of the privilege of incorporation, and the inability to check the rising power of labor unions.

The corporation, as a means to organize and finance production efficiently, is a useful device. Simons did not deny this. However, it could also serve as a vehicle to obtain massive monopoly power in the market. Thus, the right to incorporation must be carefully regulated by the government. The responsibility for this supervision had been largely abdicated in the nineteenth century. State governments passed lenient incorporation laws without any effective control of the use of that privilege. Simons favored a *federal incorporation law* to charter all corporations from the federal government. This would allow checks on monopoly power to be built into the incorporation charter. Size of the firm, assets held by the firm, and similar variables could be controlled by the terms of the charter rather than regulation. Simons recognized the old Marshallian concern with increasing returns industries.[32] Such cases, he argued, should be operated by the government as a public monopoly.

In spite of his adamant demands to eliminate monopoly, Simons was somewhat ambivalent towards the antitrust policy of the government. To the extent that its enforcement successfully undermined monopoly power, he was on the side of the "trust-busters." But he could never shake an inherent mistrust of bureaucracy. His restrained applause for the exploits of Thurmond Arnold reflects his rather jaundiced view of the Justice Department in Washington:

> Carrying the ball for free trade, he runs toward and behind his own goal line whenever he imagines an opponent in the offing; but he never gets downed behind his goal and somehow keeps on the offensive throughout. In the end he is headed squarely in the right direction and, unlike his opponents, exhausted merely from watch-

---

[32] We noted in Chapter 2 that $P = MC$ is the efficiency point. However, in the case of a decreasing cost industry, the marginal cost curve is below the average cost curve. Marginal cost pricing thus would not permit the firm to cover average costs. This firm is called a *technical monopoly*.

ing his frightened rushes, is fresh and fit at the end as at the start.[33]

Simons always preferred to see halfbacks on his team head straight down field.[34]

The presence of substantial monopoly in the industrial economy was readily admitted by Simons. But he became increasingly convinced that *labor monopoly*, not *enterprise monopoly*, was the true threat to the free market system.[35] His opposition to union monopoly was based on the fundamental nature of a politically organized monopoly. While admitting that "it was shameful to have permitted the growth of vast corporate empires," enterprise monopoly is still only a "skin disease" whose cure is "easy to correct if we will."[36] Labor "syndicalism," on the other hand, is "a different kind of animal." Here the source of monopoly power lies in coercion. Once established, Simons saw no ready check to such power. Certainly, he argued, there is no reason to expect the labor leaders to constrain themselves. Echoing Frank Knight's dictum against power he wrote: "Monopoly power must be abused. It has no use save abuse." He noted with alarm the apparent harmony of interests among the union and the industrial monopolist in attaining profits.

Such views on monopoly are, of course, wholly consistent with the neoclassical beliefs. Here Simons ran into the problem facing Chamberlin—and others—who observe a marked divergence between theoretical models and the structure of firms in the real world. Chamberlin sought to change the theory; Simons to bring reality closer to the postulates of the competitive model. He saw very clearly the dilemma of trying to argue on the one hand that the theoretical analysis is essentially correct (as he thought it was) while also maintaining that unrealistic assumptions approximated the real world (which he admitted they did not). Monopoly *did* exist in substantial amounts, and one result was to produce inflexible prices. Rigid prices undermined the degree to which Say's Law would produce full employment of all resources. Simons's antimonopoly position was therefore a crucial aspect

---

33 Simons, *Economic Policy, op. cit.,* pp. 93-94.

34 And, of course, Arnold was a member of the New Deal Team. Roosevelt's program—especially legislation such as the National Recovery Act—made Simons uneasy for this clearly created substantially *more* monopoly power.

35 The most complete treatment of his views on labor is his essay, "Some Reflections on Syndicalism," *Journal of Political Economy,* vol. LII, no. 1 (March 1944), 1-25 and reprinted in *Economic Policy, op. cit.,* pp. 121-59.

36 It should be added that Simons was extremely pessimistic that such a "will" would in fact prevail in the United States.

of his aggregate policy. Writing in the mid-forties, Simons was discussing the problem which the modern decision maker sees in the Phillips curve.[37] Simons abhorred forms of price regulation such as those embodied in "income policies" or "wage-price guidelines." His solution to the dilemma of the Phillips Curve would be to "shift" the curve by eliminating rigid prices. His shift would be accomplished by eliminating private monopoly.

Like many radicals, Simons recognized his prescriptions might be bitter medicine for the society to swallow. As he pointed out with regard to his views on labor syndicalism:

> Questioning the virtues of the organized labor movement is like attacking religion, monogamy, motherhood, or the home. Among the modern intelligentsia any doubts about collective bargaining admit of explanation only in terms of insanity, knavery, or subservience to 'the interests.'[38]

Simons was deeply pessimistic regarding the outcome of a struggle between labor and capital. Writing in 1944 he commented:

> It is easy to argue that the whole problem is so hard and ominous politically that no effort should be made to solve or even to see it— that the real choice lies between a certain, gradual death of economic democracy and an operation . . . which would cure if successful but is almost certain to kill. I am no forecaster and am not in direct communication with the Almighty. Consequently, I can only maintain that it is immoral to take such absolute dilemmas seriously. Democracy would have been dead a thousand times if it paid much attention to historical extrapolations. . . .[39]

Yet his writings at times belie his own concern over precisely this dilemma. Beneath his attacks on the policies of the depression and war years lay a gloomy prognostication of the future of the western world. As a biographer put it shortly after his death:

> Simons died before the outlines of the peace were clearly defined. Perhaps for his own state of mind, never too peaceful, it was just as well.[40]

---

[37] On the issues surrounding the Phillips Curve, see Chapters 9, 10, and 14.

[38] Simons, *Economic Policy, op. cit.,* p. 121.

[39] *Ibid.,* p. 157.

[40] John Davenport, "The Testament of Henry Simons," in *Economics and the Study of Law,* Reprint and Pamphlet Series No. 4 (Chicago: University of Chi-

Henry Simons is best known today for his outspoken views on government economic policy. This is not surprising; Simons took a dogmatic stand at a time when the traditional functions of government were being seriously challenged. His proposals also dealt with taxes, tariffs, and merchandising. On each subject he carefully thought through proposals consistent with his "old fashioned liberal" position.

On the subject of taxes—which was his academic specialty—Simons insisted that government levies be *direct* and *simple*. Apart from the obvious need for sufficient revenue, the basic aim of tax policy should be to: (a) ensure that the true cost of government is levied equitably on the citizens; and (b) that a more equitable distribution of income and wealth be obtained through taxation. Looking back on his myriad of specific proposals, one is struck by their appropriateness today as the government reviews the entangled tax structure of the postwar era. For example, Simons espoused the following proposals:[41]

1. The basic source of revenues should derive from a personal income tax.
2. The tax should be levied on *all income*, regardless of source—capital gains, dividends, gifts, and wages would be treated alike.[42]
3. The revenues from this tax should be shared with the state governments.
4. "Averaging" of incomes should be allowed where an individual's income fluctuates markedly from year to year.
5. Those with incomes below some minimum level should have no tax imposed at all.

Note that much of the foundation for these proposals lies with Simons's philosophical background rather than a detailed analysis of the taxes. They are careful extensions of his belief that government should adhere as much as possible to simple "rules of the game."

In all the arguments listed, Simons appears as the advocate of what today is described as the "conservative" position in modern economics. One would hardly expect to find him expressing a sentiment in accord-

---

cago Press, 1946); reprinted from *The University of Chicago Law Review*, vol. 14, no. 1 (December 1946).

[41] Most specific proposals were incorporated in his monograph, *Federal Tax Reform, op. cit.* His support for the personal income tax is justified in his *Personal Income Taxation, op. cit.*

[42] Simons favored a very simple definition of income: it would be the algebraic sum of (1) consumption during the period and (2) the change in the value of assets held. His discussion of income is found in Chapters II and III of *Personal Income Taxation, op. cit.* His policy aim was to remove the differential treatment given incomes from different sources.

ance with the views of (say) John Kenneth Galbraith. Yet consider the following remark in the light of our discussion of Galbraith:

> It is a commonplace that our vaunted efficiency in production is dissipated extravagantly in the wastes of merchandising. . . . Profits may be obtained either by producing what consumers want or by making consumers want what one is actually producing. The possibility of profitably utilizing resources to manipulate demand is, perhaps, the greatest source of diseconomy under the existing system. If present tendencies continue, we may soon reach a situation where most of our resources are utilized in persuading people to buy one thing rather than another, and only a minor fraction is actually employed in creating things to be bought.[43]

This is surely a statement of the *dependence effect* worthy of Galbraith himself. In fact, Simons's economic analysis closely paralleled the conclusions of Chamberlin. He foresaw a situation where most advertising expenditures would tend "only to counteract the expenditures of competitors." In the end, "all of them may wind up with about the same volume of business as if none had advertised at all." This is much the same result as Chamberlin's "monopolistic competition."

Just as he tended to accept Keynes's diagnosis of the illness and reject the cure, so it is doubtful that Simons would today be alongside his arch-foe Alvin Hansen in espousing the social imbalance hypothesis. Distortions from advertising are the least important aspect of Simons's program; he felt it was only a special case of the monopoly question. What he would say today is, of course, impossible to predict, for he said very little about the issue before his death.[44] His followers have, in general, not echoed sentiments favoring the Galbraithian quote above. But then, it was never the particular policy which Simons propounded which made him important to current thought. His legacy—like that of Knight—is written in the political philosophy which he so ably expounded in defense of his economic policy statements. Milton Friedman has summarized the impact of Simons very well:

> No man can say precisely whence his beliefs and values came—but there is no doubt that mine would be different than they are if I had not had the good fortune to be exposed to Henry Simons. If . . .

---

[43] Simons, *Economic Policy, op. cit.*, p. 71.

[44] Simons' views on advertising are very briefly put forward at two points in his work, *Ibid.*, pp. 71-73, 85-86.

I express much disagreement with him, that, too, bespeaks his influence. He taught us that an objective, critical examination of a man's ideas is a truer tribute than slavish repetition of his formulas.[45]

---

[45] Friedman, "The Monetary Theory and Policy of Henry Simons," *op. cit.*, p. 1.

CHAPTER 14

MILTON FRIEDMAN—
Classical Liberal as Economic
Scientist

*Little man whip a big man every time
if the little man's in the right and keeps
a'comin'.*
MOTTO OF THE TEXAS RANGERS

The intellectual revolutions against previously accepted thought that we have been describing in this volume were spawned from what their architects took to be empirical evidence. Pigou, Veblen, Chamberlin, and Keynes were convinced from their observations that the assumptions of neoclassical economics were unrealistic; thus, they attempted to develop new and more relevant theories for their own time.

But it should be clear that no single event in the history of the United States had more sweeping impact on economic thought than the Great Depression. Through the commentaries of Keynes, Hansen, and Lerner, academic thinking on economic matters went through an upheaval that can be compared to no other sudden change in the development of the discipline. For these men cast into doubt the quantity theory of money and Say's Law—the central core of the monetary and employment theories of neoclassicism. Moreover, it is not surprising that this should be so. The seeming inability of the Federal Reserve System to bring respite from the tragedy threw into disrepute long-accepted propositions about the role of monetary factors in economic change which the quantity theory had propounded. Idle land and capital and the destitution of millions of unemployed men seemed to belie the logical beauty of Say's Law.

The new economics of Keynes provided a diagnosis and a remedy. The problem was to increase the flow of aggregate demand, namely investment, which (through the Keynesian multiplier aided perhaps by a Hansen-Samuelson accelerator) would lead to a magnified increase in the flow of income. The quantity theorists' belief that the level of money income and the price level were largely determined by the stock of money was held to be true, if at all, only in periods of full employment. Alvin Hansen's confident prediction that the great issue of the future was to be secular stagnation led him and his influential students to advocate easy monetary policy, but only as a means of pushing interest rates down. The point was to avoid interfering with the increasing government investment that alone could offset the slide into economic maturity. In addition, Abba Lerner's functional finance provided the set of instruments needed for government to do the "fine-tuning" that would restore the economy to full employment. Almost all agreed that the stock of money was the inert companion of the real economic force of increasing investment.

At Chicago, Henry Simons demurred. Though he attacked with vitriolic fervor the notions of Keynes and Hansen, it remained for one of his students to contribute the analytical depth, scientific precision, and empirical evidence that alone could effectively challenge the Keynesian orthodoxy of the new economics.

This student was Milton Friedman, the son of Ruthenian immigrants who worked in sweat shops at the turn of the century. From such inauspicious beginnings, he was eventually to set the agenda for the major economic debates of the post-World War II era. For the movement away from the monetary implications of neoclassical economics was to be halted by the empirical research and theoretical arguments of this brilliant economist.

Today, no one testifying before congressional committees in investigating economic affairs is listened to with more respect. The accounts of his performances before sessions of the Joint Economic Committee and the Committee on Banking and Currency make fascinating reading in the art of persuasion that would have been relished by no one more than Keynes himself.

The proceedings have the aspect of a high level seminar. After one particularly difficult session, with Friedman explaining his new version of the quantity theory of money through a series of equations in the clearest possible terms to the hushed assembly of Senators and Congressmen, the following colloquy took place:

The Chairman: Mr. Friedman, the Federal Reserve Board loves to brief Senators and Congressmen on economic affairs in order to diminish our economic ignorance, and so does the Council of Economic Advisors.

I wonder if we could arrange a seminar in which you could brief these gentlemen on these equations. I will be glad to invite them and have you brief them on these equations, if you would be willing to come and, of course, we will pay you an honorarium for it.

I think an advanced course for the Federal Reserve and possibly even the Council of Economic Advisors would be very good. Could you do that possibly?

Mr. Friedman: A professor is always willing to profess.[1]

The reply was typical and apt. For Friedman has "professed" and made his influence felt not only in testimony before Congress, but through his classic articles and books, his classroom lectures, his column in *Newsweek*, but most of all through the force of his personality, which has allowed his heretical and radical ideas in defense of market capitalism to capture the imagination of scores of economists and legislators.

A short, balding man with a large intellectual head, a round face, a smiling expression and two keen eyes which gleam brightly from behind broad spectacles, Friedman charms his supporters and dismays his detractors with his buzz saw debating technique which, when combined with a cherubic appearance, is all the more devastating. Leo Rosten has taken Milton Friedman as the prototype for his character, Fenwick, and painted an accurate portrait of Friedman in action.

". . . he listens carefully to anything you tell him, and *promptly* wants to know where and how you found out whatever it is you told him—and how you know it is so. Worse, he separates inferences from proof. Fenwick enjoys following every single little chug in your train of thought—indeed, he gets right on the train with you. And you have barely begun to move before Fenwick excitedly demonstrates that: (a) you have taken the wrong train; or (b) it doesn't stop where you want to go; or (c) the tracks don't lead from your premise to your preferred conclusion; or (d) that train

[1] U.S., Congress, Joint Economic Committee, *Employment, Growth and Price Levels,* Hearings before the Joint Economic Committee, 86th Cong., 1st Sess., May 25, 1959 (Washington, D.C.: U.S. Government Printing Office, 1959), p. 634. We might note that the inquisitor was Senator Paul Douglas of Illinois, himself a highly respected economist.

will land you where you don't want to go and didn't even know you were going.[2]

It is this talent for argumentative discourse combined with his capacity to do solid research and master the deepest intricacies of economic theory that have made him the most prominent member of the new neoclassicism. Today he bids fair to challenge Keynes as the twentieth century's most influential economist.

Friedman was born in Brooklyn, New York, in 1912. He grew up in Rahway, New Jersey, and studied at Rutgers University, where he received his B.A. in 1932. There he came under the influence of Arthur F. Burns, who was to instill in Friedman an appreciation for the importance of empirical inquiry that has survived throughout his career. Later, he received a scholarship to attend the University of Chicago where he took courses from Frank Knight, Henry Simons, Jacob Viner, and Henry Shultz. From Simons and Knight, he developed his philosophy of classical liberalism and a deep skepticism about the appropriateness of most government intervention. From Viner he developed a feel for the vitality and importance of economic theory.[3] From Arthur Burns (and through him, indirectly Wesley Mitchell), Friedman received his keen appreciation for high standards of objectivity and thoroughness. From Shultz, and later from Harold Hotelling at Columbia University, he received a thorough training and developed an abiding interest in mathematical economics and mathematical statistics. The distinctiveness of his scientific work is his blending of these strands of analysis.

During the war, he worked for the Division of Tax Research at the U.S. Treasury, where he became its leading spokesman for the withholding tax and clashed frequently with Senator Robert Taft, for whom he acquired enormous respect. In 1946, Friedman received his Ph.D. from Columbia University for his dissertation on income from independent professional practice.[4]

---

[2] Leo Rosten, "An Infuriating Man," in "The World of Leo Rosten," *Look*, November 15, 1966, p. 14.

[3] "Without question, one of the greatest intellectual experiences of my life was the first quarter course in economic theory with Jacob Viner. This opened my eyes to a world I had not realized existed. I was made aware of both the beauty and the power of formal economic theory." Personal correspondence with Milton Friedman, June 22, 1967.

[4] An expanded version was later published with Simon Kuznets as *Income from Independent Professional Practice* (New York: National Bureau of Economic Research, 1954). Friedman's work for the government, from the midnineteen-thirties until after World War II, was not actually his first choice of occupations. As with

After the war, Friedman returned to Chicago where he settled into the serious business of economic theory and controversy. His work brought him early recognition. In 1951 he received the John Bates Clark medal, becoming the third recipient of that coveted award— following Paul Samuelson and Kenneth Boulding; and in 1967, he was elected President of the American Economic Association. As Paul Snowden Russell Distinguished Service Professor of Economics at Chicago, (and from his contemporary hexagonal-shaped house on his mountaintop in Ely, Vermont, where he spends half the year), Friedman has played the key part in attempting to turn the tide against the new economics.

His attack on the new economics was many-pronged. First, he painstakingly reconstructed and tested the quantity theory of money. Second, he reemphasized the power of monetary policy. Third, he questioned the Lerner view of the flexibility and potency of fiscal policy and the Lerner-Samuelson belief in the trade-offs between inflation and employment. Fourth, he argued that the orthodox interpretation of the Great Depression was incorrect and constructed his own formula for preventing such catastrophes in the future. Fifth, he challenged the logic of the Veblen and Chamberlin methodologies and, lastly, restated the classical liberal philosophy in terms pertinent to his own time.

The Quantity Theory of Money

This venerable doctrine, which, as we have seen in Chapter 2, goes back in the history of economic thought at least to David Hume and reached fullest flower at Cambridge at the hands of Alfred Marshall and A. C. Pigou, was presented in the textbooks in a highly rigid and extreme form. Without qualification, it was asserted that a change in the stock of money resulted in a proportionate change in prices and money income. In this naive version, in which the relation was considered so precise, extravagant expectations were created about the possibility of using monetary policy to produce prolonged and uninterrupted economic stability and progress. The Keynesians, in using this "straw man" version, argued that changes in velocity were so unstable as to make the effects of changes in the quantity of money largely unpredictable.

Friedman developed a much more subtle and sophisticated statement of the quantity theory of money—refining and giving precision

---

Paul Samuelson, academic anti-Semitism made it difficult for him to get a university position. See Milton Viorst, "Friedmanism," *The New York Times Magazine* (January 25, 1970), 80.

to the Henry Simons version that had been part of the oral tradition at Chicago.[5] In this version, velocity is regarded as a stable function of a few variables. In order to analyze velocity, it is necessary to look at the factors influencing the demand for money. The quantity theory attempts to answer the question: What determines the demand for money? That is, what determines velocity? Friedman's answer is that the demand for money is determined by the following factors: the rate of interest on bonds, the rate of return on stocks, the rate of change of the price level, and the amount of income received from the ownership of property that people have. In short, the demand for money is determined by the cost of holding money, which is in turn dependent on the rate of return that can be earned by holding alternative assets and the anticipated rate of change in the price level. The higher the interest rate on bonds, or yields on equities, and the greater is the anticipated rise in the price level, the greater will be the incentive to get out of cash balances.[6]

But the important question now is, how constant is the velocity of money? To the Keynesian economist, it is highly variable and unpredictably so. As we saw in Chapter 7, Keynes devised his liquidity preference schedule to show that increases in the quantity of money would be accompanied by a fall in the rate of interest which would lead to an increase in the quantity of money demanded. What is worse, in an extreme situation, there might be a liquidity trap in which case changes in the stock of money could have no effect on income since these changes could not affect interest rates and, therefore, investment and income. As we saw in the chapter on Samuelson, the latter accepted this as a distinct possibility. But Friedman postulated that the demand for money is a stable function of a limited number of variables which can be reliably specified. A sharp rise in velocity does not, therefore, discredit this version of the quantity theory. If this rise occurs, for example, during hyperinflations, the cost of holding money would be increasing and, therefore, the demand for money would be predicted to decline. The importance of Friedman's formulation is that it sharply limits the num-

---

[5] For a contrary view, see Don Patinkin, "The Chicago Tradition, The Quantity Theory, and Friedman," *Journal of Money, Credit and Banking*, vol. 1, no. 1 (February 1969), 46-67.

[6] Note the relationship between the Friedman and Keynesian formulations. In both, the demand for money is a function of the interest rate. See Milton Friedman, "Money: Quantity Theory," *International Encyclopedia of the Social Sciences* (New York: The Macmillan Company and The Free Press, 1968), p. 439. See also Richard T. Selden "Monetary Velocity in the United States," in M. Friedman, editor, *Studies in the Quantity Theory of Money* (Chicago: University of Chicago Press, 1956), 179-257.

ber of explicit variables to which monetary demand is related. In short, Friedman hypothesized that there would be a predictable response to changes in the few variables he specifies.

In order to test this hypothesis, Friedman's students in his famous Money and Banking Workshop at the University of Chicago examined the stability of the demand for money during various episodes in the United States and foreign countries. The chief result of the studies indicated that interest rates do indeed affect the demand for money, as the Friedman and Keynesian versions of the quantity theory predict, but the effect is *not very great* in magnitude. Furthermore, the rate of change in prices has a clear-cut and dramatic effect only during periods of extreme inflations and deflations.

The most significant finding was that velocity is a stable function of long-run income or what Friedman calls permanent income.[7] Since money is a luxury good, the demand for which increases as income rises, one would expect velocity to decline over time as long-run income rises. The policy implication is that the monetary authority, if it wishes to maintain price level stability, must increase the stock of money enough to offset this decline in velocity.

But the main conclusion that Friedman and his students reached was that the quantity theory is an extremely useful tool for analyzing changes in prices and money income. In Friedman's words: ". . . there is perhaps no other empirical relation in economics that has been observed to recur so uniformly under so wide a variety of circumstances as the relation between substantial changes over short periods in the stock of money and in prices; the one is invariably linked with the other and is in the same direction; this uniformity is, I suspect, of the same order as many of the uniformities that form the basis of the physical sciences."[8]

This restatement of the quantity theory went a long way toward rehabilitating the doctrine and putting it back into place as one of the key tools in the economist's tool kit.

But Friedman was not satisfied with this demonstration of the resiliency of the neoclassical monetary theory. He recognized that, in order to effect a successful counterrevolution, it would be necessary to show that the quantity theory was a more powerful instrument of analysis

---

[7] See Milton Friedman, *A Theory of the Consumption Function* (Princeton, New Jersey: National Bureau of Economic Research, Princeton University Press, 1957), pp. 7-37.

[8] Milton Friedman, "The Quantity Theory of Money—A Restatement," *Studies in the Quantity Theory of Money*, ed. author (Chicago: University of Chicago Press, 1956), pp. 20-21.

than was the Keynesian alternative. To put this more directly, it was necessary to demonstrate that the demand for money was not only a stable function, but was *more* stable than the consumption function and autonomous investment. This was his next order of business.

The Power of Money

In 1963, he presented his findings in one of the most controversial and provocative papers he has ever written. For the first time, someone had attempted directly to test the predictive power of the Keynesian as opposed to the quantity theory. His conclusion was that, contrary to the widespread belief of the new economics, monetary velocity is stabler than the investment multiplier.

In order to test the hypothesis, he and his student, David Meiselman, compared a very simple model of the Keynesian and quantity theories, and attempted to discover if there is a better correlation between money and consumption than between Keynesian "investment and consumption."[9] The results indicated that money is a more successful predictor of income than autonomous expenditures (which, for purposes of his study, he defined as the sum of net private investment expenditures plus the government deficit). The results held for year-to-year and quarter-to-quarter changes. What is more, autonomous expenditures seemed to have no explanatory power. Hence, "the critical variable for monetary policy is the stock of money, not interest rates ·or investment expenditures."[10]

Of course, this finding did not go unchallenged. Other economists, using definitions of autonomous expenditures different from that used by Friedman and Meiselman, concluded that both money and autonomous expenditures are powerful.[11] This interchange with his critics at least proved an important Friedman point. One of the central concepts of the Keynesian income-expenditure approach—autonomous ex-

---

[9] Consumption was used as a proxy variable for income. Since autonomous expenditures are a part of income, correlating this variable with income would introduce a bias since it would mean correlating income with a part of itself.

[10] Milton Friedman and David Meiselman, "The Relative Stability of Monetary Velocity and the Investment Multiplier in the United States, 1897-1958," *Stabilization Policies*, The Commission on Money and Credit (Englewood Cliffs, N.J.: Prentice-Hall, Inc., 1963), p. 166.

[11] Albert Ando and Franco Modigliani, "The Relative Stability of Monetary Velocity and the Investment Multiplier," *American Economic Review*, vol. 55 (September 1965), 693-728; Michael DePrano and Thomas Mayer, "Tests of the Relative Importance of Autonomous Expenditures and Money," *American Economic Review*, vol. 55 (September 1965), 729-52.

penditures—is not a clear-cut operational concept. Furthermore, it showed that the Keynesian Revolution had by no means produced "a carefully formulated, logically coherent theory of income determination. . . ." Regardless of the definition chosen for "autonomous investment," money turned out to be important in the determination of income, indicating that monetary policy is substantially effective.[12]

What is more, Friedman's findings have held up astonishingly well over time. In a study conducted by the Federal Reserve Bank of St. Louis, Leonall C. Andersen and Jerry L. Jordan estimated the response of total spending in the economy to changes in various measures of monetary and fiscal actions. They tested the Keynesian proposition that the response of economic activity to fiscal actions is more sensitive, relative to that of monetary actions. Their conclusion was that the evidence is not consistent with this proposition. There was no measurable net influence from fiscal actions during the first quarter 1952 to the second quarter 1968. Furthermore, the response of economic activity to monetary actions compared to fiscal actions is greater, more predictable, and faster.[13]

Moreover, Friedman's theories have been supported by other evidence. Those economists who placed major reliance on fiscal policy as a determinant of aggregate demand predicted a major slowdown in economic activity beginning in late 1968 and extending into 1969. Their predictions were based on the 10 percent surcharge on individual income taxes that went into effect in July of 1968. Friedman and his adherents denied that the surcharge would have any effect on slowing down the economy, since the money supply was growing roughly at a 10 percent annual rate.

In November, 1968, Friedman debated these issues with Walter Heller, the former Chairman of President Kennedy's and later President Johnson's Council of Economic Advisers, at the Trinity Place campus of the New York University School of Business. In the course of the discussion between these two advocates of widely divergent viewpoints on economic policy, Friedman explained his reason for believing that the surtax would not work.

As he pointed out, it certainly would seem obvious on the face that an increase in taxes would have contractionary effects. For the dispos-

[12] Milton Friedman and David Meiselman, "Reply to Ando and Modigliani and DePrano and Mayer," *American Economic Review*, vol. 55 (September 1965), 753-85.

[13] Leonall C. Andersen and Jerry L. Jordan, "Monetary and Fiscal Actions: A Test of Their Relative Importance in Economic Stabilization," *Federal Reserve Bank of St. Louis Review*, vol., 50, no. 11 (November 1968), 11-23.

able income of the taxpayers is reduced and, through the Keynesian multiplier, income should decline. But the trouble with this naive Keynesian view is that it only tells half the story. For if the federal government continues to spend the same amount of money after it imposes a surtax, that reduces the amount it has to borrow. This must mean that the people who would have loaned the government the funds with which to finance the deficit have more. Since this is the case, people have money available for other things. They can use it to lend to others or to pay their taxes or for any number of other purposes. But the result should be a fall in the interest rate, which in turn induces people to borrow those funds that would have been loaned to the government. So an increase in private investment, expenditure on consumer durables, and so on, will take place. When both sides of the story are told, the two sides offset each other, leaving fiscal policy measures with little or no effect. And that was precisely Friedman's prediction regarding the tax surcharge.

The tax surcharge episode turned out to provide a controlled experiment of the sort seldom encountered in the social sciences. If you looked at the high-employment budget[14] alone during this period, you would, if you were a Keynesian, forecast a sharp slowdown in economic activity. If you looked at monetary policy alone, as Friedman would suggest, you would predict no slowdown in the early part of '69. As it turned out, notwithstanding a tremendous movement from stimulus to restraint in the federal budget, the slowdown did not occur as the advocates of the new economics predicted. But the money supply continued to expand and so, too, did economic activity. This was completely consistent with Friedman's assertion that "the state of the budget itself has no significant effect on the course of nominal income, on inflation, on deflation, or on cyclical fluctuations.[15]

---

[14] The high-employment budget is a measure of the size of the surplus or deficit which would occur in the federal government budget if the economy were at full or *high employment*. The actual amount of tax collection is dependent upon the level of economic activity, once the government has set the tax and expenditure rates. Friedman was the first to suggest that we examine fiscal policy in terms of the high employment budget, in a paper before the Econometric Society in September 1947. The suggestion was later followed up by the CEA under Walter Heller. See Milton Friedman, "A Monetary and Fiscal Framework for Economic Stability," *American Economic Review* (June 1948).

[15] Milton Friedman, "Has Fiscal Policy Been Oversold?", *Monetary vs. Fiscal Policy, A Dialogue between Milton Friedman and Walter W. Heller* (New York: W. W. Norton and Company, Inc., 1969), p. 51. At least one reporter claimed that Heller "was torn to shreds by Friedman's arguments." (*The New York Times Magazine*, January 25, 1970, 83).

This conclusion would not have surprised a quantity theorist as much as a Keynesian. For to the quantity theorist, "money burns a hole in your pocket." That is, an increase in cash relative to other assets, will *always* cause a spillout that has effects in every nook and cranny of the economic system. No sector is safe from its impact. Thus, even if business investment is completely unresponsive to a fall in interest rates (in Hansen's sense) the increased money supply will still have its income-generating effects. So the channels through which monetary policy works are different to a Keynesian than to a quantity theorist. And Friedman takes pains to indicate precisely what those channels are. The following scenario might be likely.

If the monetary authority, through open-market purchases of government securities, increases the stock of money, the stock of cash is now high relative to other assets. Money holders may well attempt to purchase common stock to achieve a desired relationship between money and these assets. This causes the price of stock to rise and yields to fall. As this occurs, the relative prices of other assets will make them more attractive to purchase and so some of the cash spills over into these relatively tempting areas. The chain may be from government securities to stock market equities to houses, durable goods of various kinds, consumer goods, and so on. But note that the increased money supply spreads out into both investment and consumption goods and services. For as the price of, let us say, houses rises relative to the renting of apartments, the demand for and the production of dwelling units for rental purposes increase. But this in turn increases the price of such services relative to other assets, undoing the initial effects of divergencies in relative prices. So the train may be traced from relatively low yielding assets into the purchases of a wide spectrum of assets acting ultimately on services and the income stream.

Notwithstanding Friedman's belief in the potency of monetary weapons, he later felt it necessary to enter a caveat against the use of monetary policy to "fine-tune" the economy or to apply Lerner's tools of functional finance. To Friedman, the proved effectiveness of monetary policy might lead policy makers to believe that they can use this device to make minute adjustments in the economy and so always maintain price level stability and full employment simply by manipulating the stock of money.

Friedman *versus* Lerner on Functional Finance

Early in his career Friedman had warned against Lerner's functional finance principles which came to dominate the thinking of Keynesian oriented policy makers. In his review article of Lerner's *Economics of Control* which he published in 1947, Friedman referred to Lerner's functional finance as "a brilliant exercise in logic," and went on to say:

> It strips governmental fiscal instruments to their essentials: taxing and spending, borrowing and lending, and buying and selling; and throws into sharp relief the function of each. In the process it throws into discard conventional patterns of expression, verbal cliches which at times embody valid implications of more subtle reasoning but which, taken by themselves, muddle analysis of the effect of governmental actions. Reading Lerner's discussion of functional finance is almost sure to induce a much-required reorganization of the mental filing-case that one has been using to classify the factors involved in governmental fiscal operations.[16]

Although Friedman admired Lerner's dialectical skill, he expressed the opinion that the problem of maintaining economic stability is far more complex than Lerner's rules implied. The work of Arthur F. Burns and Wesley C. Mitchell on business cycles had impressed upon Friedman the unevenness and variable timing of economic activities. Economists not only find it extremely difficult to predict the course of business, but even to identify the current situation. Of course, to Lerner this difficulty would be irrelevant. The errors in forecasting are unimportant since the government can always reverse itself by changing policy. But to Friedman, this facile optimism regarding the power of government to fine-tune conflicts with the fact that "neither government action nor the effect of that action is instantaneous. There is likely to be a lag between the need for action and government recognition of this need; a further lag between recognition of the need for action and the taking of action; and a still further lag between the action and its effects."[17]

To Friedman, the time lags are a substantial proportion of the duration of cyclical activity. Since we do not have the ability to forecast correctly both the direction and the magnitude of the necessary policy, governmental attempts to use Lerner's functional finance prescriptions, far from stabilizing the economy, might very well exacerbate the fluctuations. "By the time an error is recognized and corrective action

---

16 Milton Friedman, "Lerner on the Economics of Control," *Journal of Political Economy*, vol. 55 (October 1947), 405-16. Reprinted in Milton Friedman, *Essays in Positive Economics* (Chicago: University of Chicago Press, 1953), p. 313. (Quote)

17 *Ibid.*, p. 315.

taken, the damage may be done, and corrective action may itself turn into a further error."[18]

The research findings of Friedman and his co-workers had demonstrated the power of money to influence economic activity. But this demonstration had perhaps proved too convincing. The change in opinion from reliance on fiscal policy through the use of Lerner's functional finance tools and Hansen's compensatory fiscal policy to a thoroughgoing reliance on a fine-tuning approach to monetary policy suggested that perhaps the pendulum had swung too far back to the pre-Great Depression period of thinking. Friedman devoted his presidential address at the December meetings of the American Economic Association in 1967 to the question of the limits of monetary policy.[19]

---

[18] *Ibid.*, p. 316. Friedman's analysis of the problem of the destabilizing effects of countercyclical actions in the absence of a considerable ability to forecast economic activity is contained in, "The Effects of A Full-Employment Policy on Economic Stability: A Formal Analysis," *Essays in Positive Economics, op. cit.*, pp. 117-32. A fuller statement of his "lags" hypothesis can be found in, "A Monetary and Fiscal Framework for Economic Stability," *American Economic Review* (June 1948), 245-64. Reprinted in *Essays in Positive Economics, op. cit.*, pp. 133-56.

[19] Milton Friedman, "The Role of Monetary Policy," *American Economic Review*, vol. 58 (March 1968), 1-17.

The questions of functional finance and fine-tuning of the economy were still very much in Friedman's mind at the time he delivered his farewell speech as President of the American Economic Association. Gerald R. Rosen interviewed him in his Washington hotel suite just before he presented his address. At one point, Rosen asked him how he would evaluate the new economics' accomplishments between 1961 and 1967. Friedman replied:

> It's very hard to say that the New Economics has accomplished very much of anything, except getting a great deal of publicity. I have always been amused by the fact that the New Economists emphasize fine-tuning—or changing direction of the economy within a short span of time. But if you look at what actually happened, it certainly did not occur over a short span of time. The 1964 tax cut was said to be an absolute necessity in 1962. It was stressed again in 1963, and it was finally enacted in 1964.
>
> So the fine-tuning took two years. Once again, if you take the present surtax proposal, it was first made a year ago and said to be absolutely essential then. The proposal was later, in effect, retracted and then reinstated. If a surtax is enacted, it will certainly not be before sometime in 1968. So it would seem clear that whatever the New Economics has accomplished, it is not on the side of fine-tuning through the tax route.

Friedman also took the opportunity afforded by this interview to repeat one of his favorite propositions, that "the best is often the enemy of the good" in pointing out that both monetary and fiscal policy used according to the well-intentioned precepts of functional finance prescriptions have made the economy more erratic rather than smoother. See, "Has the New Economics Failed? An Interview with Milton Friedman," *Dun's Review*, vol. 91 (February 1968), 38-39, 93-96.

Inflation and Interest Rates

Perhaps the most important conclusion reached in this address was his statement that monetary policy cannot peg interest rates or the rate of unemployment for more than limited periods. In the typical Keynesian-oriented textbook approach, an increase in the stock of money, given the negatively sloping liquidity preference schedule, would mean that at the current rate of interest there is an excess supply of money. People can be induced to hold this larger quantity of money only at lower interest rates. But in their attempts to get out of money and into bonds, the prices of securities rise and the yields fall.

Friedman agrees with this analysis only to a point. For he adds that this initial drop in interest rates is only the beginning of the process. As he demonstrated in his restatement of the quantity theory of money, and in his explanation of the channels through which monetary policy works, the increasing rate of montetary growth will have effects not only on investment markets resulting from the initially lower interest rates, but on all spending, thereby raising income. But the rising income raises the liquidity preference schedule, and the price level. These effects reverse the downward pressure on interest rates, eventually returning them to their initial level. Furthermore, if the public comes to expect that a higher rate of monetary growth will correspond with an increasing price level, borrowers will be willing to pay and lenders will insist upon higher interest rates. So Friedman sees four effects of an increasing rate of growth in the money stock:

1. The initial impact of a falling rate of interest, described above, which Friedman calls the "liquidity effect."
2. An income effect: As the increasing stock of money increases income, the demand for money increases, leading to a shift upward in the liquidity preference schedule. This will tend to send the interest rate back to its initial position.
3. A price effect: The increased spending resulting from the increased money supply will raise the price level, thus reducing the real quantity of money—also having the effect of raising interest rates back to the initial level.
4. A price expectations effect: Since the borrower, as a result of the inflation, expects to pay off his loans in dollars of reduced purchasing power, he is willing to pay more for the use of money. And since the lender has the same expectation with regard to the rising price level, he will insist on a higher price for the use of his money. This causes interest rates to rise *above* their original level.

Paradoxically, and contrary to the Keynesian teachings, Friedman concluded, "low interest rates are a sign that monetary policy *has been* tight—in the sense that the quantity of money has grown slowly; high interest rates are a sign that monetary policy *has been easy*—in the sense that the quantity of money has grown rapidly. . . . These considerations . . . explain why interest rates are such a misleading indicator of whether monetary policy is 'tight' or 'easy.' For that, it is far better to look at the rate of change of the quantity of money."[20]

This analysis of the relation between inflation and interest rates seemed to square with the situation in the United States during 1968 and 1969, when the increasing stock of money was accompanied by rising prices and interest rates. Thus, during the 1960's, the United States economy experienced one of its most severe inflations and, at the same time, record high interest rates. Furthermore, it squares with the evidence in countries that have had the most persistent inflations, such as Brazil, Chile, and Argentina where interest rates are highest.[21]

Inflation and the "Trade-Off": The Optimum Quantity of Money

Furthermore, his view of inflation leads Friedman to deny the importance of Lerner's and Samuelson's emphasis on the trade-offs between inflation and employment. First of all, in regard to Lerner's notion of "Sellers' Inflation," Friedman argues that the empirical evidence does not support the theory. In the postwar period, for example, the unadministered prices rose more rapidly than administered. As an example, Friedman noted that the wages of domestic servants rose more rapidly than the wages of steel workers.

Nevertheless, for the 1933-1937 period, Friedman admits the existence of a "sellers' inflation." But he attributed this rise in the price level to a very large rise in the stock of money resulting from a gold influx, in combination with a period of growing strength of unions, and the price regulations associated with the NRA. His main objection to

---

[20] Friedman, "Role of Monetary Policy," *op. cit.*, 7. See also, Milton Friedman, "Factors Affecting the Level of Interest Rates," *Proceedings of the 1968 Conference on Savings and Residential Financing* (Chicago: United States Saving and Loan League), pp. 10-27.

[21] An excellent discussion of the issues surrounding the Friedman vs. Keynesian view of the relation between interest rates and the price level can be found in, "A Classical Look at 'Real Cost' of Money," *Business Week*, June 28, 1969, pp. 130-31.

Lerner's thesis is that Lerner identifies stickiness in prices with administered prices. Stickiness in prices occurs when people become adjusted to rising prices. They thus become accustomed to renegotiating contracts based on their anticipation of future inflation. Even after the monetary basis for rising prices has been eliminated, there is still a tendency for prices and wages to move up. When people become accustomed to inflationary expectations, prices become sticky because of the infrequency with which they are adjusted.[22]

Because of Friedman's views on the ability of people to adjust to inflation, so that price increases become fully anticipated, he rejects the Lerner-Samuelson view that there is, in the long run, a trade-off between inflation and the level of unemployment. It is true that an increase in inflation can have the *temporary* effect of reducing unemployment. But as people begin to anticipate inflation, they start adjusting their contracts, interest rates rise, and the initial benefit proves ephemeral. In order to stimulate employment, it becomes necessary to inflate at a still faster rate. As Friedman put it, "I would be inclined to say that if a 2 percent rate of inflation is consistent with any given level of employment from the long-run point of view, then a zero percent rate of inflation is also consistent." In short, the Phillips curve becomes vertical.[23]

Moreover, in a further analysis of inflation, Friedman has come around to the rather startling position that a mildly falling price level would be most beneficial. The reason for this conclusion, which is so sharply at variance with the received doctrine, requires further elucidation.

Assume that an individual decides to add an extra dollar to his cash balances on the average over a year. Now it is quite clear that from the point of view of the individual, an extra dollar can be added only if he spends a dollar less. But in so doing, he will have a slight effect on the price level, making it possible for everyone else, taken together, to receive a dollar's more worth of goods and services, while *not* reducing

---

[22] Friedman, *Savings and Residential Financing, op. cit.*, pp. 52-59.

[23] Milton Friedman, *Proceedings of a Symposium on Money, Interest Rates and Economic Activity* (Washington, D.C.: American Bankers Association, 1967), p. 121. See also, Friedman, "Role of Monetary Policy," *op. cit.*, especially 7-11.

Paul Samuelson, as we have seen, does not completely accept Friedman's analysis of this problem. Samuelson remains skeptical of the view that there is never any money illusion. Although he believes that the long-run Phillips curve is twisted toward the more vertical, he is not certain that people make the adjustments necessary to make it completely so. Personal correspondence with Paul Samuelson, April 11, 1969.

their cash balances. Note that the result of the decision of the individual to add a dollar to his cash balance has raised *both* the real balances he holds (while reducing his consumption), and raised the consumption of everyone else while *not* reducing their cash balances. The end result is an increase in welfare in the sense that everyone is better off, and no one else is worse off. This is the Pareto-Lerner criterion as we saw in Chapter 10. Since this is the case, it would be good economic policy to induce greater holdings of cash balances on the average. But note that the old specter of Pigou's externalities raises its head. For while the individual who adds the extra dollar to his cash balances confers benefits on everyone else, he cannot receive compensation for having done so. Note how this is precisely analogous to the case of Sidgwick's lighthouse and Pigou's and Samuelson's public-goods analysis. Just as not enough lighthouses or smoke-abating equipment will be constructed by individuals in the absence of collective action (because the marginal private benefit is less than the marginal social benefit), so, too, there will be less than optimum cash balances held. So we have an inefficiency.

How might the inefficiency be eliminated? That is, what policy can government follow to induce individuals to voluntarily add to their holdings of real cash balances? Three possible policies might be followed: the monetary authorities can pursue a policy of inflation, stable prices, or deflation. Which of these three alternatives would cause the greatest inducement to individuals to add to cash balances in such a way that private and social benefits are reconciled?

Let us look at each policy. If we have an inflation—and assume along with Friedman that it is completely anticipated—what are the costs to an individual of holding an extra dollar in his cash balance? The costs are two: first, there is the cost of giving up present consumption goods now that he could otherwise have; second, there is the cost of holding money in the sense that as the price level rises, the real value of the dollar added to his cash balance declines. This is a cost that must be added to the first cost in order to get the total cost to him of holding an additional dollar during a period of completely anticipated inflation.

What about the costs of adding a dollar to one's cash balance in a period of stable prices? In such a case, only the first cost mentioned above is applicable. Since prices are not rising, there is no additional cost in the form of a depreciating dollar. So, during a period of price stability, it costs less to add an additional dollar to one's cash balances than during a period of inflation. It follows, therefore, that the inducement to do so would be greater—that the demand for cash balances will be higher in such a period.

But a situation of completely anticipated falling prices is better yet. For, although the first cost mentioned above still exists—that is, there is still the cost of abstaining from present consumption—there is not only *no* additional *cost* of a depreciating dollar, there is the *benefit* to be derived from the increased purchasing power of the appreciating dollar. The individual's real balances will, in fact, grow. So the latter situation is surely best if we wish to induce each individual to help eliminate the divergence between private and social cost. For this reason Friedman advocates a midly falling price level in opposition to the Lerner predisposition in favor of mild inflation.[24]

The Great Contraction

Perhaps the most important part of Friedman's attack on the new economics consisted of a reexamination of the orthodox interpretation of the Great Depression. As was pointed out at the beginning of this chapter, the period of the 1930's was the great watershed in the history of the private market economy, for that catastrophe caused a searching reexamination of the precepts of laissez-faire economic policy. No other series of events in America have led to such a dramatic shift in opinion regarding the role of the state in economic life. What is more, this change was recognized early.

In a paper presented to the American Economic Association in 1946, Clarence E. Ayres, one of America's leading adherents of Veblenian economics, commented on the suddenness with which economic ideas changed in the thirties, the extraordinary rapidity with which they

---

[24] See Milton Friedman, "The Optimum Quantity of Money," *The Optimum Quantity of Money and other Essays* (Chicago: Aldine Publishing Company, 1969), pp. 1-50.

The reason Friedman advocates mildly falling prices rather than prices falling at a greater rate is because, beyond some point, the individual will become so concerned about the safety of his cash that he will incur large costs in guarding and storing it so that the extra real balances that he holds use up productive resources. For some sufficiently large rate of price level decline, there will be a net loss; and for a sufficiently small rate, there will be a net gain. We shall not be concerned here with Friedman's analysis of the optimum rate of decline in prices. It should be noted, however, that an alternative to a falling price level would be payment of interest on money (including demand deposits). Friedman had earlier made this point in his *A Program for Monetary Stability* (New York: Fordham University Press, 1959), p. 73. Paul Samuelson has also lent support for Friedman's proposition that a mildly falling price level is beneficial. See Paul A. Samuelson, "Nonoptimality of Money Holding under Laissez Faire," *Canadian Journal of Economics* (May 1969), 303-8.

gained adherents, and the amazing response which was extended to Keynes's ideas. In this sense, he referred to the Keynesian revolution as being "comparable to the Darwinian revolution or even perhaps the Copernican revolution." The events of that time led to a scrutinizing reappraisal of the roles that should be assigned to the state in economic life. As Victor Abramson pointed out, "There can be no doubt that the Great Depression has had the pervasive result of stimulating an awareness of the importance of the positive contribution that government can make to the maximization of the social product."[25]

Thus, it was widely agreed that the Depression was evidence that the private market economy is inherently unstable, and that only a vigorously interventionist government can offset or prevent such episodes. Furthermore, as we have seen, monetary policy fell into disrepute because it was believed to have failed to bring about recovery. Even Henry Simons shared Keynes's view as to the causes of the Great Depression. His interpretation of the evidence led him to place greatest reliance on fiscal powers as the key weapon of economic policy.[26]

But Friedman's thoroughgoing scientific study reached almost precisely the opposite conclusion. His examination of the 1929-1933 debacle led him to conclude that it was an unnecessary episode, and that the Federal Reserve System bears the main responsibility for the Great Depression. The sharp and unprecedented decline in the stock of money was a consequence of the monetary authority's failure to provide the liquidity that would have enabled the banks which were failing (and, therefore, destroying demand and time deposits) to meet their obligations. Furthermore, far from monetary policy having failed during the contraction, the period "is in fact a tragic testimonial to the importance of monetary forces."[27]

This is an astounding conclusion. For if Friedman is right, the attitudes of many intellectuals and others who influence popular thought that government intervention, planning, and control are necessary to maintain a stable economic environment were formed on a misconception of the facts. If the Great Depression is responsible in large part for

---

[25] See Clarence E. Ayres, "The Impact of the Great Depression on Economic Thinking," *American Economic Review—Papers and Proceedings* (May 1946), 112-25; and Victor Abramson, "Discussion," *Papers and Proceedings, op. cit.,* 146-49.

[26] See Milton Friedman, "The Monetary Theory and Policy of Henry Simons," *Journal of Law and Economics,* vol. 10 (October 1967), 1-13.

[27] Milton Friedman and Anna J. Schwartz, *A Monetary History of the United States, 1867-1960,* National Bureau of Economic Research (Princeton, New Jersey: Princeton University Press, 1963), p. 300.

shaping the intellectual community's attitude not only toward economic policy, but its philosophy of government, then Friedman's research should have shattering consequences. For it indicates that economic instability, far from resulting from unfettered free enterprise, has largely resulted from inappropriate government intervention. Indeed, as Friedman put it, "Perhaps the most remarkable feature of the record is the adaptability and flexibility that the private economy has so frequently shown under such extreme provocation."[28]

The book in which Friedman presented the results of his research into America's economic history is a massive and scholarly work written in collaboration with Anna J. Schwartz and titled, *A Monetary History of the United States, 1867-1960.* This is the book that Friedman considers his most important work.[29]

In it, Friedman presents the historical experience which he considers so important in supplementing his theoretical work regarding the direction of influence between monetary change and business conditions. From the point of view of the Keynesian Revolution, the most significant part of the *History* is the section covering the period from 1929 to 1933. We shall, therefore, focus our attention on this episode.

The popular view which began to prevail after the contraction—that "money does not matter"—is not what a careful analysis of the Great Contraction reveals. Instead, Friedman and Schwartz interpret these four years as strongly implying that money is crucial. They assert that monetary policy, far from failing during the contraction, was never tried.

Friedman and Schwartz note that there might have been a business recession from 1929 to 1930. As a consequence of the Federal Reserve System's undue concern with stock market levels, monetary policy was unusually tight. From 1927 to 1929, a period of business expansion, prices were stable while the stock of money declined. From 1929 to 1930, there was a 3 percent fall in the stock of money, more than it had fallen in all except the most severe depression periods. But the stock market crash, which some economists take to have triggered the Great

---

[28] Friedman, *Program for Monetary Stability, op. cit.,* p. 9.

[29] In personal correspondence, Friedman says that the work that he thinks "most deserves to be remembered, yet which has not been much noted, are the final pages of my *Price Theory* dealing with capital theory. It has always been my intention to write a little book based essentially on those pages but whether I shall ever get around to doing so or not, I do not know." (June 22, 1967). Since these pages are highly technical contributions to the most abstruse of all subjects in economics, and have had little direct influence on policy, we shall not attempt a summary of Friedman's presentation here. The interested reader should consult Milton Friedman, *Price Theory: A Provisional Text* (Chicago: Aldine Publishing Company, 1962), pp. 244-63.

Depression,[30] would probably have led to a rather ordinary recession. There were no bank failures on any substantial scale, nor any sign of weakening of public confidence. Prior to the Federal Deposit Insurance Corporation, the best sign of public attitude toward the banking system was the ratio of deposits to currency. This ratio remained relatively high during this period. Up to September of 1930, there was no evidence of a banking crisis or a liquidity decline.

But the period 1930 to 1933 is the one for which Friedman and Schwartz feel that the monetary authorities bear the chief responsibility. A concatenation of bank failures spread across the country culminating in the failure of the Bank of the United States in New York on December 11, 1930. This bank, although an ordinary commercial bank, was widely believed by people abroad and immigrants in the United States to be a government bank. The failure of this bank precipitated an enormous liquidity crisis.

The character of the contraction changed after the failure of this large bank which had held roughly $200 million in deposits. There was a marked fall in the ratio of deposits to currency. As depositors started to withdraw deposits, a string of bank failures followed like a line of dominoes tumbling.

What role did the Federal Reserve System play during this period? One astonishing conclusion of Friedman and Schwartz's research is that the Federal Reserve System behaved impassively and inactively. They could find no evidence that the Federal Reserve engaged in open market operations or tried in any significant way to provide banks with liquidity. This is a shocking disclosure, since the System was established as "a lender of last resort" largely to provide just such liquidity during the kind of crisis that occurred during this period. Notwithstanding the pleas of George Harrison (the governor of the Federal Reserve Bank of New York) that it engage in open-market operations, the Reserve System did nothing while scores of banks failed.

The next important date is September, 1931. For in that month Great Britain went off the gold standard. This led to an external drain of gold from the United States. It is a bizarre fact that the System responded to this event by raising discount rates. Indeed, within two weeks of this event, the System raised discount rates more than it ever had before. The New York Reserve Bank raised its discount rate to 2 1/2 percent on October 9 and to 3 1/2 percent on October 16. The move

---

[30] For example, see John K. Galbraith, *The Great Crash* (Boston: Houghton Mifflin Company, 1955).

ended the gold drain within two weeks; at the same time, however, there was a spectacular rise in bank runs and failures. In October 1931, 522 commercial banks closed their doors and in the next three months, 875 more did the same. During this period (August 1931 to January 1932), the money stock fell 12 percent.

At only one time in the period were expansionary open-market operations of any significance attempted. After the second of the three banking crises, there was growing support in Congress for more government spending and monetary expansion. These views were attacked in the business and financial communities as "greenbackism" and "inflationary." Nevertheless, congressional pressure resulted in the Federal Reserve beginning large-scale open-market purchases in April 1932. By August, the Federal Reserve had raised its security holdings in an amount of roughly $1 billion. Bank failures subsided and interest rates fell; soon all general economic indicators began to rise. Wholesale prices rose in July and production in August. The figures looked like a cyclical revival was beginning.

However, the recovery was only temporary. In late 1932, with the System's lapse into passivity, there were more bank failures, the deposit-currency ratio fell, the money stock ceased to grow and began falling in January 1933, interest rates began to rise, and economic indices deteriorated. Net open-market purchases had ceased as of August 10, 1932 and net sales began in early 1933. Overall during this period, the money stock declined by over one-third.[31]

Friedman and Schwartz believe that if vigorous open-market operations had been employed in 1930, the banking crisis could have been avoided and the Depression would not have become so deep. Moreover, if Benjamin Strong, the influential Governor of the New York Reserve Bank and a staunch advocate of open-market operations, had not died one year before the stock market crash of 1929, there might have been large-scale open-market purchases by the Federal Reserve System early in the contraction.

That one man could have been so important in preventing a depression means that economic stability depends on fate, luck, or happenstance. Yet our financial history reveals that, in every banking crisis,

---

[31] These findings should have come as a revelation to established Keynesians. As late as 1958, R. F. Harrod, Keynes's biographer and one of his leading disciples, was able to write: "In the thirties, after the Wall Street crash, there were terrific nonmonetary forces making for depression. The central banks, both in Britain and the United States, did all they could to counteract them. . . . With this end in view they maintained a credit policy of ultra-ease." Roy F. Harrod, *Policy Against Inflation* (London: Macmillan & Co., Ltd., 1958), p. 63.

much has depended upon the presence of one or more outstanding individuals willing to assume leadership and responsibility. To Friedman, such a situation cries out for alternative arrangements, a system not resting on the capriciousness of nature or the whim of the gods. Friedman's most developed and far-reaching scheme for monetary reform as an alternative to this parlous situation had earlier been presented in another of his books, *A Program for Monetary Stability.*[32] To this analysis, we now turn.

Toward Monetary Reform

To Friedman, a stable monetary framework is essential for effective operation of a private market economy. In such an economy, the central tasks for the monetary authorities are to (1) set an external limit to the amount of money and (2) prevent counterfeiting. If these tasks are carried out properly, a stable monetary framework will result.

Friedman claims that economic cycles in the United States have been produced or intensified by government intervention or uncertainty. Major inflations of United States history have all been associated with war and were produced by the printing press or its equivalent. The Federal Reserve System was established with the specific responsibility of stabilizing monetary conditions and ostensibly was armed with adequate power to prevent great instability. However, Friedman charges that the 44 years since 1914 have had more instability in the stock of money and in general economic conditions than in the 47 years before 1914. Friedman traces through the evidence of various inflations and contractions to try to support this contention, and concludes that government intervention in monetary matters has proved to be a ". . . potent source of instability." His interpretation of the historical record is that ". . . the central problem is not to construct a highly sensitive instrument that can continuously offset instability introduced by other factors, but rather to prevent monetary arrangements from themselves becoming a primary source of instability." In other words, unlike Abba Lerner, Friedman does not think that the nation needs a skilled monetary driver of the economic vehicle always turning the wheel to adjust to unexpected turns in the road, but rather, a way to keep a backseat monetary passenger from occasionally leaning over and jerking the steering wheel and threatening to send the car off the road.[33]

---

[32] Friedman, *Program for Monetary Stability, op. cit.*

[33] For the rebuttal, see Abba P. Lerner, "Milton Friedman's *A Program for Monetary Stability:* A Review," *American Statistical Association Journal* (March 1962), 211-20.

In considering the tools of monetary policy, Friedman argues that open-market operations alone are sufficient to carry out monetary policy. At the same time, he convincingly argues that changing the discount rate and reserve requirements are defective tools for affecting the quantity of "high-powered money"[34] and, thus, for altering the stock of money. Both, he thinks, are blunt instruments and yield not fully predictable results.

In his views on monetary policy, Friedman was enormously influenced by Henry Simons's "Rules vs. Authorities" argument. As we noted in the last chapter, Simons favored price level stability as the general goal. However, Friedman thinks there are many problems that would arise since changes in the level of prices and changes in the money supply are uncertain at best in the short run. Besides, the Federal Reserve System does not control the price level, it controls the stock of money. Since monetary changes have their effect only after a lag, and the lag is long and variable, Friedman thinks it would be better to have a "rule" connected more directly with something the Federal Reserve System can control: the stock of money.[35]

Friedman's rule is that the stock of money be increased at a fixed rate year-in and year-out without any variation in the rate of increase to

---

[34] High-powered money is the amount of currency outside of the Treasury and Federal Reserve available for use by the public plus all deposits at the Federal Reserve Banks. The quantity of money is directly proportional to the amount of high-powered money.

[35] The notion that monetary actions affect economic conditions only after a lag that is long and variable is one of Friedman's most controversial conclusions. It has led to much debate and empirical testing. Friedman's fixed rule policy proposal rests in part on his observations regarding this lag in effect of monetary policy. To Friedman it is supported by his conception of the channels through which monetary policy works, and extensive historical studies. He also buttresses his argument with observations about the "sheer inertia" of the government decision making process and "the political costs of implicitly or explicitly admitting error by reversing course rapidly." See Milton Friedman, "The Lag in Effect of Monetary Policy," *Journal of Political Economy*, vol. 69 (October 1961), 447-66; J. M. Culbertson, "Friedman on the Lag in Effect of Monetary Policy,"*Journal of Political Economy* (December 1960), 617-21; and J. M. Culbertson, "The Lag in Effect of Monetary Policy: Reply," *Journal of Political Economy* (October 1961), 467-77. Also, John Kareken and Robert M. Solow, "Lags in Monetary Policy," *Stabilization Policies*, Commission on Money and Credit (Englewood Cliffs, N.J.: Prentice-Hall, Inc., 1963), pp. 14-96. The present state of this debate seems to have brought us to the conclusion that there is much evidence in support of a large lag in the effect of monetary policy, but not much evidence that the lag is variable. See Thomas Mayer, "The Lag in the Effect of Monetary Policy: Some Criticisms," *Western Economic Journal* (September 1967), 324-42.

meet cyclical needs. For Friedman's definition of the money supply (currency outside of commercial banks plus demand and time deposits), empirical evidence for the last 90 years indicates that an annual growth rate of a little over 4 percent per year would be most desirable.[36]

The Methodology of Positive Economics

It is important for an understanding of Friedman's contribution that his philosophical ideas be separated from his purely scientific work. As we have seen, the major body of his work has been strictly scientific and dictated by his characteristic approach. This approach stems from his methodological insistence on the extreme importance of separating the knowledge of what is, from judgments about what ought to be. It is this philosophy that shaped the character of Friedman's "positive" economics. In addition, it is clear that Friedman views economic theory as a kit of tools which is instructive in dealing with almost every problem. He agrees with Abba Lerner that it is most definitely not a work of art to be developed for its own sake.

Another distinctive feature of Friedman's philosophy is his belief that a very large fraction of differences of opinion about policy derive from differences about what is rather than from differences in values about

---

[36] In a recent work, Friedman has modified his views on this matter. In his paper, "The Optimum Quantity of Money," he suggests that a 2 percent rate of increase might prove better than the 5 per cent rule since, as we have seen, it would reduce the difference between the private and total social costs of adding to real balances. Friedman, in "a final schizophrenic note" admits that his new view contradicts his earlier position on a 5 per cent rule. In any event, either "a 5 per cent rule or a 2 per cent rule would be far superior to the monetary policy we have actually followed. . . . I shall continue to support the 5 per cent rule as an intermediate objective greatly superior to present practice." Milton Friedman, "The Optimum Quantity of Money," *Optimum Quantity of Money, op. cit.*, p. 48.

Friedman's change of mind is doubtless a result of long and hard reflection on the logical properties of a new analysis that was worked out after he had become a most persuasive champion of the 5 per cent rule. In testimony before the Committee on Banking and Currency of the House of Representatives in 1964, after Friedman strongly supported his 5 per cent rule of monetary increase, Representative Reuss of Wisconsin suggested that should Friedman prove to be wrong, he would "be the first man to come in here and confess error and say change the law tomorrow." Friedman replied: "It is a natural human quality of everyone of us that the hardest thing in the world to do . . . is to admit error." U.S. Congress, House Subcommittee on Domestic Finance, Committee on Banking and Currency, *The Federal Reserve System after Fifty Years*, 88th Cong., 2nd sess., 1961, p. 1143. Thus, Friedman's change of opinion must not have come easily.

what ought to be.[37] This means that most differences of opinion are not over ends-in-view or values, but disagreements over predictions regarding the effects of various policies. These disagreements are capable in principle of being resolved by empirical evidence. It is for this reason that Friedman places great stress on hypotheses being put into the form of conceivably refutable statements. For only in this way can disagreements be resolved. This implies, of course, a most sanguine view of human nature, since it is based on an assumed reasonableness of human beings and their ultimate commitment to rational discourse. Friedman's strong commitment to this position is reflected in his important essay, "The Methodology of Positive Economics."[38] The distinction between positive and normative economics was first developed by the father of John Maynard Keynes—John Neville Keynes who distinguished between "a *positive science* . . . a body of systematized knowledge concerning what is; a *normative* or *regulative* science . . . a body of systematized knowledge discussing criteria of what ought to be. . . ."[39]

To Friedman, this is a fundamentally useful distinction since normative policy conclusions necessarily rest on a prediction derived from positive economics about the consequences of alternative policies. So normative economics cannot be independent of positive economics. Friedman believes that a large proportion of economists would agree on policy conclusions if they agreed on the implications of alternative policies. So it is the progress of positive economics that is crucial to the resolution of normative differences. If reasonable men in a given cultural context agree about ends, they need only discover the action that will allow them to achieve these ends. If differences over fundamental basic values are so deep that they are irreconcilable, then they are "differences about which men can ultimately only fight."[40]

This is a major reason why the free market is so crucial. Friedman's view that differences in values are differences over which men must ultimately fight focuses his attention on the market mechanism as a device for reconciling value differences. For exchange to occur, it is clear that values must differ. Individual parties engaging in exchange must have different tastes. This means that all will benefit from exchange. As Friedman notes, "the essence of exchange is the reconcilia-

37 See Milton Friedman, "Why Economists Disagree," *Dollars and Deficits* (Englewood Cliffs, N.J.: Prentice-Hall, Inc., 1968), pp. 1-16, especially pp. 6-10.

38 Milton Friedman, "The Methodology of Positive Economics," *Positive Economics, op. cit.*, pp. 3-43.

39 John Neville Keynes, *The Scope and Method of Political Economy* (London: Macmillan & Co., Ltd., 1891), p. 34.

40 Friedman, *Positive Economics, op. cit.*, p. 5.

tion of divergent values; of achievement of unanimity without conformity."[41] Individuals will continue to exchange until, at the margin, each attaches the same relative value to a little more of the commodities in question. So, through the free exchange of commodities, they are brought into agreement. And throughout the whole market, all participants will come to have common values at the margin. Friedman argues that, for a society to be stable, there must be a common set of values that must be unthinkingly accepted by most of the people most of the time. One of Friedman's most original contributions is his argument that this set of commonly shared values can be developed and changed and accepted by the free market. This view of the market as a reconciler of divergent values is part and parcel of his classical liberal philosophy.

Friedman as Marshallian

It is Friedman's insistence on the importance of the predictive power or implications of theory that allows him to demur sharply from the strictures of Veblen and Chamberlin, and so to attack two other harbingers of the new economics. He explicitly refers to Veblen's criticisms regarding the "unrealism" of economics because it assumes a rational economic man. To Friedman, such criticism is entirely wide of the mark. The issue is not the realism of the assumptions, but its ability to yield predictions "for as wide a range of phenomena." To Friedman (as to Alfred Marshall), economic theory is an "engine of analysis," and economists should not seek a "photographic reproduction" of the world.

In regard to Chamberlin's "Revolution," Friedman accepted the usefulness of Alfred Marshall's grouping of firms into "industries," in which similarities among the firms were more important than their differences with each firm producing a single "product"—that is, goods that are perfect substitutes to purchasers. In the case of a monopolist, the firm *is* the industry. Obviously, the assumption of a perfectly elastic demand curve for firms in an industry is an abstraction. For some purposes, the industry can be considered perfectly competitive; for other problems, it is appropriate to treat the firms as if they had some monopolistic power. But, to Friedman, Marshall did not assume perfect competition in a descriptive sense. It simply was a useful simplification for problems "in which a group of firms is affected by common stimuli, and in which the firms can be treated *as if* they were perfect competitors."[42]

---

[41] Milton Friedman, "Value Judgments in Economics," *Human Values and Economic Policy*, ed. Sidney Hook (New York: New York University Press, 1967), pp. 85-93.

[42] Friedman, *Positive Economics, op. cit.*, pp. 37-38.

Chamberlin's attempt to construct a more general theory was in Friedman's view a failure, except in so far as he refined Marshall's monopoly analysis and enriched the economics vocabulary. The point at issue is Chamberlin's treatment of product differentiation, the distinguishing feature of his theory. For how can firms producing "similar" but differentiated products be grouped together into the same industry? If products are differentiated, doesn't this mean that each firm *is* the industry? Thus, "the theory of monopolistic competition offers no tools for the analysis of an industry and so no stopping place between the firm at one extreme and general equilibrium at the other."[43] So Friedman was able to dismiss much of Veblen and Chamberlin on the ground that their criticisms of neoclassical economics were in large measure directed at the "unreality" of neoclassical theory. Since the test of a theory is its ability to yield accurate predictions, not the realism of its assumptions, much of the Veblen and Chamberlin analysis has been largely irrelevant.[44]

Capitalism and Freedom

In the field of social philosophy, Friedman has restated the case for classical liberalism. In developing this philosophy, he was influenced by his teachers, Frank Knight and Henry Simons. To Friedman, the liberalism of the eighteenth and nineteenth centuries stressed the "doctrines

---

[43] *Ibid.*

[44] Friedman's pragmatic approach to methodology was doubtless influenced by his acquaintance with the writings of Charles Sanders Peirce, the founder of American pragmatism. Ironically, Peirce had been a teacher of Veblen at Johns Hopkins, and might have had much to do with Veblen's appreciation of Darwinism. See P. Wiener, *Evolution and the Founders of Pragmatism* (Cambridge, Mass.: Harvard University Press, 1949), pp. 70-96.

The ideas of Peirce which seem to have had most impact on Friedman are contained in Peirce's collection of philosophical essays, *Chance, Love, and Logic* (New York: Harcourt, Brace, Inc., 1923). In this work, Peirce argues that to be useful, theories must be simpler than the complex facts they seek to explain. It is convenient to employ a principle of certainty where the facts would justify only some degree of probability. Friedman's methodological prescription regarding a theory's usefulness being its test by implication is in essence the Peircian criterion of meaning. An idea, according to Peirce, is clear if we understand its conceivable effects or the logical consequences necessitated by adopting it as a premise or rule for the resolution of a problem. Just as the meaning of an idea is found not by intuition, but by working out its implications, the usefulness of a theory is found not by considering its assumptions, but by examining its implications. As we saw in Chapter 12, Frank Knight would reject the view that economic theory is a system for prediction. Thus, Knight did not much influence Friedman's methodological approach.

relating to a 'free man' which are diametrically opposed to the modern day concept which stresses 'welfare' and equality over freedom. Freedom is the highest value and is the opposite of coercion. It implies the right to make and act on one's own decisions."[45]

In society, the basic problem of social organization is the coordination of the economic activities of large numbers of people. This coordination can be carried out in only two ways: through voluntary means, such as a market; or through central control or political coercion. The classical liberal is not indifferent between these two choices. Economic freedom is an important part of overall freedom and "an indispensable means toward the achievement of political freedom."[46] For only if one's livelihood is independent of government control is one able to express his true political opinions.

Friedman's views on the proper role of government are little different from those of Adam Smith: (1) To provide a framework for law and order by protecting individuals from external enemies (national defense) and from coercion by their fellow citizens. (2) To promote economic freedom by providing, interpreting, and enforcing the rules of the game. In effect, this means the enforcement of voluntary contracts, the definition and enforcement of property rights, and the provision of a stable monetary framework. (3) Although coercive, government action may be justified in the case of Pigovian externalities (or market failure) and where there are technical monopolies. (4) The government may be coercive on paternalistic grounds by supplementing private charity and the family in order to protect irresponsible children and madmen.

In *Capitalism and Freedom*,[47] Friedman advocated that a subsidy

---

[45] Note, for instance, the definition of John Stuart Mill in *On Liberty*: "The only freedom which deserves the name is that of pursuing our own good in our own way, so long as we do not attempt to deprive others of theirs, or impede their efforts to obtain it." John Stuart Mill, *On Liberty* in *The Utilitarians* (Garden City, New York: Dolphin Books, Doubleday and Company, Inc., 1961), p. 487.

To Friedman the goal of liberalism is "to preserve the maximum degree of freedom for each individual separately that is compatible with one man's freedom not interfering with other men's freedom." Milton Friedman, *Capitalism and Freedom* (Chicago: University of Chicago Press, 1962), p. 39. Note how this attitude toward the value of individual liberty contrasts with that of Galbraith. In an interview which Galbraith gave the West German newspaper *Der Zeit*, he is reported to have said that he believed the Berlin Wall to be a good thing since it contributed to peace. His chief objection to it seemed to be that it was not aesthetically pleasing. *Der Zeit*, July 5, 1968.

[46] Friedman, *Capitalism and Freedom, op. cit.*, p. 12.

[47] *Ibid.*, pp. 191-95.

be paid to individuals whose income fell below some socially accept-able level of poverty. The proposal, which Friedman labeled a "nega-tive income tax" would set a limit beneath which no family income could fall. It would allow us to eliminate all other social welfare schemes such as Social Security, farm price supports, unemployment compensation, public housing, and the whole "rag-bag" of welfare pro-grams that, according to Friedman, have not only not helped the poor, but have impoverished them further. So as to minimize the adverse effects on incentives, Friedman's proposal involved a sliding scale fea-ture. Assume, for example, that we agree that the poverty line is $3000 and the rate of subsidy is, say, 50 percent. If an individual re-ceives an income of $2000, in excess of his exemptions and deductions, he would be $1000 below our poverty line. With a 50 percent negative income tax rate, he would receive a subsidy of $500. Although it still reduces the incentives of those helped to help themselves, this program does not eliminate them entirely, since an extra dollar earned would always leave the individual with more income.[48] But it should be clear that Friedman is not in favor of the negative income tax in order to redistribute income. He advocates it because he believes that an over-whelming majority of the upper income groups would be willing to im-pose taxes on themselves for this purpose. His argument really rests on his belief that charity is a collective good involving Pigovian externality problems. People want to eliminate dire distress and poverty and can do so optimally only collectively.[49] However, Friedman warns that any government action beyond promoting freedom and providing the rules creates a dangerous negative externality. This is true because "every act of government intervention limits the area of individual freedom di-rectly and threatens the preservation of freedom. . . ."

This means that government intervention has neighborhood effects of its own which should be weighed against those that it is designed to remove. But how large a weight the classical liberal attaches to the negative effects of additional government intervention depends on the scope of existing government control. "This is an important reason why many earlier liberals, like Henry Simons, writing at a time when gov-ernment was small by today's standards, were willing to have govern-ment undertake activities that today's liberals would not accept now that government has become so overgrown."[50]

---

[48] For a fuller discussion of the issues surrounding the negative income tax and the various alternatives proposed, see Christopher Green, *Negative Taxes and the Poverty Problem* (Washington, D.C.: The Brookings Institution, June 1967).

[49] Friedman, *Savings and Residential Financing, op. cit.*, p. 54.

[50] Friedman, *Capitalism and Freedom, op. cit.*, p. 32.

Thus, for example, where Simons would advocate government ownership in the case of technical monopolies—monopolies that arise because it is efficient to have a single enterprise—Friedman would choose private monopoly. He would do so not only because the powers of government have grown so large in recent times, but because technological changes are so rapid that what is a technical monopoly today might not be one tomorrow. But if government ownership or regulation is chosen, there is little chance that future technological considerations will lead to a removal of government from this sphere.

Friedman argues that democracy is the appropriate form of government to foster political freedom. But the necessary prerequisite to democracy is a free market, that is, a capitalistic, free enterprise system. This is so because, in order for a political decision to be freely made, the act must be severed from connection with one's livelihood. If the government is the sole employer and the only source from which the requisite instruments of effective political advocacy can be had, then the individual hostile to the existing government but dependent on it for his livelihood, would have to hope that the government is indeed self-denying. For this government would not only have to be imagined to continue to employ this advocate of its destruction, but would have to be willing to supply the paper, presses, and halls for the dissenter to propagandize for its overthrow. What's more, even if the government were to continue to employ this hostile critic and to stand ready to sell him the services of printing presses, paper, and halls, it surely could not afford to provide these services to all free of charge. Thus, the political advocate in the socialistic state would have to raise funds. But those with the most funds are likely to be those in greatest positions of power in the government with the most to lose in the event of a political overthrow. Radical minority movements in capitalistic countries have indeed often been financed by millionaire angels. The underground newspapers of the radical left, which have become so much a part of the scene at many American universities in recent years, could hardly be expected in a socialist state. According to Friedman, only a capitalistic system separates economic and political power, allowing one to offset the other. It was not by chance that capitalism and democracy grew up together in a limited corner of the world:

> Historical evidence speaks with a single voice on the relation between political freedom and a free market. I know of no example in time or place of a society that has been marked by a large measure of political freedom and that has not also used something comparable to a free market to organize the bulk of economic activity.

Because we live in a largely free society, we tend to forget how limited is the span of time and the part of the globe for which there has ever been anything like political freedom: the typical state of mankind is tyranny, servitude, and misery.[51]

It can be seen that Friedman has restated for his time the relevance of the classical liberal philosophy of Adam Smith and John Stuart Mill. On this basis, he has developed policy proposals which would return our economy to a largely laissez-faire system. But the classical liberal is not an anarchist. For a government which maintained law and order, protected property rights, defined and adjudicated the rules of the economic game, enforced contracts, promoted competition, provided a stable monetary framework, dissolved monopolies, overcame the important Pigovian externalities, and protected lunatics and children would have valuable functions. But most of our departures from the free market are not justified. In *Capitalism and Freedom*, Friedman lists 14 activities of government that he feels violate classical liberal principles. All of them, though well-intentioned, do not produce the results intended. Indeed, in most cases, they produce the opposite result. Among those listed are tariffs and quotas in foreign trade and interferences with international payments; the fixing of prices and wages; the control of entry into occupations through licensure; the regulation of output, such as the prorationing of oil by the Texas Railroad Commission; conscription to man the armed services; the compulsory social security program.

We shall not have space to develop in detail Friedman's specific proposals for removing government from these activities in which it is now engaged. But, because our society has come to take so many of these functions for granted, Friedman's advocacy of alternative arrangements seems shocking.[52]

---

[51] *Ibid.*, p. 9. For a dissenting view of Friedman's position that capitalism is a necessary (albeit not sufficient) condition for political freedom from the point of view of a political scientist, see C. B. Macpherson, "Elegant Tombstones: A Note on Friedman's Freedom," *Canadian Journal of Political Science*, vol. 1, (March 1968), 95-106.

[52] The reader desiring to see Friedman's arguments on these issues should consult: "The Case for Flexible Exchange Rates," *Positive Economics, op. cit.*, pp. 157-203; Milton Friedman and Robert V. Roosa, *The Balance of Payments: Free versus Fixed Exchange Rates*, Rational Debate Seminars (Washington, D.C.: American Enterprise Institute for Public Policy Research, 1967); Milton Friedman, "An All Volunteer Army," *New York Times Magazine*, May 14, 1967; Milton Friedman, "Why Not a Volunteer Army?", *New Individualist Review*, vol. 4, no. 4 (Spring

The Achievement of Milton Friedman

Friedman's success in rehabilitating classical monetary theory and in defending competitive capitalism has begun to have its effects. Some echo of the noise his ideas were making in the academy began to reach politicians and the general public in the early 1960's. Senator Barry Goldwater was so impressed with *Capitalism and Freedom* that Friedman became his unofficial advisor on economics during the 1964 campaign. In 1968 Friedman played a similar role in the successful campaign of Richard M. Nixon. But like Paul A. Samuelson, he has preferred to remain in the university rather than accept an official governmental position.[53]

The 1969 *Report* of the Joint Economic Committee on the *Economic Report of the President* provides striking evidence of the pervasive influence of Friedman's views on monetary policy. The majority report recommended that the Federal Reserve Board set a rate of increase in the money supply ranging from 2 percent to 6 percent, and accused the Federal Reserve of being an engine of inflation in 1967 and 1968. The only difference that the minority report expressed with regard to this recommendation was that the "money supply should grow at the lower end of the 2 to 6 percent band consistent with economic stablity."[54]

Even economists with whom Friedman had had most disagreement in earlier years over the question of "rules" versus "authorities" in monetary policy seemed to be capitulating. Thus, in 1969 Professor J. M. Culbertson of the University of Wisconsin, testified before the Joint Economic Committee that the Federal Reserve's erratic application of monetary policy may be termed "a threat to the security of the Nation." Furthermore, he suggested that Congress order the Federal Reserve Board to "make the Nation's money supply behave in a stabilizing man-

---

1967), 3-9; Milton Friedman, "A Volunteer Army," *Newsweek*, December 19, 1966, p. 100; Milton Friedman, "Occupational Licensure," *Capitalism and Freedom, op. cit.,* chap. IX, pp. 137-60; Milton Friedman, "Social Security," *Newsweek*, April 3, 1967, p. 81; Milton Friedman, "Social Welfare Measures," *Capitalism and Freedom, op. cit.,* chap. XI, pp. 177-89.

[53] On this fact, *Business Week* commented, "Friedman . . . has not been called to Washington—because he is too brilliant, too idiosyncratic, too iconoclastic, too right wing in his politics, or too uninterested, depending on whom you talk to. . . . And what the Administration is really saying about the causes and cures of inflation bear a distinct Friedmanship stamp, although officials are sometimes inclined to hide the fact behind a facade of middle-of-the-road blandness." *Business Week*, June 28, 1969, p. 130.

[54] U. S., Congress, Joint Economic Committee, *January 1969 Report of the President*, 92nd Cong., 1st sess., April 1, 1969, pp. 22-24, p. 91.

ner, and provide it with presumptive guidelines."[55] And Paul Samuelson, in an advertising brochure discussing his plans for the eighth edition of his famous textbook, said that his book "will go from one-and-a-half cheers for Friedman up to two."

Perhaps the best testimony to Friedman's impact in America in the latter part of the 1960's is that he began to find his public lectures picketed by student dissidents carrying placards with such slogans as "The Free Market Won't Solve Everything."[56] What's more, his picture appeared on the cover of *Time* magazine for December 19, 1969, and he was the subject of a cover story in *The New York Times Magazine* for January 25, 1970. Such exposure is rare for these academic economists whose chief contributions are of a highly technical character.

Friedman's remarkable success in putting across his once unpopular ideas—in seeing so much of what he had for so long alone advocated become respectable opinion on economic matters—is a tribute to his intellect, his courage, his dazzling scholarship, and his indefatigable energy. No economist of his time, with the exception of Keynes, and certainly no American, can match him in the power of persuasion, and in the black art of debate.[57] What Mencken once said of Nietzsche can most appropriately be said of Friedman, "When he took to the floor to argue it was time to send for ambulances." Perhaps not all have been persuaded, but at the very least, as the editor of one influential magazine recently stated:

> Thanks largely to Friedman's long and at first lonely labors, there has been a classical revival. The result is that for the first time in history the classicists and the Keynesians possess equal intellectual force. The healthy effect is that argument must now proceed by analysis rather than ridicule.[58]

---

[55] "Inflationary Policy Is Charge Against Fed," *Washington Post*, February 26, 1969. For Culbertson's earlier and more hopeful views on the efficacy of an activist fine-tuning monetary policy, see J. M. Culbertson, "Friedman on Lag in Effect of Monetary Policy," *op. cit.*

[56] John Davenport, "The Radical Economics of Milton Friedman," *Fortune*, June 1, 1967, pp. 130-31, 147-54.

[57] Friedman's lack of immediate results in convincing fellow economists has been blamed on his early habit of extreme aggressiveness in debate. But, as Milton Viorst has noted, "If he was once considered a pushy Jewish kid from New Jersey, [Friedman] is now acknowledged to be unfailingly thoughtful and courteous. Desisting from the technique of withering insult, he couches his arguments . . . in the most sweetly reasonable terms, though without ever sacrificing a cutting edge." (Milton Viorst, "Friedmanism," *op. cit.*, 83.)

[58] *Business Week*, November 23, 1968, p. 152.

CHAPTER 15

CONCLUSION

Those intrepid enough to write a volume summarizing the policy controversies that divide contemporary economists are surely free of any obligation to provide a guide to the future. At least we have resisted mightily our recognition of this duty. A chapter titled, "What of the Future?", would doubtless lend a proper air of contemplativeness to the study and provide a (short-run) reputation for profundity to its authors. But such prognostication is not for us. The history of economics suggests prudence in this regard. When and how the next revolution in economic thought and policy will come about are best left to the future to decide. Our excursion is over. It remains only to see where we are.

The Economic Revolutionaries

The doctrine of the need for an activist government to control economic affairs was constructed upon the rubble of the neoclassical structure. The demolition of the House of Marshall was carried out, in the main, by Veblen, Pigou, Chamberlin, and Keynes. These writers stressed the existence of consumer irrationality, divergencies between private and social costs, the wastes of competition, and the inadequacy of aggregate demand under laissez-faire. So the chief pillars of the Marshallian temple were undermined: the economic man, the quantity theory of money, Say's Law, and the unmitigated benefits of competition. These doctrines together had provided the intellectual gantry for a laissez-faire economic policy.

The New Economics

Alvin Hansen's work carried on the attack in two areas: first, he helped carry the Keynesian message to America and taught it to the generation of students at Harvard who were to help form the economic policy of post-World War II America. His second and less influential effort came late in his career when he began to speak out on questions that arose in the wake of Veblen, Pigou, and Chamberlin: What are the implications of the abrogation of consumer sovereignty and the existence of advertising and product differentiation? In answer, he developed in embryonic form some of the themes that were later fully developed in the work of his colleague, Galbraith. One of Hansen's most brilliant pupils, Paul A. Samuelson, was to replace Hansen as the leading teacher of the young men who would eventually inspire macroeconomic policy. His best-selling introductory textbook reached more tyro economists than had any such book before. In it, the Keynesian system was reduced to precise arithmetic and geometry so that the elements of the analysis and its policy suggestions could be grasped by the undergraduate. In his more arcane contributions, and at the suggestion of his mentor Hansen, he combined the Keynesian multiplier with the accelerator into an elegant mathematical model that gave a theoretical underpinning to the business cycle and stimulated much work in the development of growth models. Furthermore, his interests were catholic. He fashioned from the Pigovian analysis of externalities and public-goods, the logical analytics supporting a theory of government expenditure. And in his more "popular" moods, he spoke out on policy questions, particularly those regarding discretionary monetary and fiscal policy to control employment and the price level, lending his prestige to specific recommendations.

The contributions of Abba P. Lerner to economic thought and policy in America should be appreciated at least as much as those of Hansen's and Samuelson's. Lerner's functional finance analysis provided a neat set of directions for use with Keynes's monetary and fiscal tool kit. With Lerner's functional finance rules in front of him, the policy maker could, in a moment, tell what is needed in the event of any contingency from inflation to unemployment. Unfortunately, as it later turned out, the two extremes were not mutually exclusive. And so Lerner, in conceding the inappropriateness of his instruments for attacking the new inflation of the late 1950's, developed his theory of Sellers' Inflation and suggested remedies.

Playing to a much larger audience than the American Economic Association, John Kenneth Galbraith became the most noticed of social critics. His brilliantly sophisticated cynicism and writing style, with which he satirized the "conventional wisdom," gave a voice to those who inarticulately sensed a malaise in an opulent society. Galbraith's Veblen-like concern with consumer irrationalities and the technological imperatives of the second half of the twentieth century suggested new meanings in the patterns of industrial organization that far transcended Chamberlin's concerns. What's more, his association with famous movie stars, artists, and political figures, and his widely publicized leisure class postures, provided the economics profession with a public celebrity that lent it glamour. Even the most hopeless drudge of an academic scribbler could derive positive externalities generated by Galbraith's fame.

The New Neoclassicism

When Alfred Marshall, in an uncharacteristic moment of despondency regarding the vitality of his contributions, expressed his fear that his *"Principles* will be waste paper" in 50 years, he could not have foretold his good luck in having men the calibre of Knight, Simons, and Friedman to carry on. Frank Knight completed the neoclassical structure with his analysis of the role of profit in economic life. In doing so, he provided a formidable armor for protection against the attacks on consumer sovereignty. More important, he firmly grasped the nettle offered by Pigou's charge of "market failure" under laissez-faire by showing the importance of clearly defined property rights in a neoclassical framework. This contribution provided the battleground for future campaigns over the issue of the necessity of government intervention to reconcile the divergencies between private and social costs. In addition, he was Hansen's counterpart at Chicago, where he stimulated his colleagues and students to accept a largely free market philosophy that ran counter to the trend of the times.

Knight's colleague, Henry Simons, provided the ideological bearings for the counterattack on Keynes and Hansen. His stress on the rule of law rather than authorities in economic affairs and his brilliantly-reasoned defense of a positive program for a laissez-faire society inspired many disciples.

By far the most influential of these has been Milton Friedman. Friedman donned the white robes of science to demonstrate the singular relevancy of neoclassical economics for contemporary problems. Friedman amassed empirical evidence to demonstrate the inappropriateness of much economic policy that had been promoted by the new economics, and he carried the main burden of the new neoclassicism's counterattack. Pragmatists like Samuelson and Lerner were met on their own ground by an economist of at least equal brilliance and persuasiveness. If a refurnished and reformed market economy survives the onslaught of the new economics, much of the credit will go to Friedman and the new neoclassicism. As Veblen said at the end of his *Theory of Business Enterprise*: "Which of the two antagonistic factors may prove stronger in the long run is something of a blind guess; but the calculable future seems to belong to the one or the other."

Index